MW00777906

Media in the Global Context

"Once again, the irrepressible intellectual Emmanuel Ngwainmbi has brought us another one of his outstanding books, Global Media Representation and International Community Perception, with a steady hand on organization, choice of chapter writers and a sharp focus on the worldwide nature of media representation as the international community sees it. Ngwainmbi is clearly one of the leaders in communication and this book, edited by him, shows his mastery."
—Prof. Molefi Kete Asante, *author of* Revolutionary Pedagogy

"A timely book which brings together insightful contributions, especially from Asia and Africa, which will contribute to debate on key global media issues in areas as journalism reporting and the representation of issues as conflict, extremism and terrorism, as well as important matters of our time as social media and fake news practice and their implications."
—Salvatore Scifo, Ph.D., *Bournemouth University, United Kingdom*

"An insightful volume which interrogates the nuances of representation within cultural and comparative contexts, and illuminates some historical perceptions through contemporary prisms."
—Prof. Nosa Owens-Ibie, *Acting Vice Chancellor, Caleb University, Lagos, Nigeria, and Secretary General, Association of Communication Scholars & Professionals of Nigeria (ACSPN)*

"This book strikes at the core of media representation in a global context. Through bold and insightful articles from scholars from different part of the world, it examines critical historical and contemporary issues in media representation. Clearly, it is a great resource for those interested in the interplay between the media and the global society."
—Bumni Makinwa, Ph.D., CEO, *AUNIQUEI Communication for Leadership, and formerly Africa Regional Director, United Nations Population Fund (UNFPA)*

"This book brings refreshing perspectives on perennial and emerging concerns about media and communication in societies from different parts of the world. The writers contend with these global imperatives from their peculiar local contexts. They shine a light on new opportunities for democratised access to the media, appraise prospects offered to otherwise marginalised demographic groups, and focus on the pressing issues of reliable reporting as a means of tackling diverse forms of insecurities. Through this volume, Ngwainmbi and the team of writers confront the techno-glorious promises of a more equitable global media scape. The conditions under which these promises are feasible are left for you to find out. An insightful read!"

—Oluyinka Esan, Ph.D., *Reader in Media & Film, School of Media and Film,*
University of Winchester

"This book offers a timely contribution to the understanding of the dynamics of global media representation and perception in a new era undermined by the unprecedented connectivity, both symbolically and physically, in human history. Instead of repeating a technical-driven globalization illusion, this book offers a collection of wonderful works to map the diversity of localization in which technological adoption interacts with the changing cultural and social patterns... It is indeed an inspiring work for international communication research and practice across the globe."

—Deqiang Ji, *Associate Professor at Communication University of China;*
Vice Chair, International Communication Section, IAMCR;
Editor-in-chief, China Media Research,
www.ChinaMediaResearch.cn

"A very welcome addition to the literature on globalization of media and communication. What distinguishes this valuable collection is its focus on the global South."

—Daya Thussu, *author of* International Communication: Continuity and Change
& *Professor of International Communication, Hong Kong Baptist University*

Emmanuel K. Ngwainmbi
Editor

Media in the Global Context

Applications and Interventions

Editor
Emmanuel K. Ngwainmbi
Charlotte, NC, USA

ISBN 978-3-030-26449-9   ISBN 978-3-030-26450-5   (eBook)
https://doi.org/10.1007/978-3-030-26450-5

This Palgrave Macmillan imprint is published by the registered company Springer Nature
Switzerland AG
The registered company address is: Gewerbestrasse 11, 6330 Cham, Switzerland

FOREWORD

Various media are the conduits through which we gain access to the world around us. Consider this, without media we would have no idea what is happening with the elections of world leaders. We would be virtually clueless about the full value and expanse of commercial products created in other countries. Our knowledge of cultural nuances throughout the world would be limited to whatever was brought back from individual journeys to other countries. Media are our portals to knowledge and information across the globe. Even still, that information is steeped in the political, socioeconomic, communal, cultural, and communicative complexities of the convergent media that bring us the stories about these other worlds.

Emmanuel Ngwainmbi's book *Media in the Global Context: Applications and Interventions* is an ambitious undertaking that seeks to explore uses of global media globalization for a range of purposes. To appreciate the scope of this volume one merely needs to contemplate the intricacies of media in each respective country. Each nation has thousands of traditional, and exponentially more, contemporary social media channels. These include television, radio, film, and print journalism. They also include digital media channels that prior to the 1990s had not been a factor. Some have restrictions on what can and cannot be publicly said about the government. Those countries with a totalitarian regime constrict how or whether the truth reaches citizens. Even still, there are those who use the tool of the internet as an apparatus to terrify others. Regardless of the teleological ends, media are imbued with certain key characteristics. It is designed to be an open and neutral system that is used for distributing dedicated and therefore socially, politically, and relationally particular information. There are distinctive features of contemporary global media that make it far more compelling than the media of the 1970s and 1980s.

Specifically there are three distinct aspects of contemporary global media that inhabit the core of the text you hold in your hands. These features of a mediated information society might be best described as functions:

- Global Media as neutral and diffuse
- Global Media as transformative
- Global Media as a global germ

GLOBAL MEDIA AS NEUTRAL AND DIFFUSE

It seems odd in a book like this one to even form one's lips to say that global media is neutral given the sociopolitical and economic tensions at work in media development, policy, and distribution. The debates on global media endlessly situate government, corporation, and personal interests in an impossible triangle of consumerism and politics. This reminds me of the old debate about firearms that starts something like this: "Guns don't kill people. People kill people." Even as a gun owner it is hard to say this with a straight face, knowing that the absence of guns owned by citizens may not end violence but it will significantly stem everyday senseless violence among citizens. The mere presence of global media permits the spreading of information at rates that are fast and often out of the control of otherwise hegemonic fascist states. On the one hand, to say that global media is neutral is to say that information or truth is also neutral. On the other hand, it can be argued that the global media's tug of war with truth and propaganda is because of the government-corporation-personal interest triangle rather than something that is endemic within media as a conduit for sharing the truths of lived experiences. In other words, we just use media that way. No matter what perspective aligns with your own it is clear that the real issue is, what people do with media rather than what media does to them. Media is an institution whose agenda is set by the ongoing priorities and politics. As you read this book and are introduced to the discussions about terrorism and media, it is striking that media are used as conduits for multiple discourses that seek to convey meanings to specified audiences, some-times for nefarious purposes intended to dominate others. The conver-gence of media via different media channels such as radio, internet, and television can intensify the rhetoric in a way that regularizes privilege and dominance. Global media are only as neutral as the people who regulate it, and yet media are always widely distributed once information hits the internet.

GLOBAL MEDIA AS TRANSFORMATIVE

Media is not always used for dispatching misbehavior, violence, or terror. It may also be used to inspire, uplift, or bring hope. Although this book examines global media and fake news, community disintegration, terror, and contested space, there is also a countervailing set of messages here about the yearning for an ethical space that normalizes and embraces humanity and equity. There is a transformative quality to global media, perhaps more so than any other kind of media. The global media offer a portal for seeing the rest of the world. It awakens curiosity about how other individuals and families live, how regimes operate, how global business functions, and how other cultures sustain their identities. To the individual, no matter where one lives in the world, digital media is the synecdoche for the great expanse of opportunity and technological abun-dance, often implying the question, "If I could share a message with the whole world what would I say." The transformative capacity of the global media is awe-inspiring, especially when used to improve life.

GLOBAL MEDIA AS A GERM

When the media does not improve life, it is like a germ. A germ is a seedling. It is something that is innocuous until placed within conditions that help it to spread. In the same way that germs are invasive and often invisible, the stealth qualities of global media can often leave us wonder-ing whose intrusive agenda is being proposed. A prime example of this is the way in which US President Donald Trump has used media to sig-nal his hyperactive conservative, misogynist, and racially xenophobic val-ues. Even as US citizens seek, refuge from the vile nature of President Trump's discourse the global media constantly reminds us that the more egregious politics of Trump's regime seem to have been heavily influ-enced by Trump's relationship with Russian president Vladimir Putin.

It is through the global media's setting of its agenda that any chance of focusing on any of Trump's redeeming qualities is intercepted by the barrage of press coverage and political standpoints concerning Trump's private meetings with Putin. Without repeated coverage of this relationship, the average citizen would have either forgotten or moved on from further curiosities about this clandestine meeting. Now, with the stoking of this fire, Americans are stirred up about Trump's alleged disloyalties, or at least his suspicious dealings with one of the United States' known enemies. Of course, President Trump would like US citizens to believe there is no Russian interference of the US presidential election and that any relationship with Putin is non-consequential and miscellaneous. Naturally, the socioeconomic implications of a Russian alliance leave citizens less than satisfied with Trump's casual dismissal of the meetings. Nonetheless, the influence of global media makes it virtually impossible for Trump to escape scrutiny over this decision. We are reminded once again that the information society that is principally responsible for the success of global media has shifted power to citizens to directly and forcefully interrogate the state apparatus. That is a powerful tool in a democratic society, but not so much in an autocratic one where citizens are disallowed from questioning authority. The differing geopolitical contexts must not be lost on the reader. What *Media in the Global Context: Applications and Interventions* shows us is how the changing conditions from one global media habitat to another shapes the discourse and outcomes for citizens.

CONCLUSION

When operating at its optimum global media are useful for intercepting and/or troubling institutional processes that undermine or debilitate communities.

The most powerful aspect of the internet is its ability to be used as a multifaceted instrument. The Global media have been an economic growth engine stimulated by a world economy constantly in search of consumers. It is also often a space unfettered by localized restraints. Consequently, it can be used for any and every kind of personal, political, social, and economic interest. The three functions of global media listed here are clearly not an exhaustive set. A citizenry that is able to use global media to retrieve custody over meanings, to take agency in deciding its future, and to interrogate dominance is a privileged one.

This book shows us that not all citizens are this fortunate. Some are terrorized and some live within the bounds of contested spaces on a daily basis. Some do their best to manage the impacts on their families, communities, and identities via media. Unfortunately, the sober reality is that there are technological deficits as there are deficits in our lived experience that continue to limit the embrace of our humanity.

Cincinati, USA   Ronald L. Jackson II

Dr. Ronald L. Jackson II is an immediate past President of the National Communication Association, Professor of communication, former Dean of the McMicken College of Arts & Sciences at the University of Cincinnati (UC), and an internationally renowned identity scholar and sought after speaker. He is an award-winning author of more than 75 publications related to the study of masculinity, identity negotiation, race, and culture. He has published 15 books including his most recent books *Interpreting Tyler Perry* (with Jamel Bell) and the 2014 International Comic-con Will Eisner award-winning book *Black Comics: Politics of Race and Representation* (with Sheena Howard). His book with Kimberly Moffitt and Simone Puff about the award-winning TV show Scandal—*Gladiators in Suits: Race, Gender, and the Politics of Representation in Scandal*—is forthcoming with Syracuse University Press in Summer 2019. Ron earned all degrees in communication (with a specialty in organizational and cultural communication). He received a B.A. and M.A. from University of Cincinnati, In addition, a Ph.D. from Howard University. He has held faculty appointments at Penn State University and University of Illinois prior to joining the faculty at University of Cincinnati.

CONTENTS

xi

NOTES ON CONTRIBUTORS

Adebayo Fayoyin is a Senior Lecturer at the School of Public Health, University of the Witwatersrand, Johannesburg South Africa. He has 30 years of professional experience in media relations, policy advocacy and health communication having worked for development agencies such as UNFPA, UNICEF and USAID at national and international levels, and over 20 years of full-time and honorary teaching and research experience in tertiary institutions and professional organizations in Nigeria, Malawi, Kenya, and South Africa. Fayoyin has vast experience in high-level policy advocacy and has implemented public and political outreaches during national, regional and global conferences. A certified trainer, the author has designed and implemented over 100 professional training courses in public communication and social and behavior change communication, he has designed and implemented nearly 100 professional training courses in public communication and social and behavior change communication and published up to 50 case studies on various health and development issues. He is on the editorial board of several journals including *Communication Cultures in Africa*, *Journal of Population Studies*, *Communication Cultures in Africa* and *African Journal of Opinion*. He has a Ph.D. in Communication and Language Arts, and other degrees in international law and diplomacy, public policy and management and strategic management.

Mahmoud M. Galander is an Associate Professor of communication in the Mass Communication Department of Qatar University. He is the founding member of the Arab European Association of Communication Educators (AREACORE), and the chair of the Islam and Media Working Group of the International Association of Media and Communication Research (IAMCR). He has contributed to the World Journalism Project, which researches journalism status around the world, and remains an active member of the Arab-US Association of Communication Education (AUSACE). Dr. Galander is the author of several English and Arabic mass media books, including *Mass Media in Sudan: Towards a History of Media Politics Interplay*, and has contributed chapters and articles on media and politics in Arabic and English books and journals.

Kehbuma Langmia is a Fulbright Scholar and Chair in the Department of Strategic, Legal and Management Communication, School of Communications, Howard University. Langmia who received the doctorate from the Mass Communication and Media Studies Program at Howard University in 2006 has extensive knowledge in Information Communication Technology, Intercultural Communication and Social Media. He has published 11 books, 14 books chapters, and 9 peer-reviewed journal articles nationally and internationally. Professor Langmia's books include *Globalization and Cyber Culture: An Afrocentric Perspective* and *Social Media: Culture and Identity* and *Social Media: Pedagogy and Practice* co-edited with Tia Tyree. He has written on topics such as media and technology in emerging African democracies, rhetorical traditions of communication within 'Black Thinking', learning techniques, globalization, and traditional cultures.

Seseer Mou-Danha is a doctoral student and instructor at North Dakota State University. She is an expert in media analyses and her research focuses specifically on crisis and terrorism reports, as well as how organizations use external media strategically. Seseer holds a Master's degree in Media Studies from Western Michigan University and a Bachelor's degree in Human Communication from Bowen University Nigeria. She is a member of the National Communication Association, Central States Communication Association, and Kentucky Conference on Health Communication. She has co-authored publications including Communication for development: Strategic adaptations and historical iterations in *Journal of Development Communication*, and Peace, security and sustainable national development in Nigeria in the *International Journal of Peace and Conflict Studies*. She is the recipient of academic awards including 3-Minute Thesis Competition, Preliminary Round at

North Dakota State University and an Honorary Student Leadership Award from Western Michigan University. Seseer has worked as a research consultant for several organizations, in public relations and event planning roles, and as a reporter.

Muiru Ngugi teaches at the School of Journalism and Mass Communication, University of Nairobi. He studied at the Kenya Institute of Mass Communication (KIMC), University of Wales Cardiff, UK, George Mason University and at Emory University where he obtained a Ph.D. in Liberal Arts. A former Carnahan Post-Doctoral Teaching Fellow at Washington and Jefferson College, Pennsylvania, United States, he is also a former Chevening Scholar at the University of Wales, Cardiff. He has taught at Daystar University, George Mason University, Emory University, Washington and Jefferson College, Truman State University, St Paul's University and at the University of Nairobi. He is a former board member of the Media Council of Kenya and Chair of its Training and Accreditation Committee and has been a consulting editor for numerous organizations including the World Bank and the Kenya government. A former journalist with the Kenya News Agency and at the Weekly Review, his journalism has appeared in many publications around the world. His articles have been published in numerous refereed academic journals including *Africa Media Review*, *Queen: Journal of Rhetoric*, *Equid Novi: African Journalism Studies*, *Media Development*, amongst others. He has been a co-editor of two books and has contributed chapters in more than five books, including an encyclopedia.

Emmanuel K. Ngwainmbi who has a Ph.D. in Human Communication Studies currently teaches global media studies, mass communication, and media law in the Department of Communication Studies at the University of North Carolina, Charlotte (UNCC). Prior to joining UNCC, he has held faculty appointments at the George Washington University, St. Thomas University, Morgan State University, Jackson State University, Grambling State University, Elizabeth City State University, Florida Memorial College among others. An international communication expert with some 40 years' experience in teaching, management, media, and cultural awareness training, he has successfully managed communication projects for more than twelve inter-governmental organizations, international development, and financial institutions such as Bank of America, African Development Bank, Bank of America, and Wells Fargo. A tenured full professor in several universities in the United States, he often lectures in Asia, Africa, Central America, and Europe. Professor Ngwainmbi has authored 16 books and over 200 white papers, scholarly articles, and his works have been translated into eight major languages. He has contributed content in media handbooks and encyclopedia. He serves on 12 boards dedicated to global peace and on the Editorial Boards of 15 peer-reviewed academic journals, including the Global Listening Center, the Journal of Media and Society, Journal of Development & Communication Studies, and Athens Journal of Media and Communication. He is considered as one of the leading scholars in strategic communication and public advocacy pertaining to emerging global economies and development institutions.

Blessing E. Okafor is an instructor in the Department of Communication at North Dakota State University. Okafor holds a master's degree in the English Language from the University of Lagos and a bachelor's degree in English Language and Literature from Nnamdi Azikiwe University (Nigeria). She is a member of the National Communication Association, Central States Communication Association, and Mixed Methods International Research Association. Her research interests include workplace relationships, organizational dissent, organizational leadership, employee wellbeing, and strategic communication. Her research on the influence of temperament and leader-member-exchange quality on employees' use of upward dissent strategies received a top four paper award in the Organizational and Professional Communication Division of the Central States Communication Association 2019 conference, and her research on Recent research on dissent in organizational settings: She continues to explore various expressions of dissent in verbal expressions and violent actions by individuals and groups including terrorists.

Charles Okigbo who has a Ph.D. in Journalism and a Ph.D. in Educational Leadership from Southern Illinois University, Carbondale, teaches journalism and strategic communication in the Department of Communication at North Dakota State University, Fargo, ND, where he also directs research in media coverage of election campaigns and the uses of advertising and public relations in corporate and political communication. His other academic interests are in mixed methods applications in studying social problems, explorations of framing in crisis reporting, and the broader applications of communication in national development. His recent publications are on strategic health communication in urban contexts and strategic political communication in Africa. His teaching experiences include full or part-time instructional positions at the University of Nigeria, the University of Lagos, and Daystar University (Nairobi). Professor Okigbo had been the Registrar of the Advertising Practitioners Council of Nigeria (APCON) (Lagos) and the Executive Coordinator of the African Council for Communication Education (ACCE) (Nairobi). His publications have featured in *Africa Media Review, Communication Educator, Communication Yearbook, International Communication Gazette, Journal of Communication* (Germany), and *Journal of Development Communication, Journalism Quarterly* now *Journalism and Mass Communication Quarterly* (JMCQ), and *Media Development*, among others. Professor Okigbo was Executive Coordinator of the African Council for Communication Education (ACCE) and Registrar of the Advertising Practitioners Council of Nigeria (APCON). He is passionate about promoting collaborative programs that bring communication scholars and practitioners together to address pressing problems of society, using both theoretical knowledge and experiential learning. Echoing Curt Lewin, he avers there is nothing more practical than a good theory.

Wei Sun is an Assistant Professor in the Department of Communication, Culture and Media Studies at Howard University, Washington, DC. Her research interests include intercultural communication, new media studies, and health communication. Dr. Sun teaches doctoral seminars in Intercultural Communication, Qualitative Research Methods, Social Media, Communication and Culture, Diversity & Leadership, Community & Public Health, etc. Her publications have appeared on *The Howard Journal of Communications, Intercultural Communication Studies*, and *World Communication*. Her scholarly works have been included in several books, such as Bilge, Nurhayat, and María Inés Marino (Eds.). *Reconceptualizing New Media and Intercultural Communication in a Networked Society.* IGI Global, 2018; William, Keisha M., and Morant, Frances S. (Eds.). *Reifying Women's Experiences with Invisible Illness: Illusion, Delusions, Reality.* Lexington Books, 2017; Cheong, Pauline H., J. Martin, Judith N., and McFadden, Leah (Eds.). *New Media and Intercultural Communication.* Peter Lang, 2012.

Janice Hua Xu is an associate professor of Communication at Holy Family University, Pennsylvania. She holds a Ph.D. in communication from University of Illinois at Urbana-Champaign. Before college teaching in the United States, she worked as a lecturer of international communication in Peking University in China, a news assistant at *New York Times* Beijing Bureau, and radio broadcaster at Voice of America, Washington, DC. Her research interests include culture and communication technology, media globalization, and grassroots activism. She has published articles in *Media, Culture, & Society*, *Global Media Journal* (Canadian Edition), *Journalism Studies, International Journal of Communication, Telematics and Informatics, Studies in Visual Arts and Communication*, and contributed chapters to multiple communication studies books, published by Routledge, Sage, Peter Lang, Taylor & Francis, Indiana University Press, Hong Kong University Press among others. She is a recipient of the Pennsylvania State University Authur W. Page Center Legacy Scholar Grant for multimedia teaching in public communication, and served as expert witness in US District Court Southern District of New York.

LIST OF FIGURES

LIST OF TABLES

PART I

Online Media, Political Change and Nationalism

CHAPTER 1

Terrorism as Media Propaganda: A Theoretical Approach

Charles Okigbo and Blessing E. Okafor

INTRODUCTION

Terrorism, derived from the Latin term terrere, *to frighten*, refers to the strategic use of intentionally perpetrated violence through lethal instruments of warfare with the ostensible goal of creating fear and panic to achieve predetermined political, religious, and ethnically oriented goals. Its typical method is the unleashing of violence against vulnerable or soft targets, although military posts have not been spared, as was the case with the Beirut 1983 bombing that claimed the lives of 241 US and 58 French soldiers who were peacekeepers. The primary goal of terrorism is to attract public attention by the violent acts as well as media pronouncements that precede or come after the attacks. Terrorism is primarily a communication of an unusual nature because there is always a sender or messenger, a message, a target audience, and some feedback. Schmid and de Graaf (1982) are convinced that terrorism is not only an act of

C. Okigbo (✉) · B. E. Okafor
Department of Communication, North Dakota State University,
Fargo, ND, USA
e-mail: charles.okigbo@ndsu.edu

B. E. Okafor
e-mail: blessing.okafor@ndsu.edu

© The Author(s) 2019
E. K. Ngwainmbi (ed.), *Media in the Global Context*,
https://doi.org/10.1007/978-3-030-26450-5_1

communication but that for the terrorist, what matters the most is the message, not the victims.

Because terrorists care more about the message they transmit through their attacks, and how the public or groups interpret this message, they pay considerable attention to the dramatic and visual impacts of their attacks. Many terrorist attacks are staged to achieve a high visual effect and command full attention from the public. Alex Schmid (2005) averred that terrorism is fundamentally a communicative act whereby the victims of the violence serve as a channel for the message. Terrorist communicators perceive that the louder and more impactful the news, the more successful the attack. Victims are usually people, as such within the context of communication they can be considered as message or messenger (channel). According to Argomaniz and Lynch (2018, p. 491), the victims of terrorism are the messengers for the violent act even if they are rarely the focus of our investigative efforts. When Boko Haram terrorists attacked a Nigerian high school and kidnapped 220 female students, these victims were messengers, also a message from the terrorists who were preaching that Western education is "haram" (evil) with life and death consequences for young people going to school.

Whether victims of terrorist attacks are messengers or messages, the goals are usually fear, intimidation, anxiety, and insecurity. There is always a clear strategy on how to maximize the impact of the message through the messenger for Crenshaw (1998) has explained that terrorists do not communicate nonsensically. Terrorists are strategic and careful in their plans and actions, even when the end may be suicidal. Communication has an intrinsic value for terrorists whose aim, according to Bocksette (2008, p. 8) "is to exploit the media to achieve maximum attainable publicity as an amplifying force multiplier to influence the targeted audiences." The mission of terrorists is to influence target audiences through their attacks on the victims. Addressing their mission through communication qualifies terrorists as strategic communicators. If we accept strategic communication as the "purposeful use of communication by an organization to fulfill its missions" (Hallahan et al. 2007), it is easy to agree with Rothenberger (2015, p. 487) that strategic communication can be applied to terrorism discourse. Terrorist attacks portend significant communication messages not only in the terrorist act itself but also in "the continued communication about it, (and) the interpretations and explanations (that) are important issues for terrorist groups." In attaching meaning to terrorist acts, these acts become symbols laden with powerful messages for specific members of the target audience. The discourse of terrorism as strategic communication touches on many aspects of the phenomenon, and not surprisingly, it continues to attract interdisciplinary attention worldwide.

CONTEXT

Terrorism is so widely perceived by different groups that it defies consensual definitions. It is perpetrated by actors without any ideologies, suicide groups without clear directions, well-organized global networks of highly trained professionals, and occasionally by sovereign states that want to teach their enemies lessons of life and death. A common effect of many terrorist attacks is the crisis that ensues from attacks and resulting discussions and interpretations by the media and influencers. Terrorists rely on violent attacks to communicate fear, intimidation, and insecurity. As the cumulative evidence from the National Consortium for the Study of Terrorism and Responses to Terrorism (START) has shown, terrorist violence remains extraordinarily high compared to historical trends. Ending or curtailing terrorism will require more communication than military intervention, hence the need to understand terrorism as strategic communication.

Terrorism is a complex phenomenon to unravel, and its discourse deserves more attention than researchers, governments and the media have accorded so far. It is an age-old problem which continues to evolve even in disciplines such as political science, security studies, and communication. The wide-ranging definitions, explanations, and exemplars of terrorism are commonly encountered in many subjects.

The complexity of the concept of terrorism underlines some of the current discussions of "the complex relationship between radicalization, narratives of victimhood, and political violence" (Argomaniz and Lynch 2018, p. 491). Terrorism is not a monopoly of non-state actors, and thus we need to pay closer attention to "state targeting of combatants – for states can act as terrorists just as non-state actors can" (Taylor 2018, p. 591). As a complex phenomenon, terrorism takes on different features, and it continues to evolve depending on the driving motives of perpetrators, some of who are local individuals, lone attackers, or members of international networks. Although ever-growing and changing, it still has some robust features. The National Consortium for the Study of Terrorism and Responses to Terrorism (START 2018) reported three consecutive years (2015–2017) of declining numbers of attacks and deaths worldwide since terrorist violence reached its peak of nearly 17,000 attacks and 45,000 total deaths in 2014. The scenario of incidents was complicated by the deadliest terrorist incident in 2017 that took place in Mogadishu, Somalia and claimed more than 580 lives and wounded 300 people. Since 1970, more than 180,000 terrorist attacks have been recorded since 9/11 (START 2018). Despite concerted efforts by some countries and global coalitions to prevent and counteract terrorism through military and public diplomacy operations, the results are not inspiring. Overall, terrorist attacks remain extraordinarily high when compared to historical trends dating back to the decade before the 9/11 attack in the United States.

An essential justification for examining terrorism as strategic communication is the reality that terrorist attacks have become part of our contemporary political, sociocultural, and communication landscape. We cannot undermine terror-based violence because it represents the assailant's "aspirations" even if these are warped. Barlow (2016) has shown that even when there seems to be a military victory over terrorist groups, it is often temporary, as they usually regroup, rebrand, take on new names, transform themselves, and become even more dangerous. Understanding terrorism as strategic communication prepares us to employ more communication strategies as counteractive measures and think beyond military tactics. To this end, Barlow (2016, p. 20) recommends that successful counter-terrorist strategies must include methods and means which are "political and economical in nature, as you cannot kill an aspiration" with mere physical force.

Overview of Recent Global Terrorist Acts

There is an undeniable religious favor as well as a geographical dimension to recent terrorist attacks. The data from the Global Terrorism Database (START 2018) show that there are about two dozen terrorist groups worldwide and of these, 11 are the most active; six of these most active accounted for more than 3800 attacks that killed about 16,000 people in 2017. The Middle East (with North Africa) and South Asia accounted for more than 7200 of the 10,900 terrorist attacks of 2017.

The Global Terrorism Data Base (START 2018) further shows that more than half of the recent attacks took place in four countries: Iraq (23%), Afghanistan (13%), India (9%), and Pakistan (7%). More than half of all deaths from terrorist attacks occurred in three countries: Iraq (24%), Afghanistan (23%), and Syria (8%). There were 17 lethal terrorist attacks in the United States in 2017, with the deadliest being the Las Vegas incident involving an extremist individual who shot and killed 58 people and wounded 850 others at a country music festival. Lethal terrorist attacks have taken place in these US states California, Colorado, Florida, Kansas, Maryland, Louisiana, New Mexico, New York, Oregon, Tennessee, and Virginia. These incidents and their variability underline the value of seeing terrorism as strategic communication because terrorist acts are local, national, regional, and global phenomena, commanding interdisciplinary and worldwide interests leading to new conceptualizations and reimagining.

TERRORISM REIMAGINED IN ACADEMIA

The burgeoning interest in the field of terrorism scholarship has attracted multidisciplinary approaches that underline the importance that various groups of people, especially researchers, policymakers, non-profit organizational leaders, and journalists, among others, have attributed to this complex subject. It is indeed a complex area where such difficult concepts as counter-radicalization, de-radicalization, resistance, disengagement, perpetrators, radicalization, reborn anew, victims et cetera, reign supreme. Although terrorism is a common term in popular discussions and academic writing these days, it has not become more comfortable to have consensual meanings for it because different users of the term understand it differently depending on their contexts and situations. Three ways of reimagining terrorism today involve the standard approach, the first of which is seeing it in the violent acts of intimidation and instilling fear by perpetrators; secondly, in the borderless reach of the media in making terrorism potentially ubiquitous; and thirdly in the expanded view of using the term as a metaphor for adverse effects as when we say that some financial reporting is terrorism. All these reimagining scenarios are relevant in explaining terrorism as strategic communication.

Terrorism as Violent Behavior

Another key needed to unlock the mystery behind terrorist behavior has been offered by Krueger (2007) who explained it as intentional, politically motivated violence that is carried out by sub-state organizations and individuals to sway an audience other than the immediate victims. The US Federal Bureau of Investigation (FBI) defined terrorism as the illegal utilization of force or brutality against a target audience or property to instill fear and intimidation for some political or social gain (Tiefenbrun 2003).

Victims of terrorist attacks are an important party to the tragedy, and so are all those associated with them, particularly their families, communities, and governments. Thus, understanding the experience of victimhood in this context is vital if we are to comprehend the entirety of the complexity of terrorism (Argomaniz and Lynch 2018, p. 492; Hanle 1989).

Some Sources of Terrorism

The root causes of terrorism are poverty, political extremism, lack of education, economic deprivation, racism, fanaticism, extremism (Krueger 2007). Following the unprecedented terrorist attacks on American soil on September 11, 2001 (known as 9/11) some well-known public figures including President George W. Bush had reported that the root of terrorism is economical and political development, but much of the extant literature shows that there is no significant connection between terrorism and the different income measures (Enders et al. 2014). Remarkably, Krueger (2007) explains that developing countries do not have higher terrorism attacks than rich countries. Wealthy countries such as the United States, Germany, and France have cases of internal or localized terrorism, of which one of the most serious and lethal was the Timothy McVeigh bombing of the Federal Building in Oklahoma City on April 19, 1995, which killed 165 people, including 19 children. However, rich countries seem to be the focal point of transnational terrorist attacks (Abadie 2006) because the greatest danger is from the enemies outside rather than the dissidents within. In this age of global media, the enemies outside a country try to maximize the communicative impact of their actions, hence global and virtual press is a new way to understand terrorism as a form of strategic communication.

TERRORISM AND VIRTUAL MEDIA

Since the infamous 9/11 attack by Al Qaida, and more recently the tragic exploits of ISIS in Syria, Boko Haram in Nigeria, and the bombing of Charlie Hebdo Magazine in Paris, we have seen terrorists taking advantage of virtual reality to extend their reach to the global audience. Terrorism is now virtual reality, and terrorist groups have become very adept at using virtual media with its promise of instant global reach and making communication borderless and ubiquitous.

The digital dimension makes the new age of terrorism a virtual reality because of the speed at which terrorist attacks can be reported and the fear of further attacks. Not only can terrorist attacks spread to other locations like a virus, we are faced with the possibility of computer viruses shutting down electric grids and financial infrastructures in many countries. Our mechanical apparatus and the complex infrastructure of urban living are now more vulnerable to terrorist attacks than ever before because of the possibility of staging attacks from remote locations. The threats and accompanying fears are more devastating because some of the suspects are not individual terrorists but in some cases are state actors who have turned perpetrators, supposedly in the interests of their government. This new reality is more frightening because of the real danger of attacking from remote and distant locations, the reality of unimaginable global reach, and the high possibility of the involvement of state actors. This new reality has taken terrorism to a new level.

The malicious cyberattacks at Sony's film and television studio in November 2014, which was believed to be related to its planned release of a politically sensitive movie "The Interview" was believed to have been masterminded and carried out by North Korea. The movie was a raunchy comedy about an attempt to assassinate the North Korean leader Kim Jung Un. Another example of high-tech terrorism by a state is the Russian attack on the 2016 US presidential election system, which is the equivalent of an "information warfare."

Terrorism as a Metaphor: The third way of reimagining terrorism is the expanded use of the term to denote unpalatable experiences that do not necessarily imply physical or tangible harm as in the reference by Tracy (2012) to the "financial terrorism" that was perpetrated on Greece by the US media. This was during the financial crisis that arose from Greek Premier George Papandreou's handling of the economy. Angered by the alleged conspiracy by international financial institutions and the media against Greece, a criminal complaint of fraud was filed with Greece's Attorney General, likening the Greek debt crisis to a coordinated act of financial terrorism (Tracy 2012, p. 515).

Although the financial crisis and credit problem in Greece in late 2009 and early 2010 was not worse than the terrorist acts in The Netherlands, Ireland, Belgium, Spain, Portugal, and Italy, the major credit agencies colluded to undermine Greek government finances (Tracy 2012, p. 515) and the media framed one of the crisis incorrectly as "Greek contagion," "Greek disease," and Greek people as "Incorrigible." By heightening fears about the Greek financial situation, the media engaged in a kind of journalistic terrorism that did not employ a physically violent act or infrastructural disruption from a remote location.

The society is ill served and indeed suffers when mainstream journalism fails to provide enlightened and ethical coverage, as was the case in the Enron and WorldCom scandals in the United States (McChesney 2004), although that was not financial terrorism. The poor reporting and cooperation in the Greek financial crisis resulted in severe acts of economic terrorism. In this new guise, terrorism is no longer just those destructive acts by rebellious dissidents or lone-wolf attackers but it now applies to how the media can plant fear and anxiety in people's minds depending on the way journalists frame their coverage. International media coverage of Africa falls under this mode of deliberate adverse reporting to paint the subject in a negative light—journalistic terrorism. No wonder the standard journalistic practices by the Western media provide a distorted view of Africa (Hawk 1992; Bunce et al. 2017). This failure of journalism has significant consequences for how essential members of the public, locally and internationally, perceive the situation. The results can be as lethal as the effects of some terrorist attacks.

Reimagined terrorism, which provides an expanded interpretation of the term, deserves a more creative strategic approach in the package of response tools and mechanisms. The meaning of terrorism in society is increasing, hence we should reassess our approaches to containing and countering terrorism in all its forms and ramifications. Unfortunately, as Max Taylor (2018, p. 590) observed, "our collective response to the management of terrorism has not been strikingly successful, given that terrorism seems to flourish and grow despite the enormous resources devoted to countering it." Terrorists have become stunningly strategic, and they display high levels of technical sophistication, patience, discipline, and ingenuity, as the 9/11 Commission Report showed. They are increasingly becoming more adept at utilizing strategic communication to achieve their nefarious goals. The situation calls for strategic dialogue to be deployed in counter-terrorism initiatives and organizational-management efforts to prevent terrorist attacks, and equally importantly, to contain any crises arising from terrorist attacks. In the next section, we explain strategic communication in more detail before providing an outline for crisis communication that can be useful in managing situations that arise from terrorist attacks.

STRATEGIC COMMUNICATION

Many terrorists are admittedly strategic because their activities show long-term planning, patience, expert skills, networking acumen, disguises and subterfuge, decoy, and ploy; indeed, their actions show both an "art and a science," which are the hallmarks of strategy (Okigbo 2014). If terrorists are unabashedly strategic because of their uses of planning and targeting techniques, their employment of communication approaches is without doubt strategic too because their messages and channels are pre-selected to deliver maximal communication results.

Most human communication is strategic, just as terrorism is planned and not serendipitous. Kellermann (1992, p. 288) explained this by arguing that all communication is strategic because "communication by its very nature, can*not* be strategic." If all communication is strategic, "strategic communication" is "hyper strategic." This is because strategic communication is more explicitly chosen, intentional, thoughtful, and controlled. By nature, our discussion usually has an aim or goal, with possibilities of adjustments in message design and delivery, and some measure of anticipation of response or reaction. Even the purest forms of communication usually have aspects of forethought and control, which make them undeniably planned and not done on the basis of trial and error. The purest forms of terrorism, even when lone-wolf perpetrators execute them have the hallmarks of premeditation and strategic planning. It is unlikely that terrorist groups would engage in violent attacks if there were no media to relay their activities to their target audience.

Terrorist groups strategically attract attention by using "inhumane strategies and daring tactics," "new skills and abilities," even local and international media, in advancing their course" (Polonska-Kimunguyi and Gillespiem 2017, p. 246). Many terrorist groups are adept at using social media to advance their perceptions and gain legitimacy, broaden their support, and appeal emotionally to their target audience, all reflecting mastery of strategic communication skills (Neumann and Smith 2005). Although some international media, such as *France 24* and *Deutsche Welle* may "fall victim to extremists' objectives" and unwittingly become tools in terrorists' propaganda machinery (Polonska-Kimunguyi and Gillespiem 2017, p. 269), local and national media as well as influencers in society are not immune to such exploitation by terrorists who employ strategic communication tactics. Such tactics require research, preplanning, and careful forethought, which are all associated with terrorist operations.

Strategic Communication as Process

Strategic communication involves purposeful messaging to achieve predetermined objectives. It starts with research or surveillance that leads to the selection of message content for packaging and delivery. Evaluation of effectiveness or performance comes at the end, before a new cycle of communication may be reenacted. This is the typical pattern and sequence in communication campaigns, which are the step-by-step implementation of designs aimed at achieving predetermined objectives. Planning, forethought, and research underline strategic communication and communication campaigns. Concerning communication campaigns and the place of research in them, Botan (2006) defined strategic communication as planned communication campaigns that begin and end with research to learn about and understand an organization's public. In addition to learning about the public or targets, people who use strategic communication must be mindful of the best level for pitching or locating their efforts, knowing that there are differences among the levels. Similarly, communication strategists are cognizant of the audience targeted and the impact of communication activities on them.

In discussing the levels used in strategic communication, Okigbo and Onoja (2017, p. 66) explained that "strategic communication applies at the three levels of the interpersonal, group, and mass communication, each involving the setting of goals and the selection of appropriate verbal and nonverbal messages to achieve predetermined targets." Terrorist attacks that are personalized fall within the framework of interpersonal or small group communication; for example, the attack on Charlie Hebdo Magazine in Paris was meant to communicate intimidation to its publisher and his staff at the interpersonal and small group level.

Terrorist groups have mastered what makes for dramatic international news coverage that the global news networks crave, so they capitalize on those to heighten the communication impact referred to as "The CNN Effect." This phenomenon has many interpretations, depending on the context and the user. One interpretation is that it involves live and continuous TV coverage of foreign events capable of influencing government policies, public officials and public opinion (Hess and Kalb 2003). By being strategic in their manipulative use of real-time international journalism, terrorist groups knowingly exercise some influence on governments, business corporations, and public opinion. We can, therefore, state that terrorism is a form of strategic communication.

Indeed, although terrorism is communication, it lacks such desirable attributes as social responsibility and widespread public recognition of its value; hence, it cannot be open or corporate communication (Rada 1985). There are grey areas such as when terrorism can be seen as public or organizational communication. Here are a few examples: North Korea and Russia engaged in undisguised use of terror to strike fear among their enemies abroad by assassinating enemies of the state. In February 2017, two female operatives assassinated Kim Jong-Nam, the half-brother of North Korean leader Kim Jong-un in Kuala Lumpur through poisoning; in March 2018, there was an assassination attempt allegedly by the Russian Government on double agent Sergei Skripal (aged 66) and his daughter Yulia Skripal (aged 33) in Salisbury, a sleepy village in England. By operating so openly and brazenly, those two governments deliberately wanted to send a message to their target, hence they were engaging in some form of public communication. That sort of terrorism by state actors is as strategic as when terrorist groups engage in violent acts against their carefully chosen victims.

STRATEGIC COMMUNICATION'S TWO PARADIGMS: PRESCRIPTIVE AND EMERGENT

Strategic communication is best explained with recourse to two approaches that are the prescriptive approach and the new approach—both of which apply to terrorism as communication. The normative approach is based on the idea that we define our objectives in advance and then select the best communication packages to achieve them, while the new approach holds that we cannot always foresee the path to achieving our objectives ahead of time. These two approaches arose from seeing strategic communication as an aspect of strategic management or the deployment of communication in addressing organizational and institutional objectives and missions.

These two approaches also reflect the two parallel methods of strategy formation, which are (1) deliberate, planned, analytical, and top-down, and (2) more natural, emergent, visionary, and bottom-up process (Cornelissen 2011). In discussing terrorism as strategic communication, the prescriptive approach appears more relevant because terrorist groups engage in extensive planning, with clearly defined objectives, targets, victims, and publicity apparatus. Borrowing from Mintzberg and Waters (1985), Kirk Hallahan (2015, p. 246) explained the prescriptive approach as involving deliberate strategies where "outcomes are clearly specified, and activities are painstakingly planned…." This is the typical method of terrorist groups, with their heavy reliance on careful planning, audience targeting, and media publicity.

With the new approach, we acknowledge that strategies are not always developed according to a master plan but often come from adjustments, adaptations, new threats, and opportunities or even accidental actions (Frandsen and Johansen 2015; Lynch 2012). This is not an absence of a strategy, as much as it is the reliance on our wits and instant learning from unfolding circumstances. It is a new strategy when actions, responses, and new moves evolve as the group engages in strategic education and adjusts to changing conditions (Hallahan 2015). Barlow (2016, p. 16) has recounted how the Boko Haram terrorist group in West Africa having been weakened by superior Nigerian Army firepower "rebranded itself as the Islamic State's West Africa Province (ISWAP)." Boko Haram also adjusted its operational tactics and reached out to the Islamist groups in the Central African Republic and Al-Shabaab in Somalia and the Islamist Allied Defense Force in the Democratic Republic of Congo in response to the changing circumstances of their weakening potency. Those adjustments were made because of their changing fortunes following their routing from their base in Nigeria. That behavior is consistent with Hallahan's belief that terrorist groups have the ability to change their tactics and circumstances on the spur of the moment.

The normative approach is "much more widespread than the emergent perspective," and it represents "what we might call the *archetype…*" (Frandsen and Johansen 2015, p. 231), even though new strategies are now getting due recognition in such areas of communication as public relations, corporate communication, and crisis communication. Since there are no guaranteed results in using strategic communication, one should plan for emergent situations where resulting consequences may not be realized, and make necessary adjustments that fit into new, unexpected realities.

Both prescriptive and emergent strategic communication are relevant in terrorism communication discourse. Terrorists understand that even with all their efforts to plan for maximum damage and maximum publicity some situations are beyond their control, so they are often ready to use a different approach to unleash terror on their victims. Terrorist attacks result in crises of varying degrees of seriousness that range from simple incidents to more complicated conditions such as the 9/11 attacks which had long-lasting repercussions. Terrorism is not only strategic communication, but it is also a special kind of crisis communication because terrorists crave crises at personal/individual and societal levels.

THE COMMUNICATION OF TERRORISM

Crisis communication is inherently strategic because it involves systematically planned and timely dissemination of verbal and nonverbal messages about an unexpected event to the public, to reduce fear and anxiety or to stabilize a situation of disequilibrium. It is known that terrorist attacks usually lead to one form of crisis or another. Sparks et al. (2005) defined crisis communication as the process of using strategically designed messages transmitted through mediated or interpersonal channels to pass across vital information to particular members of the public during a crisis.

Crisis communication enables the audience to become conscious of the evolving situation and consequently to take steps to ensure safety and security. For instance, the specter of unpredictable terrorist attacks in parts of Israel that include Jerusalem and the West Bank has placed the residents in a perpetual state of crisis anticipation. Residents are trained to know how to use emergency communication channels to alert citizens of an incipient danger. As a partner in crisis communication, the government has a towering responsibility to alert its citizens. Governments have specialized roles in mitigating the harmful effects of terrorist attacks from a crisis communication point of view. How about situations where the government or the state is the perpetrator of terror, as the cases with North Korea, Russia, or with the Saudi killing of the *Washington Post* journalist, Jamal Khashoggi? Here, governments must respond strategically to terrorist attacks, which are indeed crisis communication.

Canel and Sanders (2010) studied the response of the government shortly after the terrorist attacks that took place in Madrid (2004) and London (2005) and concluded that terrorist attacks can be crisis communication in three different ways. In the first place, terrorist attacks are vivid crises in that they often command spectacular imagery. Secondly, they have substantial communicative dimensions because terrorists are interested in the impact of their attacks, always aiming at maximal disruption, fear, and, terror. Thirdly, terrorist attacks are aimed at hurting the reputation of specific groups, institutions, and organizations. Terrorist attacks like communication, are a form of crisis communication. Terrorists aim specifically to create panic and crisis while governments work assiduously to assuage the fears and anxiety that those attacks engender.

One of the most enduring images of the 9/11 Terrorist Attack on the World Trade Center was President Bush addressing survivors and sympathizers (and indeed, the whole world, including the terrorists themselves) on the rubbles with these courageous words:

> I can hear you! I can hear you! The rest of the world hears you! Moreover, the people – and the people who knocked these buildings down will hear all of us soon!

This was in response to a rescue worker shouting "I can't hear you!" when the President was speaking to sympathizers and rescue workers, which suggests that certain responses in crises cannot be scripted in advance. President Bush's unscripted but reassuring response to the rescue worker illustrated new strategic connection that was created at the spur of the moment in a crisis.

Crisis communication involves designs for relating to the public before, during and after an adverse event has occurred. Terrorist attacks incite the media and consequently dissemination of information about the attacks in both social and traditional media (Sparks et al. 2005). The widely accepted strategies for crisis communication planning are relevant in using communication for the management of terrorist attacks. The models involve situation analysis, setting clear goals and objectives, selecting communication elements, choosing the appropriate media, developing the messages, planning for feedback and evaluation, and acknowledging the necessity for adjustments following formative assessments, as the implementation unfolds (Fink 2013; Wilcox and Cameron

2012; Wilson and Ogden 2016). Terrorist attacks are designed to create crises that attract as much full attention as possible. Terrorist acts
behoove governments, security agencies, and the media to know how to
counter expected negative impacts of terrorism by employing diplomatic
crises communication planning and management methods. The US
Department of Homeland Security and law enforcement offices across
the US often stage rehearsals to address terrorist attacks.

Having now established that terrorism is strategic communication
because it is prescriptive (planned to achieve predetermined objectives)
but can also be emergent (when it is adjusted on the fly to suit changing
circumstances), we add that terrorism belongs to the area of crisis communication because terrorist groups aim to create fear and tension. It is
the responsibility of governments and civic organizations to mitigate the
harmful consequences of terrorist activities with crises communication
interventions.

We explained the critical steps in communication interventions,
emphasizing the place of research to assess the situation, and establish
what could be achieved.

CONCLUSION

Based on the arguments advanced in this chapter, we deliver these conclusions, (1) Terrorism is a global phenomenon, which is pervasive and
widespread, with no region of the world safe from its devilish clutches,
(2) that terrorist attacks are designed to be strategically communicative
as disrupters of peace and security, and messengers of tension, fear, and
crises, which must be addressed with appropriate strategic communication, prescriptively or emergently, (3) that in strategic communication
verbal and symbolic messages are employed to achieve predetermined
objectives, (4) prescriptive and emergent, strategic communication is
apposite in discussions of terrorism because terrorists are strategic, they
purposefully select their targets, time of attacks, the methods, and the
means that offer them the best opportunities for maximal communication impact, and (5) the terrorist's mantra is often maximum harm, fear,
and publicity.

Terrorist groups are becoming ever more adept in their uses of communication tactics by capitalizing on violence and dramatic events that
meet journalists' criteria for news reporting. Many terrorist groups
choose strategies that ensure media coverage of their attacks, which are

staged ostensibly with predetermined publicity in mind. Terrorist strategists realize that the violence acts they unleash on their targets is an instrument of media publicity and that "the more horrible the atrocity, the more expansive the media coverage" (Rothenberger 2015, p. 488). Terrorist groups use the mass media and other channels of information and influence to get their messages of fear and terror across, capitalizing on the psychological impact of their violent acts. The media and those who comment about, interpret, and explain the physical violence create this psychological impact.

In many cases, the psychological impact is more damaging and fear inducing than the physical abuse itself (Picard 1993). In their clever uses of the mass media and other vehicles for their propaganda and campaign of fear (Gerrits 1992), terrorist groups heighten insecurity and crisis in their target environments. Terrorism is instrumental violence which is designed to induce fear and create crises, hence the need to adopt crises management techniques in preventing and containing it.

It is essential to see that because terrorist groups are strategic in their uses of communication and propaganda, governments and relevant organizations should include strategic communication techniques when designing counter-terrorism interventions. Our understanding and interpretations of terrorism will continue to change with the times, and so should the strategies for addressing it. The recent cases of sovereign states (such as North Korea, Russia, and Saudi Arabia) "terrorizing" their supposed enemies underline the need for continual interrogation of the concept and phenomenon since some of the existing interpretations are inadequate. In this chapter, we have shown that terrorism is pervasive and afflicts all world regions, even if not unilaterally and equivalently. Being such a global phenomenon and of a persistent nature, it is an interdisciplinary concept that is a pertinent subject in communication, political science, security studies, and sociology, among others. We agree with many scholars who argue that terrorists are far from being nonsensical or arbitrary in their use of violence as effective communication to engender fear and create crises. Having laid this foundation for showing that terrorism is prescriptive and emergent strategic communication, future research in this area can more easily explore how different terrorist groups have employed different communication strategies and tactics. Another critical area of future research can be the uses of crisis communication strategies and tactics in counter-terrorism and post-terrorist attack situations.

QUESTIONS FOR DISCUSSION

1. Define and describe various types of terrorism?
2. Which is the most and least impactful form of terrorism in a community and how can the press help minimize the spread of terrorist doctrine?
3. In which ways can terrorism be considered a strategic reporting mechanism?
4. If you were a senior administrator in an organization that is in charge of maintaining homeland security, how would you apply a communication program to prevent terrorist acts around the organization?

Assignment on Terrorism as Strategic Communication: *Working in a small group or by yourself, identify a recent media report of a terrorist attack and summarize the story in 200 words. Identify the aspects of this story and the attack that support the view that terrorists are strategic communicators. Use references from this chapter, where appropriate.*

REFERENCES

Abadie, A. (2006). Poverty, Political Freedom, and the Roots of Terrorism. *The American Economic Review, 96*(2), 50–56.

Argomaniz, J., & Lynch, O. (2018). Introduction to the Special Issue: The Complexity of Terrorism—Victims, Perpetrators, and Radicalization. *Studies in Conflict & Terrorism, 41*(7), 491–506.

Barlow, E. (2016). The Rise and Fall—And Rise Again of Boko Haram. *Harvard International Review, 37*(4), 16–20.

Bocksette, C. (2008, December). *Jihadist Terrorist Use of Strategic Communication Management Techniques.* The George C. Marshall European Center for Security Studies, The Marshall Center Occasional Paper Series, Number 20. Garmisch-Partenkirchen, Germany.

Botan, C. (2006). Grand Strategy, Strategy, and Tactics in Public Relations. In C. Botan & V. Hazleton (Eds.), *Public Relations Theory II* (pp. 223–247). New York and London: Routledge.

Bunce, M., Franks, S., & Paterson, C. (Eds.). (2017). *Africa's Media Image in the 21st Century: From the 'Heart of Darkness' to 'Africa Rising'.* London: Routledge.

Canel, M. J., & Sanders, K. (2010). Crisis Communication and Terrorist Attacks: Framing a Response to the 2004 Madrid Bombings and 2005 London

Bombings. In W. T. Coombs & S. J. Holladay (Eds.), *The Handbook of Crisis Communication* (pp. 449–466). Chichester: Wiley-Blackwell.

Cornelissen, J. (2011). *Corporate Communication: A Guide to Theory and Practice* (3rd ed.). London: Sage.

Crenshaw, M. (1998). The Logic of Terrorism: Terrorist Behavior as a Product of Strategic Choice. In W. Reich (Ed.), *Origins of Terrorism: Psychologies, Ideologies, Theologies, States of Mind* (pp. 7–24). Washington, DC: The Woodrow Wilson Center Press.

Enders, W., Hoover, G., & Sandler, T. (2014). The Changing Nonlinear Relationship Between Income and Terrorism. *The Journal of Conflict Resolution, 60*(2), 195–225.

Fink, S. (2013). *Crisis Communication: The Definitive Guide to Managing the Message*. New York: McGraw-Hill.

Frandsen, F., & Johansen, W. (2015). The Role of Communication Executives in Strategy and Strategizing. In D. Holtzhausen & A. Zerfass (Eds.), *The Routledge Handbook of Strategic Communication* (pp. 229–243). New York: Routledge.

Gerrits, R. P. J. M. (1992). Terrorists' Perspectives: Memoirs. In D. L. Paletz & A. P. Schmid (Eds.), *Terrorism and the Media* (pp. 29–61). Newbury Park, CA: Sage.

Hallahan, K. (2015). Organizational Goals and Communication Objectives in Strategic Communication. In D. Holtzhausen & A. Zerfass (Eds.), *The Routledge Handbook of Strategic Communication* (pp. 244–266). New York: Routledge.

Hallahan, K., Holtzhausen, D., Van Ruler, B., Verčič, D., & Sriramesh, K. (2007). Defining Strategic Communication. *International Journal of Strategic Communication, 1*(1), 3–35.

Hanle, D. J. (1989). *Terrorism: The Newest Face of Warfare*. Elmsford, NY: Pergamon Press.

Hawk, B. G. (Ed.). (1992). *Africa's Media Image*. Westport, CT and London: Praeger.

Hess, S., & Kalb, M. (Eds.). (2003). *Media and the War on Terrorism*. Washington, DC: The Brookings Institution.

Kellermann, K. (1992). Communication: Inherently Strategic and Primarily Automatic. *Communication Monographs, 59*(3), 288–300.

Krueger, A. (2007). *What Makes a Terrorist: Economics and the Roots of Terrorism*. Lionel Robbins Lectures. Princeton: Princeton University Press.

Lynch, R. (2012). *Strategic Management* (6th ed.). Harlow, England: Pearson.

McChesney, R. W. (2004). *The Problem of the Media: US Communication Politics in the Twenty-First Century*. New York: Monthly Review Press.

Mintzberg, H., & Waters, J. A. (1985). Of Strategies, Deliberate and Emergent. *Strategic Management Journal, 6*, 257–272.

Neumann, P., & Smith, M. (2005). Strategic Terrorism: The Framework and Its Fallacies. *Journal of Strategic Studies, 28*(4), 571–595.

Nine-Eleven (9/11) Commission Report. (2004). *Final Report of the National Commission on Terrorist Attacks upon the United States*. New York: Barnes & Noble Books.

Okigbo, C. C. (2014). Strategy: What It Is. In C. C. Okigbo (Ed.), *Strategic Urban Health Communication* (pp. 1–10). New York: Springer.

Okigbo, C., & Onoja, B. (2017). Strategic Political Communication in Africa. In A. Olukotun & R. G. Picard. (1993). *Media Portrayals of Terrorism: Functions and Meaning of News Coverage*. Ames, IA: Iowa State University Press.

Picard, R. G. (1993). *Media Portrayals of Terrorism: Functions and Meaning of News Coverage*. Ames, IA: Iowa State University Press.

Polonska-Kimunguyi, E., & Gillespiem, M. (2017). European International Broadcasting and Islamist Terrorism in Africa: The Case of Boko Haram on France 24 and Deutsche Welle. *The International Communication Gazette, 79*(3), 245–275.

Rada, S. E. (1985). Transnational Terrorism as Public Relations? *Public Relations Review, 11*(3), 26–33.

Rothenberger, L. (2015). Terrorism as Strategic Communication. In D. Holtzhausen & A. Zerfass (Eds.), *The Routledge Handbook of Strategic Communication* (pp. 481–496). New York: Routledge.

Schmid, A. P. (2005). Terrorism as Psychological Warfare. *Democracy, and Security, 1*(2), 137–146 [in Argomaniz and Lynch (2018)].

Schmid, A. P., & de Graaf, J. (1982). *Violence as Communication: Insurgent Terrorism and the Western News Media*. Beverly Hills: Sage.

Sparks, L., Kreps, G., Botan, C., & Rowan, K. (2005). Responding to Terrorism: Translating Communication Research into Practice. *Communication Research Reports, 22*(1), 1–5.

START. (2018, August). *Global Terrorism in 2017: Background Report*. The National Consortium for the Study of Terrorism and Responses to Terrorism. University of Maryland. www.start.umd.edu/gtd.

Taylor, M. (2018). Commentary: Rebalancing the Agenda. *Studies in Conflict & Terrorism, 41*(7), 589–593.

Tiefenbrun, S. (2003). A Semiotic Approach to a Legal Definition of Terrorism. *ILSA Journal of International and Comparative Law, 9*(2), 357–390.

Tracy, J. (2012). Covering "Financial Terrorism": The Greek Debt Crisis in US News Media. *Journalism Practice, 6*(4), 513.

Wilcox, D. L., & Cameron, G. T. (2012). *Public Relations: Strategies and Tactics*. Boston: Allyn & Bacon.

Wilson, L. J., & Ogden, J. (2016). *Strategic Communications: Planning for Public Relations and Marketing*. Dubuque, IA: Kendall/Hunt.

Additional Resources

Ahmad, J. (2018). *The BBC, The War on Terror and the Discursive Construction of Terrorism Representing al-Qaeda.* Cham: Springer International Publishing and Palgrave Macmillan.

Bilgen, A. (2012, July 22). *Terrorism and the Media: A Dangerous Symbiosis.* E-International Relations. https://www.e-ir.info/2012/07/22/terrorism-and-the-media-a-dangerous-symbiosis/.

Freedman, D., & Thussu, D. K. (Eds.). (2011). *Media and Terrorism: Global Perspectives.* Thousand Oaks, CA: Sage.

Greenberg, B. S. (Ed.). (2002). *Communication and Terrorism: Public and Media Responses to 9/11.* Cresskill, NJ: Hampton Press.

Hess, S., & Kalb, M. L. (Eds.). (2003). *The Media and the War on Terrorism.* Washington, DC: Brookings Institution.

Paletz, D. L., & Schmid, A. P. (1992). *Terrorism and the Media.* London/Thousand Oaks: Sage Publications.

Terrorism and Media. (2008). *Transnational Terrorism, Security, and the Rule of Law.*

Vergani, M. (2018). *How is Terrorism Changing US? Threat Perception and Political Attitudes in the Age of Terror.* Singapore: Springer/Palgrave Macmillan.

CHAPTER 2

Online Radicalisation and Africa's Youth: Implications for Peacebuilding Programmes

Adebayo Fayoyin

INTRODUCTION

The media–security nexus has been the subject of intense academic and political discourse since the war on terrorism started in 2001, and global security was placed under the spotlight in the media. A study on cyber-terrorism and the internet by Grishman (2010, p. 22) found that insurgent groups use different images and messaging formats to raise the visibility of their profiles. This study also expressed concern over the use of social media for terrorist-inspired communication, hate messaging and radicalization. Similarly, Dartnell (2006, p. 45), Liang (2015, p. 2), and Stanley and Guru (2015, p. 355) investigated the various activism tools and insurgency techniques around global conflicts that are featured on the World Wide Web (www). This author established a variety of processes and approaches deployed by terrorist groups in mobilizing support for their cause. They also propose strategies for countering jihadist

A. Fayoyin (✉)
School of Public Health, University of Witwatersrand,
Johannesburg, South Africa

E. K. Ngwainmbi (ed.), *Media in the Global Context*,
https://doi.org/10.1007/978-3-030-26450-5_2

propaganda including addressing the roots of radicalization and building international cooperation to support the creation of credible content.

A research review of extremism on the internet by Hale (2012) showed, amongst others, that terrorist groups use online platforms to promote their agenda and deploy rhetorical tactics, including selected facts, misleading statements, and smear campaigns, to attract attention to their cause. These findings are similar to those of Omotoyinbo (2014), who established significant online radicalization through websites, online games, chat rooms, and multimedia messaging. This author also highlighted concerns about offline indoctrination, which constitutes a significant part of the package of radicalization.

The consensus is that the relationships between the media, security, and terrorism are multifaceted. However, they also underscore the need for fresh evidence and ongoing empirical investigation concerning different groups, especially among the young people, to determine the emerging risks of and vulnerabilities to radicalization. This is critical for effective programming for peacebuilding and development.

Understandably, the risk and vulnerability of young people to radical messaging through their use of digital platforms have become a significant global and continental challenge. This is because most of the people involved in radical and extremist activities tend to be the youth. The United Nations Resolution 2250 of 2015 recognizes the risk of the radicalization of the youth through the application of information and communication technologies. The Preamble of the Resolution reads as follows:

[Expressing concern over the increased use in a globalised society by terrorists and their supporters of new information and communication technologies, in particular, the Internet, for the purpose of recruitment and the incitement of the youth to commit terrorist acts, as well as for the financing, planning and preparation of their activities...

The Preamble then continues by "underlining the need for the Member States to act cooperatively to prevent terrorists from exploiting technology, communication and resources to incite support for terrorists' acts, while respecting human rights and fundamental freedoms, and in compliance with other obligations under International Law." (UN Resolution 2250 2015)

The problem of the radicalization of the youth is a major issue in Africa. The continent is plagued by various terrorist activities and the fallout of radicalization from the many theaters of war and conflict on the continent (Shodipo 2013, p. 6; Worcester 2015, p. 1). A few examples of the crises help to prove the point:

- The Horn of Africa has been experiencing several political upheavals, and most of the combatants are young people.
- The political crisis in Somalia that is already in its third decade has led to the emergence of the Al-Shabab terrorist group—a principal non-state actor incorporating combatants, many of whom are unemployed and unengaged young people.
- The multifaceted conflicts in Sudan have influenced several countries in both West and East Africa. Most of the soldiers and combatants also belong to the youth.
- Some West African countries have been havens for insurgency groups. In particular, Nigeria, which is the most populous nation in the region, has been confronted with the Boko Haram insurgency, which has also spread to the surrounding regions (Alao 2013; Onuoha 2014). According to these authors, the majority of the actors in the Boko Haram crisis are mainly children and young people.
- The Sahel region, including many North African countries, has also been affected by political crises involving terrorist groups from the Middle East and Yemen such as al-Queda and the Islamic State—ISIL.

Undoubtedly, no part of Africa is immune to the potential risk of terrorist activities. International agencies and analysts argue that the continent continues to be a fertile ground for violent extremism and radicalization given its social, political and economic context (WANEP 2014, p. 1; UNDP 2015, p. 5). Africa's youth are connected through the various forms of media and communication. The ubiquity of social media is one of the phenomenal changes that has taken place on the continent. Social media present grand avenues for networking, the customization of information, and multidirectional communication among young people. Nevertheless, given the global radicalization of young people and the propagation of hate messaging on the media, especially in this current age of misinformation, concerns have been raised as to the risk of radicalization and online extremism among Africa's youth (UNDP 2015, p. 5).

In light of these trends, this paper investigates the nexus between digital media and the radicalism of the youth in Africa. This study is being carried out after much of the euphoria, hyperactivity, panic measures and hypersensitivity—so reminiscent of the media professionals, policymakers and the public that have characterized the war on terror—have subsided. This timing allows for fresh insights and a balanced perspective on the reality of the risks and vulnerability of the radicalization of the youth on the continent. This study aims to explore the nature of the vulnerabilities and the potential impact of digital media on hate messaging and radicalization in the case of young people.

It steps away from the historical, political, and philosophical arguments concerning the media and security that have been caused by the war on terror. Instead, this paper concentrates on the more practical elements of the risk of radicalization and hate messaging, and the exposure of the recipients to it, through access to and the use of social media. Thus, this study helps to enhance the contemporary perspective on the media–security nexus through an exploration of the correlation between the social media and the radicalization of the youth and its impact in Africa that extends beyond the euphoria on the war on terror. The implications for peace-focused education and an evidence-based program for social cohesion are also provided.

Conceptual Underpinning—Radicalisation and Its Pathways

Understanding Radicalization

Several concepts have been bandied about in the media–security debate. These include radicalization, hate messaging, extremist ideologies, great radicalization, de-radicalization, counter-radicalization, terrorism, and counter-terrorism. These concepts have become an essential part of contemporary discourses on political, media, security and terrorist issues. However, most commentators agree that there are conflicting and divergent perspectives concerning their philosophical roots, interpretations, and meaning (Hoskins and O'Loughlin 2009; Tinnes 2013; Onuoha 2014).

In this study, we focus on two concepts, which form the basis of the research and the analysis of its findings, namely radicalization and hate messages.

Schmid (2013, p. 6) argues that radicalization is a process of rejecting the status quo at the group or individual level, or of adopting an extremely political, social or religious ideology; and condoning violence as a means to achieving an ideological goal. This is consistent with the conclusions of Onuoha (2014, pp. 2–4), who defines radicalisation "as the process by which an individual or group transition from the passive reception of revolutionary, militant or extremist views, ideas and beliefs, to active pursuit of these ideals, especially through supporting, promoting or adopting violent actions to realise such intentions."

Interestingly, one of the transitions to radicalization is the verbal articulation of an ingrained ideology, in this case, verbal violence through hate speech. This is why some commentators arguably associate hate messaging with radicalization. Warner and Hirschberg (2012) conceptualize hate speech as a particular form of offensive language that makes use of stereotypes to express an ideology of hate. From this viewpoint, Egunike and Ihebuzor (2018, p. 250) lament the spate of online hate messaging among young people in Africa. Nevertheless, the pathway to radicalization is a complex one.

The Complex Pathway

Several approaches have been generated from different disciplines—economics, psychology, political science, and the behavioral studies—to analyze, explain, and understand the process of radicalization. One of the standard frameworks is the notion of the "pull-and-push" risk factors. According to Bjorgo (2005, pp. 3–4), the push risk factors include emotional vulnerability behind joining up with a radical group such as feelings of anger and a disconnection from the supporting structures in society, as well as disempowerment.

On the other hand, pull risk factors include the incentives and motivation for joining such a group. The combination of these forces offers a slippery slope into radicalization. Thus, programmers need to continuously examine the interrelationships among the facilitator and the motivational and triggering causes encouraging a person to join such a group for a better understanding of the level of causation in the radicalization processes.

Moghaddam (2004, 2005) applies a psychological lens in developing a model on the "Staircase to Terrorism." The six steps in the model are briefly described below:

1. Ground Floor: This relates to the psychological interpretation of material conditions by individuals. Here, it is noted that material deprivation is the groundswell on which the disposition to radicalization is built.
2. First Floor: This relates to the perceived options to fight unfair treatment. These entail actions by different individuals in seeking solutions to the perceived injustices and inequities that they experience. It is argued that once a solution has been found, progress to the next stage does not take place.
3. Second Floor: This relates to the displacement of aggression. At this stage, those trapped in material deprivation tend to manifest displaced aggression, which is mostly verbal. It is at this stage that hates messaging, or verbal attacks occur. However, this step also sets the stage for readiness for displaced aggression, which comes next.
4. Third Floor: This relates to moral engagement. The readiness for engaging in terrorist activities is acted upon at this stage when the individual actively seeks and finds radical groups with which to ally himself/herself.
5. Fourth Floor: This relates to categorical thinking and the perceived legitimacy of the terrorist organization. It is at this stage that the individual becomes part of the radical group as a recruit or member of a cell group. Interaction with the group also strengthens the commitment to the terrorist ethos and the values that are held.
6. Fifth Floor: This relates to the terrorist act and the sidestepping of inhibitory mechanisms. At this stage, the individual is now a full a member of the group and carries out terrorist attacks either as an individual or as part of the group.

From this analysis, Moghaddam proposes policy options, which include prioritizing the prevention of such terrorism, procedural justice toward contextualized democracy, educating against categorical stratification ("us and them" thinking), and inter-objectivity and justice.

However, several authors have challenged the linear, stepwise process to radicalization. From a review of the 2564 publications, Lygre et al. (2011)

did not support the transitional mechanisms proposed by Moghaddam. Nevertheless, they support most of the theories and the processes linked to the model.

Schmid (2013) adopted principles from the ecological approach (the micro- meso- and macro-analytical framework) in explaining the challenge of radicalization. The three conditions are summarized as follows:

- Micro-level—these are individual conditions such as identity problems, failed integration, and feelings of alienation, humiliation, and deprivation.
- Meso-level—these are conditions emanating from the broader milieu that serve as the rally point for stepping into radical ideologies. It involves aspects of the political context of and the power dynamics within society.
- Macro-level—these relate to actions from the much broader society, including the role of governments, the radicalization of public opinion, tense majority and minority relations, and opportunities which reinforce individual and personal motivations for radicalization.

The author argues that each of the levels would help in the proper understanding of the complexity of radicalization and offers proposals as to how to design and implement programs for peace-focused education.

From the preceding, it is clear that concerns about the increasing incidence and prevalence of radicalization among young people in society are no longer the question. It is apparent that the pathway to extremism and radicalization is complex and multidimensional (Hoskins and O'Loughlin 2009, p. 109; Alao 2013, p. 127; Onuoha 2014). While the phenomenon is a consequence of multiple factors, the role of the social media in the radicalization and promotion of extremist ideologies has continued to be a significant concern (Omotoyinbo 2014; Bolt 2012; Hale 2012). Thus, we argue that the ever-present challenge of radicalization presents an opportunity for fresh evidence to inform programs and policies that contribute to peace and cohesion. It is thus hypothesized that the social media are contributing to the exposure of Africa's young people to radical ideologies and hate messaging, regardless of age and gender, and that programmers need to develop a comprehensive response for peace-focused education.

METHODS

This study was conducted among the African youth, using members of the African Youth and Adolescent Network for Population and Development (African), a platform for young people to promote health and development, and that also strives for meaningful youth participation and advocacy in policy and decision-making processes at the national, regional, and global levels (Afriyan 2016, p. 3). Data were gathered through a self-administered questionnaire and interviews conducted with key informants.

The first step, taken in 2017, was a self-administered questionnaire, which was presented to participants. The questionnaires were emailed to all countries affiliated with the network in Africa. The questionnaire explored the extent of risk exposure, the type of negative messaging that the participants were being exposed to, and the potential consequences that they would be expected to suffer.

A total of 80 questionnaires were returned. Fischer's Exact Test was conducted to demonstrate the connection between age and gender and other indicators. In 2018, this researcher also conducted structured interviews with key informants amongst youth leaders from 10 countries—South Africa, Nigeria, Botswana, Uganda, Kenya, Ghana, Malawi, Zambia, Senegal, and Benin. Each interview lasted 45 minutes to one hour. The findings, gleaned from the key informants, were used to supplement the quantitative findings.

FINDINGS

Eighty participants completed the self-administered questionnaire. The majority were males (55.1%) as against the 44.9% who were females. Their ages ranged from 15 to over 35 years.

The age segmentation of the respondents is outlined in the following graph (Fig. 2.1).

Geographical Distribution of the Respondents

Sixteen African countries participated in the study, but the majority of the interviewees were from Nigeria (33.8%) and South Africa (28.8%) (Fig. 2.2).

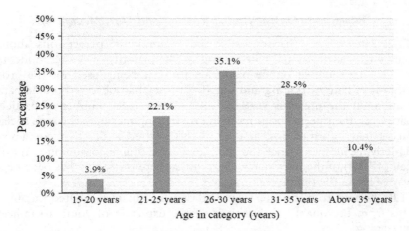

Fig. 2.1   Response rate about radicalization by age and percentages

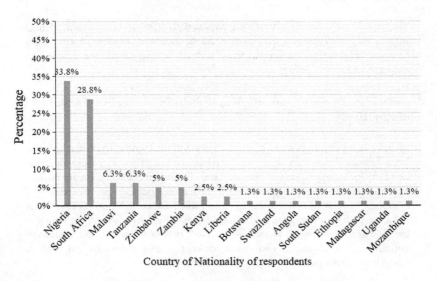

Fig. 2.2   Geographical distribution of study participants on radicalization

Exposure to Online Radicalization and Hate Messaging

Table 2.1 presents the results of the respondents' perceptions about online radicalization and hate messages. The majority of the respondents (72.2%) agreed that online platforms are now being used for the promotion of hate messaging and stated that they had observed online hate content in the previous year (82.6%). Of the total number of participants, 62, their peers about receiving underlying messages through social media had informed 5%, and 52.6% had visited a site that contained underlying messages since they had joined the online community. About half (47.3%) of the respondents agreed that hate messaging has become a way of life in the online community.

Responses from the interviews with key informants validated the findings from the quantitative analysis of the exposure of youth to radical messaging.

A male member of the South Africa Youth Advisory Panel made the following statement:

Yes, the youth in South Africa are exposed to hate messaging and radical messages. I have seen stories of beheading online. Moreover, I am aware of youth who have seen similar posts. Indeed, young people are exposed to radical ideas. No kidding.

A crucial female informant, an Afriyan member from Botswana, had the following to say:

"I have been exposed to radical messages online. I know friends who have been exposed too. People are anonymous online. They can post all kinds of stuff, including homophobic material. Social media work on meta-data and are able to connect people to a web of connectedness. Therefore, if someone in your network is exposed to radical ideas, this could expand the network of hate messaging and radical ideas. Therefore, we are all vulnerable. We are all exposed. We are all at risk", two informants, one Malawian and another, a Ugandan, did not agree that young people are exposed to underlying messages.

In Malawi, I am not aware that the youth are exposed to radical messages. Maybe I have don't paid attention to it. But I have not seen any exposure

Table 2.1 Perceptions of hate messaging

Statement	Strongly disagree	Disagree	Neutral	Agree	Strongly agree
Online platforms are now being used for promoting hate messaging against different groups of people or institutions (n=79)	2 (2.5)	7 (8.9)	13 (16.5)	38 (48.1)	19 (24.1)
I have seen online content with radical and extremist ideas over the past year (n=80)	1 (1.3)	3 (3.8)	10 (12.5)	39 (48.8)	27 (33.8)
Some of my peers have informed me that they received radical messages through the social media over the past year (n=80)	4 (5)	10 (12.5)	16 (20)	27 (33.8)	23 (28.7)
I have visited a site that contains radical messages since I joined the online community (n=80)	6 (7.5)	22 (27.5)	10 (12.5)	29 (36.3)	13 (16.3)
I am aware of peers who have visited sites that contain hate messages (n=79)	2 (2.5)	18 (22.8)	19 (24.1)	29 (36.7)	11 (13.9)
Some of my associates have received extremist messages (n=79)	7 (8.9)	17 (21.5)	18 (22.8)	27 (34.2)	10 (12.7)
My online associates suggested that I visit sites that I eventually found to contain extremist and hate messages (n=77)	14 (18.2)	25 (32.5)	16 (20.8)	16 (20.8)	6 (7.8)
My peers and I discuss the problem of hatred amongst young people (n=79)	5 (6.3)	9 (11.4)	9 (11.4)	31 (39.2)	25 (31.6)
Reducing exposure to radical messages is difficult to achieve among the African youth (n=72)	5 (6.9)	13 (18.1)	18 (25)	20 (27.8)	16 (22.2)
Hate messaging has become a way of life in the online community (n=74)	3 (4.1)	13 (17.6)	23	18 (24.3)	17 (23)

to extremist messages. None of my peers has seen that. (Lilongwe Youth Club, Malawi)

A young Ugandan female said:

Most social media work on algorithms. I do not think we are exposed to radical messages, especially if you are not looking for it. (Afriyan, Uganda)

Sources of Online Radicalization and Hate Messaging

The majority of the participants identified Facebook (80%) and Twitter (62.5%) as the most common source of online hate messaging or extremism. Blogs, Wikipedia and YouTube, were also perceived as sources of such messaging (Fig. 2.3).

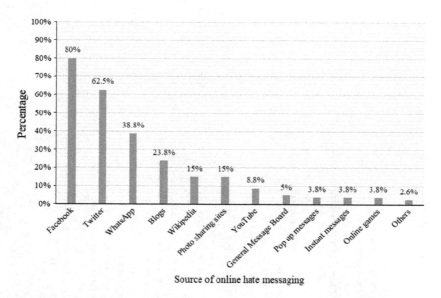

Fig. 2.3 Social media sources of hate messaging in percentages

COMMENTS ON ONLINE RADICALIZATION
AND HATE MESSAGING ($N=80$)

Some of the key informants described their experiences with the platforms as follows:

> I have seen messages from supposed terrorists, especially on YouTube, with 16 million views and 100,000 shares. Links of hate messaging and radical ideas - which have gone viral - have also been shared with me. Moreover,... just to be part of the discussions when your friends are discussing such issues, you tend to visit [such sites] to see for yourself. (Male, Youth Advisory Panel, South Africa)

> There are also different Facebook pages for different issues, good and bad. Individuals have the right to determine the type of pages or the content that they want to see. In the past, it might have been possible for stray radical messages to be posted on the walls of our Facebook pages. But such incidents seem to have decreased. (Female, Afriyan Uganda)

Causes of Online Hate Messaging

Respondents identified the various causes of online hate messaging. Ignorance (62.5%) and unwillingness to recognize diversity/differences (51.2%) were found to be the most common causes of online hate messaging. This was followed by immaturity (40%) and political loyalty (38.8%) (Fig. 2.4).

People with opposing religions (52.5%) and political affiliations (42.5%) and different sexual orientations (42.5%) were considered the most frequently targeted groups for online hate messages.

Effects of exposure to online extremism and hate messaging

Table 2.2 shows the percentages of the effects of exposure to online extremism and hate messaging.

The majority of the participants indicated that they believe that exposure to online extremism and hate messaging would lead to:

- Increased hatred and tensions (65%).
- People undervaluing themselves (57.5%).
- People adopting extremist positions (42.5%).

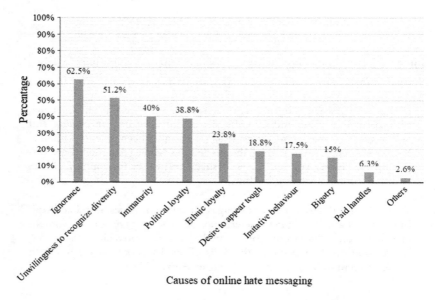

Fig. 2.4   Causes of online hate messaging

Table 2.2   Effects of exposure to online extremism and hate messaging

Effects of exposure to online extremism and hate messaging	N	%
Lead to an increase in hatred and tensions	52	65
Lead people to undervalue others	46	57.5
Lead people to extremist positions	34	42.5
Lead to the homogenization of views because of the fear of being bullied	25	31.3
Lead to radicalization	22	27.5
Lead to a breakdown in group cohesion	22	27.5
Lead people to peddle inaccuracies	11	13.8
Lead to muffling/suffocation of legitimate dissent	5	6.3

Only 6.3% of the participants believe that exposure to online extremism would lead to the muffling of legitimate dissent. On the other hand, 27.5% of the respondents believe that exposure to online extremism would result in radicalization and a breakdown group cohesion.

Most of the informants agreed with the findings from the questionnaire.

I agree that exposure to radical messaging can promote radical views. Young people can be radicalized by negative messages from digital media and could join extremist groups. We are vulnerable. But, it is our responsibility to determine what we want. (Youth Advisory Panel, South Africa)

Another informant was of the following opinion:

People catfish others with different messages. I think the reason why xenophobic attacks spread fast in South Africa is that of the social media. I also know that youth z mobilization for violence spreads fast because of the social media. (Youth, Botswana)

But some key informants did not agree that exposure to radical messages would make young people engage in radical behavior. This group believed that it is not the media but how people use the platforms that is crucial.

A male informant from South Africa made the following statement:

I do not think exposure to radical ideas will cause any reasonable young person to follow extremist ideas. Social media is a platform for different messages, both positive and negative. It cannot be the only reason why those who join radical groups become radicalized. There are other underlying causes beyond social media. (Afriyan, Kenya)

This position is consistent with that of another young female from Ghana who said:

You are not forced to believe or try everything you see on the social media. Exposure to radical messages should not turn all of us into extremists. Exposure to hate messaging should not make us haters.

Gender Differences

According to our male respondents, the targets of hate messaging are people with different religious beliefs (65.1%) and political affiliations (51.2%) and the members of different ethnic groups (39.5%). Female respondents, however, perceived that the targets of hate messaging are people of different sexual orientation (65.6%) and a different gender (34.4%).

Table 2.3 Association targets of hate messaging and gender (Fischer's Exact Test)

Targets of hate messaging	Gender
People with opposing/different religious beliefs	0.073
People with different political affiliations	0.198
People with different sexual orientations	0.049
People from different ethnic groups	0.000
People of different genders	0.019
People with a physical disability	0.107
Minority population groups	0.238

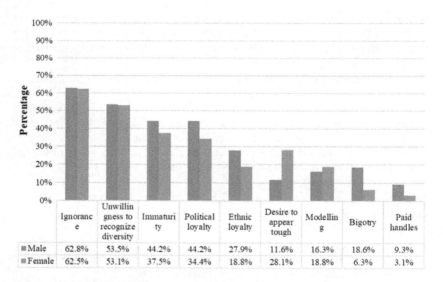

	Ignoranc e	Unwillin gness to recognize diversity	Immaturi ty	Political loyalty	Ethnic loyalty	Desire to appear tough	Modellin g	Bigotry	Paid handles
▪ Male	62.8%	53.5%	44.2%	44.2%	27.9%	11.6%	16.3%	18.6%	9.3%
▪ Female	62.5%	53.1%	37.5%	34.4%	18.8%	28.1%	18.8%	6.3%	3.1%

Fig. 2.5 Gender distribution on causes of online hate messaging

Testing for associations between gender and the targets of hate messaging showed a significant correlation when it came to people of different gender and members of different ethnic groups ($p < 0.05$) (Table 2.3)

Both male and female respondents identified ignorance, unwillingness, immaturity, and political loyalty as the most common causes of online hate messaging (Fig. 2.5). Bigotry showed a significant association with gender ($p < 0.05$) (Table 2.4). There was an association

Table 2.4 Gender distribution of exposure to online extremism and hate messaging

Causes of online hate messaging	Gender
Ignorance	0.698
Unwillingness to recognize diversity and difference	0.857
Immaturity	0.361
Political loyalty	0.291
Ethnic loyalty	0.491
The desire to appear tough and "macho"	0.125
Modeling and imitative behavior	0.655
Bigotry	0.026
Paid handles	0.498

Table 2.5 Association between effects of exposure to online extremism and gender (Fischer's Exact Test)

Effects of exposure to online extremism and hate messaging	Gender
Lead to increased hatred and tensions	0.415
Lead people to undervalue others	0.332
Lead people to extremist positions	0.339
Lead to the homogenization of views because of the fear of being bullied	0.097
Lead to radicalization	0.048
Lead to a breakdown in group cohesion	0.823
Lead people to peddle inaccuracies	0.135
Lead to muffling/suffocation of legitimate dissent	0.238

between causes of hate messaging and the demographic variable, gender as dictated by the Fischer's Exact Test.

Males reported that exposure to online extremism would result in an undervaluation of people (60.5%), extremist positions (51.2%) and radicalization (39.5%). Females reported that exposure to online extremism would result in increased hatred and tensions (68.8%) and the homogenization of views (43.8%) (Fig. 2.5). There was a significant association between gender and the radicalization of views as a resultant effect of online extremism (Table 2.5).

METHODS LIMITING OR STOPPING EXPOSURE
TO EXTREMISM AND HATE MESSAGING

Media education (76.3%) and strategic communication on the positive use of social media (53.8%) were most commonly identified as methods to limit or to stop exposure to extremism and hate messaging (Fig. 2.6).

To assess the extent of action to address extremism and hate messaging, the key informants reported as follows:

> We are not doing enough in managing the challenges posed by online radical and hate messaging in our society. Change should not start from the social media; change should start with us. The problem is not so much with the social media; the problem is with how we use the platforms. Social media would not make us safer than we want to be. It all starts with

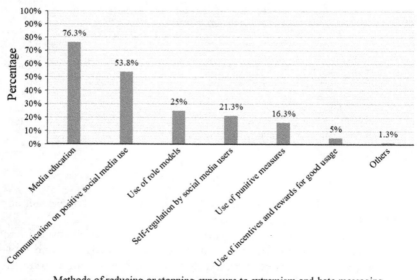

Methods of reducing or stopping exposure to extremism and hate messaging

Fig. 2.6 How to limit or stop exposure to extremism and hate messaging

the individual. We should avoid panic measures and focus on providing and creating an empowering environment for every young person is fully developed as a human being with dignity. (YAP, South Africa)

However, others had different views based on the need to focus on individual responsibility and authority in preventing stray information on individual platforms.

A female respondent from Botswana said:

> It depends so much on individuals. There is sufficient protection in the hands of all users of social media to avoid radical messages. If you look for it, you will not find it. Technology is not intrinsically bad; it depends on how we use it.

GENDER DISTRIBUTION OF METHODS FOR LIMITING OR STOPPING EXPOSURE TO EXTREMISM AND HATE MESSAGING

Male respondents reported that media education (79.1%) and self-regulation by social media users would be useful in limiting exposure to online extremism. Female respondents reported that strategic communication (56.3%) and the use of role models (31.3%) would be the most effective methods of reducing exposure to online extremism. There was no significant association between gender and the methods of limiting exposure to extremism and hate messaging ($p > 0.05$) (Table 2.6).

Table 2.6 Association between methods of limiting or stopping exposure extremism and hate messaging and gender (Fischer's Exact Test)

Methods of limiting or stopping exposure to extremism and hate messaging	Gender
Media education	0.897
Strategic communication on the positive use of social media	0.850
Use of role models	0.686
Self-regulation by social media users	0.822
Use of punitive measures	0.586
Use of incentives and rewards for proper usage	0.127

DISCUSSION

Our study affirmed that young people are exposed to digital and online hate messaging, irrespective of age and gender. This is consistent with other studies that have examined similar issues. Young people aged 20–25 years are most susceptible, which also aligns with the UN Resolution 2250 of 2015, which identifies age 18–29 as the critical age for intervention in the process of radicalization. Thus, age-appropriate communications would be needed in the process of peace-focused education and social mobilization for social cohesion. Several online channels have the potential for exposing young people to the risk of hate messaging and radicalization. Most of the platforms that Africa's youth use—Facebook and YouTube—are significant sources of hate messaging and online radicalization.

However, some of the critical informants argued that individual youths should be able to exercise discipline in their use of digital devices and to avoid exposure to negative messaging online.

Our study demonstrated a variety of underlying causes of hate messaging and potential radicalization. There is a multiplicity of determinants for hate messaging and for exposing young people to radical messaging. However, more research is needed to explore the causal relationship between exposure and radicalization.

The relationship between exposure to violent messaging and behavior is inconclusive (Ferguson 2016). This study provides a range of solutions towards addressing hate messaging and extremist ideologies among young people. Two dominant approaches are media education and strategic communication. Action research would also be necessary for compelling programming.

CONCLUSION

Our study demonstrated the reality of the risks and vulnerability of Africa's youth to different types of hate messaging through various online channels. Our hypothesis that the exposure of the African youth to digital media increases the risk of online radicalization and the exposure to hate messaging can thus be supported. Therefore, we conclude that digital platforms and media technologies contribute to the exposure of the African youth to radicalization and extremism. However, it should also be noted that the pathway to radicalization is complex, multidimensional and not linear. The media–security nexus is a complex phenomenon and thus requires a more nuanced approach to analysis and programming. Effective peace-focused educational programs and policy initiatives to respond to the situation would require program-related research. New approaches to security and peace-focused education need to be pursued at all levels.

Way Forward

1. It is vital to promote a counter-narrative strategy to support peace-focused education (Ferguson 2016): Integrated continental peacebuilding activism—within the context of the Sustainable Development Goals (SDGs) and Africa's Agenda 2063 would require a combination of online and offline processes for peace-focused education. Since young people represent a generation that "lives" for their devices, creativity and the extensive use of the digital media in achieving social cohesion should be explored.

2. Stories of change about young people who are contributing to peace and development in various African countries need to be collated and shared. This would contribute to a change in the perceptions of the youth: The more mature members of society, labeled by the youth as "deficit adults," should be perceived as the more positive "agents of change." New ways should be identified for the more mature to tell the untold stories of their youth when they were considered to be "peacebuilders" and "peace activists" so that the term "deficit adults" should become redundant.

3. An evidence-based approach to peace-focused education and strategic communication programs is necessary to enhance group cohesion and maximize the social capital of Africa's youth. The need for a theory of change for peacebuilding and resilience is essential. An age-appropriate approach to messaging needs to be developed.

4. It is essential to engage young people in Africa in endeavors to pursue sustainable peace and security. Africa's young people have always said: "Nothing for us without us!" (Mabala 2011). Whether it will be through their children and the Youth Parliament, or through their networks—as in the case of the African Network for Population and Development—they have always requested the space for meaningful and productive participation in Africa's

development. It would be essential to open up multiple platforms to pursue and engage in meaningful conversations and to conduct genuine dialogues for change and social cohesion. Such engagements should not be limited to national platforms alone but should be at the continental level.

QUESTIONS FOR DISCUSSION

1. Briefly describe what the literature says on the "media–security nexus." To what extent can the media undermine global security?
2. Do the findings from this study validate or repudiate the fears that exposure of young people to digital media could lead to online radicalization?
3. Based on the literature and findings from the study, develop three possible hypotheses for further research on the topic.
4. Examine the authors' conclusions and propose three additional conclusions that could be drawn from the study.
5. "Nothing for us without us!" Why is this conclusion critical for meaningful and productive of Africa youth on the development and implementation of programs to promote peace on the continent?

REFERENCES

Afriyan. (2016). *African Youth and Adolescent Network on Population and Development, Annual Report 2016/2017.* Johannesburg: UNFPA.

Alao, A. (2013). Islamic Radicalization and Violent Extremism in Nigeria. *Conflict, Security and Development, 13*(2), 127–147.

Bjorgo, T. (2005). *Root Causes of Terrorism: Myths, Realities, and Ways Forward* (pp. 3–4). London: Routledge.

Bolt, N. (2012). *The Violent Image: Insurgent Propaganda and the New Revolutionaries.* New York: Columbia University Press.

Dartnell, M. Y. (2006). *Insurgency Online: Web Activism and Global Conflict.* Toronto: University of Toronto Press.

Egunike, N., & Ihebuzor, I. (2018). Online Ethnocentric Hate Speech Among Nigerian Youth. In K. A. Omenugha, A. Fayoyin, & M. C. Ngugi (Eds.), *New Media and African Society.* Nairobi, Kenya: Nairobi Academic Press.

Grishman, P. (2010). *Cyber Terrorism: The Use of the Internet for Terrorist Purposes.* New Delhi: Axis Publications.

Ferguson, K. (2016). *Countering Violent Extremism Through Media and Communication Strategies.* http://gsdrc.org/document-library/countering-violent-extremism-through-media-and-communication-strategies-a-review-of-the-evidence/.

Hale, C. W. (2012). Extremism on the World Wide Web: A Research Review. *Criminal Justice Studies, 25*(4), 343–356.

Hoskins, A., & O'Loughlin, B. (2009). Media, and the Myth of Radicalization. *Media, War and Conflict, 2*(2), 107–110.

Liang, C. S. (2015). *Cyber-Jihad: Understanding and Islamic State Propaganda.* https://www.gcsp.ch/News-Knowledge/Publications/Cyber-Jihad-Understanding-and-Countering-Islamic-State-Propaganda.

Lygre, R. B., Eid, J., Larsson, G., & Ranstorp, M. (2011). Terrorism as a Process: A Critical Review of Moghaddam's "Staircase to Terrorism". *Scandinavian Journal of Psychology, 52,* 609–616.

Mabala, R. (2011). Youth and "The Hood"—Livelihoods and Neighbourhoods. *Environment & Urbanization, 23*(1), 157–181. http://www.lime3.eu/setup-data-science-solution-method/.

Moghaddam, F. M. (2004). Cultural Continuities Beneath the Conflict Between Radical Islam and Pro-Western Forces: The Case of Iran. In Y. T. Lee, C. McCauley, F. M. Moghaddam, & S. Worchel (Eds.), *The Psychology of Ethnic and Cultural Conflict* (pp. 115–132). Westport, CT: Praeger.

Moghaddam, F. M. (2005, February–March). "The Staircase to Terrorism: A Psychological Exploration". *American Psychologist, 60*(2), 161–169.

Onuoha, F. (2014). *Special Report: Why Do Youth Join Boko Haram.* Washington, DC: United States Institute for Peace.

Omotoyinbo, F. R. (2014). Online Radicalisation: The Net or the Netizen. *Social Sciences Technologies, 4*(1), 51–61.

Tinnes, J. (2013). Terrorism and the Media (Including the Internet): An Extensive Bibliography. *Perspectives on Terrorism, 7*(1, Suppl. S1–S3), 145–147.

Schmid, P. A. (2013). *Radicalisation, De-Radicalisation, Counter-Radicalisation: A Conceptual Discussion and Literature Review.* ICCT Research Paper. https://www.icct.nl/download/file/ICCT-Schmid-Radicalisation-De-Radicalisation-Counter-Radicalisation-March-2013.pdf.

Shodipo, M. O. (2013). *Mitigating Radicalism in Northern Nigeria.* https://africacenter.org/publication/mitigating-radicalism-in-northern-nigeria/.

Stanley, T., & Guru, S. (2015). Childhood Radicalisation Risk: An Emerging Practice Issue. *Practice, 27*(5), 353–366. https://doi.org/10.1080/09503153.2015.1053858.

UNDP. (2015). *Preventing and Responding to Violent Extremism in Africa.* http://www.undp.org/content/dam/undp/library/Democratic%20Governance/Local%20Governance/UNDP-RBA-Preventing-Extremism-2015.pdf.

United Nations Resolution 2250. (2015). https://www.un.org/development/desa/youth/international-youth-day-2017/resources-on-youth-peace-and-security.html.

WANEP. (2014). *Incorporating Strategies for Countering Violent Extremism in Peace*. Report by the West Africa Network for Peace Building, WANEP, 11–12 Accra, Ghana.

Warner, W., & Hirschberg, J. (2012, June 7). Detecting Hate Speech on the World Wide Web. In *Proceedings of the 2012 Workshop on Language in Social Media (LSM 2012)* (pp. 19–26), Montreal, Canada.

Worcester, M. (2015). *Combatting Terrorism in Africa*. https://www.files.ethz.ch/isn/50103/Combating_Terrorism_Africa.pdf.

Additional Resources

Ayedun-Aluma, V. (Ed.). *Digital Media or New Order, Emergent Practices in the Nigerian Media Environment*. Toronto, ON: Canada University Press.

Omenugha, K. A., Fayoyin, A., & Ngugi, M. C. (2018). *New Media and African Society: Essays, Reviews and Case Studies*. Nairobi: Nairobi Academic Press.

Gustin, J. F. (2004). *Cyber Terrorism: A Guide for Facility Managers*. Lilburn: Fairmont Press.

Lappin, Y. (2011). *Virtual Caliphate: Exposing the Islamist State on the Internet*. Washington, DC: Potomac Books.

Lewis, J. (2005). *Language Wars: The Role of Media and Culture in Global Terror and Political Violence*. London: Pluto Press.

PART II

Social Media and the Globalization of Local Cultures

Social Media Use Among the Youth and Working Class: Conditions for Remediating Globalization and Cultural Space

Emmanuel K. Ngwainmbi

INTRODUCTION

When rich countries opened up access to information and communication technology (ICT) for all types of people and countries around the world several decades ago, it did not appear clear to leaders of developing nations that the technology could transform the cultural fabric of their fragile communities and impact the socioeconomic aspirations of young people in those countries. The imbalance in cash flows between IT users in industrialized regions and those in marginalized

---

While the African Youth Charter defines youth as any person ages of 15 and 35 years, this chapter considers the youth as the transitional period of a child's interdependence with family and peers to independence and the awareness of being a member of a community. "Working class" refers to educated and trained persons 20–55.

E. K. Ngwainmbi (✉)
Charlotte, NC, USA

E. K. Ngwainmbi (ed.), *Media in the Global Context*,
https://doi.org/10.1007/978-3-030-26450-5_3

communities cannot be compared to the frequency of the use of social media gadgets. Studies show that more people around the world are now turning to multiple social media sites for news and information or to communicate their identity than a few years ago.

Together, the iconic devices iPhone and internet have changed the way people process information, learn, work, communicate, and entertain themselves and others. The iPhone, Apple's bestselling product the digital camera, the cell phone, and touchscreen interface features allow users from any linguistic background, intellectual capacity, socioeconomic class, nationality, age, or ethnocultural to store and share data is arguably the most important invention of the twenty-first century. The internet through its ability to provide data to various information and communication facilities and interconnected networks is touted as the driving force behind a vibrant global digital economy. However, some micro-economists, ethnographers, rural sociologists, development communication scholars, and world governing bodies such as UNESCO are concerned about inequality between the rich nations in the northern hemisphere (global North) and developing countries in the southern region (global South), particularly in Africa. They argue that not everyone or every nation gets the same benefits from the internet users because the countries in the North have stronger economies and more wealthy people to invest on the internet and receive accompanying gratifications than in the South. The internet has its place in the sociology of communications, from the spoken word to writing, print and broadcast media. Moreover, anthropologists and Professor Emeritus Keith Hart at the Goldsmiths College of the University of London has succinctly stated that people have brought their offline circumstances to behavior online. However, social-anthropology studies leave us wondering how access or lack to communication channels such as the iPhone and internet may be negatively affecting the capacity for the productive population in the global South to optimize their use of the communication tools in question, hence probably limiting their ability to influence globalization. Further, accessible technology such as the internet and phone may provide the same benefits full social and economic interests in every country.

Studies have also determined that using the social media space in parts of Africa lowered learners' threshold to accessing educational resources, prompting the research community and marketing experts to ask whether the same situation exists from a social and cultural perspective. While communications in developing countries have focused on policy change and aimed at building advocacy and designing policy using traditional broadcast media the radio, television, and newspaper, the African media landscape now offers a broader range of choices, including social media networks and systems—mainly the internet and iPhone.

According to a report published in the Science Technology section of Africanews, between 2017 and January 2018 alone, there were 4.2 billion internet users globally reflecting a 53% penetration rate; with 5.1 billion mobile phone users reflecting a 68% penetration, and 3.196 billion social media users up 13% year-on-year. Hootsuite, a Canada-based social media management platform, reports that internet penetration in North Africa is 49%, West Africa 39%, Central Africa 12%, Eastern Africa 27%, and Southern Africa 51%. *The Guardian* (2018) asserts that Africa's claim to be the "mobile continent" is even stronger than previously thought, and researchers predicting internet use on mobile phones will increase 20-fold in the next five years—double the rate of growth in the rest of the world. Market analysts expect that mobile data usage will grow at least five times faster than mobile voice and smartphone penetration will double that of internet use by 2020. With more people young finding the IT products a good distraction in African communities, the telecom market can grow exponentially in the next years.

Also in Africa, social media has become vital space for retrieving and sharing news, local information and entertainment as most people have been accessing WhatsApp, Viber WeChat, Facebook and Twitter. However, not at the same rate as in America. Although television is still a significant source of news and information to some 70 million households in sub-Saharan Africa with a population of one billion (est. 1,050,135,841), mobile phones have higher penetration and smartphone use more than doubled, and young people are not only using that technology to share funny hashtags or selfies. In fact, over the past few years, social media has been so influential and consequential in the lives of young Africans that some governments block social media around elections and political protests per Reuters and Associated Press reports. The transformation of "social media" to plain old "media" is happening fast in advanced economies, but in emerging countries, particularly in Africa, the impact of that transformation may already be apparent,[1] uniquely as the GSM Association predicts the number of unique mobile

---

[1] *Quartz* Africa Editor, Yinka Adegoke's article was published in *Quartz* online on March 6, 2017 in collaboration with the World Economic Forum.

subscribers will reach 5.9 billion by 2025, equivalent to 71% of the world's population.[2] During that period developing countries, particularly sub-Saharan Africa, India, China, Pakistan, Indonesia, and Bangladesh, and Latin America will drive growth (The Mobile Economy 2018 Report).

SOCIAL MEDIA PENETRATION IN BROADER MARKETS

Published reports show that social media penetration is growing in developing countries faster than in industrialized countries. Based on Poushter et al.'s analysis (2018) internet use among 17 advanced economies surveyed remained relatively flat in 2017, with a median of 87% across these nations, similar to 86% that used the portal in 2015 in 2016.

Conversely, another Pew Research Center report published in 2017 revealed that one-quarter of all US adults got news from two or more social media sites, up from 15% in 2013 and 18% in 2016 (Greico 2017), while 66% of people who had Facebook accounts used the site to harvest news. Smith and Anderson's report released by the same center in March 2018 showed Facebook and YouTube dominate the social media landscape, as majorities of United States adults use each of these sites. At the same time, 78% of 18–24-year-olds use Snapchat, and a sizeable majority of these users visit the platform multiple times per day, and 71% of Americans in this age group now use Instagram, and close to half (45%) are Twitter users.[3]

A GLOBAL PERSPECTIVE OF SOCIAL MEDIA USE AMONG YOUNG PEOPLE AND EMPLOYEES

The uses of social media can be measured based on the tolerance level and spending ability of a community. Since the worldwide web reached Africa in the early 1990s, social media have become the favorite tools for information sharing, meditation, and socialization among young people. Studies describe social media as a platform for market research and

[2] The GSMA is the trade body that represents the interests of mobile network operators worldwide.   https://www.gsma.com/mobileeconomy/wp-content/uploads/2018/05/The-Mobile-Economy-2018.pdf.

[3] http://www.pewinternet.org/2018/03/01/social-media-use-in-2018/. Retrieved September 30, 2018.

decision-making process. Billions of people use social media for learning, marketing, shopping, and decision-making, and more young people are having access to Android phones and the internet. However, it is not clear whether overtime their use of such technology has a positive or negative impact on their communications skills; whether increased use of the technology is preventing them from following their local customs or advancing the drive to compete for other opportunities in the world. For example, an online survey of 791 US undergraduates has found that the platform does not necessarily promote irrelevant, conflicting, outdated, and non-credible information (Sin 2016). Another study concluded in 2014 found that 72% of American teens spend an entire day on cell phones; 17% on the handheld gaming device, 13% on tablet computers, 25% on a gaming console (Baran 2017).

The study conducted by the Pew Research Center in Spring 2015 revealed that 80% of mobile phone owners used it for texting while only 14% accessed it to get consumer information (see Fig. 3.1).

Another survey of user attitudes carried out in Cameroon, Nigeria, South Africa, and Kenya in mid-2017 (Ngwainmbi 2017) showed a similar sense of gratification among African youth who use social media technology (see Tables 3.1 and 3.2).[4]

Meanwhile, internet usage had a positive influence on education as more young, well-educated and English speakers use it. It is not clear whether that trend has continued since the study was conducted. Nor do we know the impact of its use on the moral values of the young people (see Fig. 3.2).

Social Media and Culture

The internet and social media are powerful tools that can influence and shape human behavior. The social media has played a significant role in recent outbreaks of social protest and resistance in industrially advanced and less technologically equipped nations. Observers have concluded that in a networked world social media has the potential to promote public participation, engagement, and democratization. We recall the social transformations in Tunisia, Libya, the United States, and other countries when young people used Facebook and iPhones to mobilize

---

[4]This author found that there was a limited number of bloggers with an average of 50 per country.

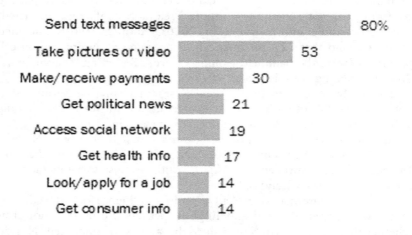

Texting Most Common Use of Cell Phones in Africa

Median adult cell phone owners who used a cell phone in the past 12 months to ...

Send text messages	80%
Take pictures or video	53
Make/receive payments	30
Get political news	21
Access social network	19
Get health info	17
Look/apply for a job	14
Get consumer info	14

Note: Median percentages across seven African countries.

Source: Spring 2014 Global Attitudes survey. Q74a-h.

PEW RESEARCH CENTER

Fig. 3.1 Why people use cell phones in Africa (*Source* Pew Research Center 2015)

themselves and hold public demonstrations that led to new governments being set up. However, as the sociologist Frank Furedi (2015) has argued, it is not the internet and the social media that mobilize people, but the creative use of the social media in responding to aspirations and needs that preexist.

Table 3.1   Why people use social media

- To reach acquaintances, friends, family, and even strangers within their communities and abroad, and share sentiments and productive information
- To mobilize groups for a cause
- To influence public opinion
- Mobile phone users send and receive money or text messages and take pictures or video
- Mobile phones result in "informationalization of poverty" through the "creation or recreation of economic disambiguation"
- To send money meant for pressing family needs, including buying airtime and phones

Table 3.2   Investment in iPhones and internet café in Africa

i. Participants spend approximately per day $1 on internet café
ii. Small scale business owners spend approximately $2 per day on iPhones in texting or retrieving stock information and currency exchange rates
iii. Secondary school people spend 50 cents or less per day on internet and iPhone while non-schoolers do not access the internet at all
iv. Non-schoolers spend 50 cents to 75 cents per day on telephone calls

Just as the invention of writing and reading has transformed the human thought process and local culture, so as communication technology been a fierce agent persuading our thoughts and actions. In fact, since the introduction of the commercial internet in the early 1990s, companies, and organizations have taken advantage of the internet and other cyber communication systems to market their products and services to millions of consumers around the world.

If this technology is to be perceived as a resource that can be utilized to gauge social and political movements, its role in channeling new information needs some attention.

Social Media as a News Channel

Social media has paved the way for anyone to report any event, no matter whether it is potentially useful or meaningless. News sites and social media feeds are updated every second with new data from regular users who share news, events experienced, photos, gossip, scoops and the latest hot topics (Garlick 2015). The process of creating and publishing news on social media is so easy that it has made social media the

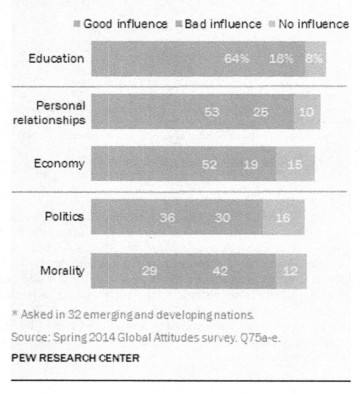

Internet Has Most Positive Influence on Education, Least Positive on Morality

*Median saying increasing use of internet has had a ___ on ... ***

■ Good influence   ■ Bad influence   ■ No influence

	Good influence	Bad influence	No influence
Education	64%	18%	8%
Personal relationships	53	25	10
Economy	52	19	15
Politics	36	30	16
Morality	29	42	12

* Asked in 32 emerging and developing nations.

Source: Spring 2014 Global Attitudes survey. Q75a-e.

PEW RESEARCH CENTER

Fig. 3.2 Impact of internet on education

fastest news channel compared to traditional broadcasting. By merely a message and clicking post or share, we can reach the world network. Unlike in the common room, there are no editors, no fact-checkers nor mechanisms put in place to proofread, edit or crosscheck for stylistic corrections.

Extensive data including pictures can be sent from a phone or camera, and social media networks are not optimized to provide factual news accounts, as Bob Garlick, owner of the Garlick Marketing and DB Communications has stated on his LinkedIn page www.linkedin.com/ Bob Garlick. Equally, because the sender has access to millions of receivers, any amount or type of content can be shared, and the sender has the power to choose and share the content he intends the audience to receive. However, on social media human relationships are easily influenced, manipulated, controlled or managed for predetermined outcomes, making the medium an untrustworthy mechanism for getting news. According to intensive research, the credibility of social media channels has been negatively affected by organizations seeking anonymously to influence search engine results, amend entries on widely accessed sources like Wikipedia and Trip Advisor.

Anyone with a credit card can access and leave comments on the pages of the world's most influential online markets such as Amazon or Barnes and Noble, thereby allowing fake reviews and false impressions about the products. Further, it is likely that some public relations firms, in a bid to keep all parties happy, could be manipulating online news coverage to reduce the impact of devastating consequences of issues and happenings on the image of businesses, governments, and public figures.

SOCIAL MEDIA AS A PREFERRED CONSUMER BRAND

In recent years, social media has not only played a central role in global converging cultures through significant data sharing (photos, languages, and ideas), it is a brand with a strategic position in the information marketplace and leverage in bringing social change. As a cyber-platform, social media can build stronger communities. One can argue that through social media consumers' aspirations are advanced on an emotional or psychological level. So if we agree that successful brand in convergence cultures engages consumers to meet their aspirations through interactivity (Arvidson 2006) engagement of their senses and emotions, we can also consider that public agencies and private corporations can utilize the brand—strong image—of social media in engaging their respective publics. Marc Gobe (2001), in his popular book *Emotional Branding*, argues that focusing on people's interest in transcending material and experience fulfillment allows marketers to tap into their aspirational drives, thereby motivating their actions. Specific messages in the form of blogs, tweets and Facebook postings timely delivered to specific audiences could make social media the preferred channel of for-profit and non-profit organizations including governments to brand their image shortly.

Branding is as much an integral part of nation-building as it is for sustaining the security of a product in the marketplace. Similarly, product advertising has much to do with selling a culture since a product is developed based on the perceived taste and values of the potential market.

SOCIAL MEDIA AND SOCIAL TRANSFORMATION

The primary purpose of social media is to share acquaintances, friends, family, and even strangers within their communities and abroad, just to share sentiments and productive information; mobilize groups for a cause; influence public opinion; advocate for change; mobile phones results in "informationalization of poverty" through the "creation or recreation of economic disambiguation." The medium can be seen as a moral and immoral compass depending on the user's intentions. For example, Ghana sometimes diverts money meant for pressing family needs and welfare into buying airtime and expensive phones.

Some studies show various ways in which social media has transformed the world. It affords us a collective marketplace of ideas and products. We can reach anyone on the planet when we need to thereby expose us to diversity and inclusion. According to Lisa Galarneau (2017), social media is changing our world in many ways:

- We support things we like.
- We learn from each other. You can find everything from make-up tips to channeled extraterrestrial messages on YouTube. Moreover, if you have ever doubted that kids are learning things these days, check out this fascinating exchange between a student and his English teacher.
- Crowd Sourced Wisdom—We share our knowledge, wisdom, and experiences. Quora is a place where you can ask any question in the world, and expect a reasonable answer.
- We unleash our more creativity and inspiration—We share our creative ideas and inspirations. Pinterest has redefined the digital portfolio/catalog.
- Increased Appreciation of the Unique and Handmade—We still have respect for the unique and the handmade. Etsy has enabled

many a domestic entrepreneur and infused our culture with a beautiful richness of creativity.

- Truth is exposed—We still haunt Twitter waiting for a cause or idea to support. Retweets are our weapon to expose information and transform thinking. It is still an incredibly powerful tool, as its signal cannot be easily stopped (following censorship laws or not). 'Can't stop the signal!'
- We are More Authentic—People in the social media space are finally talking more about authenticity, which might help minimize some of the junkier parts of our lovely information city.
- Anyone can contribute—We acknowledge that everyone has something to contribute, as long as you are careful about it. http://www.jeffbullas.com/10-ways-social-media-is-transforming-our-world/.

Globalization offers clear economic and development opportunities and benefits but comes with significant social costs that often appear to have significant consequences on young people, given their uncertain transitional status within an increasingly uncertain and rapidly evolving global context. Being in a tenuous transitional stage—their chronological development—young people do not have the resources to control its speed or the direction of social change, even though as future occupants of the world, they should play an integral role in charting course of their futures. In the World Youth Report published by the United Nations Department of Economic and Social Change (2004), analysts mention that globalization can intensify social divisions. As young people struggling to establish themselves in a new social context (the often intimidating adult world), they may be vulnerable to the threat of segregation or exclusion (p. 293). Their perceived fear of the present—the "insecure world"—and the tomorrow's world—the unknown—calls to question the notion that continued globalization may produce intended and unintended local consequences, the most worrying ones being psycho-social deprivation, social alienation, and social segregation.

THE CONFLUENCE OF CULTURE AND GLOBALIZATION

There is an offline and online culture with the latter evolving at a terrific pace, mainly because of the materials posted, retrieved, stored, and shared by commercial businesses, organizations and individuals. The internet serves as the channel through which broader social and cultural anxieties are communicated. While critics have described the internet as the single agency responsible for destroying local cultures and creating a homogenous global culture led by powerful and industrially advanced nations, technophile advocates glorify it for converging cultures—literarily bring world cultures and people together. As Marshall McLuhan ([1964] 1994) predicted his groundbreaking book, *Understanding Media* creating a "global village," McLuhan's view of one world interconnected by an electronic nervous system is indeed today part of our popular culture. McLuhan's insights about media, technology, and communication fundamentally have changed how everyone thinks about media, technology, and communications ever since. Using that stance, this chapter has so far attempted to explain that the interconnection of electronic systems or global village has stifled human creativity and as a consequence stalled the socioeconomic aspirations of those "villagers" without equal opportunity—the capacity or resources to manage and control the technology through which they are persuaded.

ASSUMPTIONS

This author assumes that (a) all communities have developed and experienced political, socioeconomic, and cultural processes, and (b) mass media content and message flows can transform urban communities. Cyber-mediated communications transform global cultures through the following prisms. Stereotyping—a widely held but fixed and oversimplified image or the idea of a particular type of person or thing. Perception—ability to see, hear, or become aware of something through the senses; a way of regarding, understanding, or interpreting something or giving a mental impression: Creativity—developing content to change sociocultural perspectives.

Based on those arguments, it can be argued that: (1) the creators of the social media technology consciously or cause cultural colonialism and hence destroy national identities; (2) that cultural colonialism drains socioeconomic capacities; and (3) ruptures the solidarity of communities, and as James Petras (2000) states, decades of cultural imperialism promote the cult of 'modernity' as conformity with external symbols. Equally, media content negotiates, ruptures, attacks social bonds and reshapes personalities are according to terms of media messaging while imperial media provide individuals with escapist identities (Petras 2000).

The mechanisms of cultural globalization include exported and shared film, literature and theater; while cultural and economic relations developed between nations as well as migration, immigration, and selected news coverage of incidents within nations have shaped how information flows on social media platforms.

To get a sense of the degree of the magnitude and depth of information circulation, its pervasiveness, and scope of persuasion, we propose a review of social media and international influence.

Social Media on Identity Construction Among the Youth

Istanbul University professor, Uğur Gündüz (2017), has appropriately defined social media as platforms where all virtual users with internet access can share content, express opinions about a topic and where communication and interaction process intensely take place without any time or place limitation. He has further argued that social media allows people to express themselves; on the other hand, it takes their believability and reliabilities away, trivializes them by objectifying (p. 91). Adolescents, teenagers, and people in their 20s and mid-thirties are now being described in media, family circles, and cosmopolitan communities as the lost generation (junkies) because of their heavy use and dependence on the internet and social media for information, advice, and instruction, or a place to obtain validation and personal gratification. The majority seem to be moving away from practicing local customs, spending time in the villages, taking instructions from their parents or elders—values generally associated with good moral upbringing. The massive exodus of young people into the towns and cities, even migration to foreign countries, the West- and East-based educational programs, widespread unemployment, and their increasing use of portable information and communication devices and access to internet-enhanced social networks all influence their culture.

There is increasing popularity of social media platforms and the internet in developing countries, and their widespread use affects the social strata, local contexts, impacts cultural norms, and group dynamics. According to a study conducted by the Royal Society for Public Health an independent, a multidisciplinary charity in the United Kingdom dedicated to the improvement of the public's health and wellbeing, 90%

of young people use social media more than any other age group.[5] Moreover, that rates of anxiety and depression in the UK have increased by 70% in the last 25 years. Social media has become the space where people form and build relationships, express themselves, shape self-identity, and learn about the world around us. Social media is linked to increased rates of anxiety, depression and poor sleep. The report also revealed that 91% of 16–24-year-olds use the internet for social networking; 70% in the past 25 years have experienced high rates of anxiety and depression. Prepared under the auspices of the United Kingdom's Royal Society for Public Health the report showed YouTube tops as the most positive with Instagram and Snapchat the most detrimental to young people's mental health and wellbeing (https://www.rsph.org.uk/our-work/policy/social-media-and-young-people-s-mental-health-and-wellbeing.html).

In some regions, internet cafés play critical sociopolitical roles in local civic life; there have been deep anxieties over the risks posed by the pubic techno-social space to young people. The digital divide has revealed that internet cafés functions as desirable social space for entertainment among young women from different socioeconomic backgrounds in China.

While most consumers prefer to use social media mainly to socialize, some institutions are gradually increasing their use of the internet and social media platforms to reach targeted groups or to disseminate messages for social change. For example, Wong et al. (2015) have discussed methods to engage adolescents and young adults on topics related to their health and how social media can be used to supplement or streamline the care public institutions provide to adolescents and young adults in the clinic. They report that a successful enrollment of more young adults for health care insurance in America depends in part on outreach efforts, including via social media. Meanwhile, other researchers have proposed further investigations to establish a framework for researching health outcomes from social media use in chronic disease management. Merolli et al. (2013) propose various uses of social media that may prove valuable for understanding social media's effect on individual health outcomes. The same framework can apply in surveying African young people's perceptions of social media use to determine the level of their

---

[5] Article titled Parliamentary Group launched to tackle health impact of social media on young people (written April 18, 2018) published at https://www.rsph.org.uk.

in participation in the globalization process and using the outcomes to engage the youth in social change.

SOCIAL MEDIA PENETRATION IN AFRICA

Overall, there has been a lower penetration rate in Africa compared to the rest of the world in the past two decades. According to a report published online by the Internet World Stats, a source that provides country and regional **stats** as well as online market research, of the 1 billion people in Africa in 2000, there were some 4,514,400 internet users and 453,329,534 by December 2018, while 177,005,700 people had used Facebook in sub-Sahara Africa. That reflects 35.2% population penetration and a 9.942% growth in internet growth between 2000 and 2017. According to the IDC markets for smartphones dropped from 44.6 to 39% in 2017, but there has since been a growth in feature phones with the introduction of Transsion, the Shenzhen, China-based handset maker of the Intel and Techno brands that started operations in some of Africa's largest markets. The mobile phone markets are likely to grow in 1 countries with large urban populations such as Nigeria, South Africa, Ethiopia, and DR Congo. The growth in the use of the internet, the iPhone and Facebook is creating employment for persons outside the traditional workplace, including the elderly and handicapped, women, and young people including college graduates. While in industrialized countries like the United States and Germany online shopping accounts for a measured increase in iPhone penetration, growing confidence and reliance on the product for interpersonal and group communication could lead to a growth in its use. In sub-Saharan Africa, other divergent factors such as data sharing on internal political crises might account for the increase in social media penetration.

Furthermore, the speed of the internet connection has accelerated faster in urban areas (allowing access to video material) than in rural areas.[6] Further, the African telecom market is projected to grow on average by at least 6.5% during the next few years. The CEO of the Chinese smartphone company Huawei CEO has reportedly stated that the company expects to double smartphone shipments to South Africa to two

[6]https://www.balancingact-africa.com/docs/reports/SSA-Media-Landscape.pdf.

Table 3.3   Most used social media networks in Africa as of June 2018

Social media platform	Role and reach in Africa
Facebook	13 million (1.79 billion worldwide)
LinkedIn	Users create a network of people they know and trust professionally
Instagram	2.7 million
Google+	Hosts Facebook and Twitters
Video sharing (Zoom)	The most engaging way of sharing video content
YouTube	8.28 million (1.5 billion worldwide)
Vimeo	Offered 4k video data in 2016, according to a post by Katy Takaoka. Vimeo's community is mainly video professionals and indie filmmakers
Live to stream	Platforms for users to broadcast and watch live video from their computers and smartphones
Twitter	7.5 million (allows only 140 characters per tweet)
Blab	Allows four people on air and others to interact
Periscope	Used to replay videos. Launched 2015

million devices and invest in Angola, Egypt, Mozambique, and Nigeria.[7] News sources such as Trendforce see the penetration rate of full-screen smartphone surge to 45% in 2018 alone (Table 3.3).[8]

Personal networks and interest-based sites are the most used social media agents for social change in Africa. In Kenya, there is increased accessibility of smartphones and mobile internet; social media are becoming an integral part of everyday life for young people. According to the second Julisha report, 59% of internet users in Kenya access the web to download movies, images, and music, as well as watch television, while 33% access information on goods and services, with just 8% utilizing it for the purchase of goods and services.[9] The low numbers could be a concern for the government that expects users to access the internet for business and education (Genrwot 2013). Conversely, the use of new social media tools like Facebook, Twitter, and WhatsApp, are quickly changing in the country. Previous research on new media, however,

[7] https://www.qelp.com/insights/africa-smartphone.

[8] Contify Telecom News, March 8, 2018.

[9] https://pctechmag.com/2013/03/main-uses-of-internet-in-kenya-a-cause-for-concern/.

Table 3.4 Internet penetration in Central America and South America (December 2011 stats)

- 50.1 million internet users in Central America; 173.1 million internet users in South America
- Internet penetration in the Central and South America region was 36%, demonstrating the massive growth potential in the region
- In some countries, internet connectivity is still patchy. For example, a blogger from an indigenous community in Bolivia may have to travel three and a half hours by bus to reach the nearest city and upload his blog posts
- 5 out of the top 20 nations spending the most time on social networks are in South America
- South America—one of the fastest growing regions for Facebook
- Brazil-over 53 million Facebook users, Guatemala has over two million
- Over 825,000 Argentinians are on Google+
- Brazil, Venezuela and Argentina—in the top 10 Twitter penetration list for March alone in 2011
- https://www.translatemedia.com/translation-services/south-america-social-media

---

indicates socio-demographic differences in the access, appropriation, and use of new technologies (Ndlela and Mulwo 2017).

The ultimate question is whether social media is the newest agent of colonization in Africa, after centuries of European presence and multinational corporations or a new resource that is capable of mobilizing the African population to chart its future in the twenty-first century and not rely on support from other continents. To put this into context let us compare the overall use of social media in Africa, Central, and South America to the rest of the world in these tables (Tables 3.4, 3.5, 3.6, and 3.7).

The Relevance of Social Media Uses to Local Culture

Arguably, social media gadgets mainly, the internet and iPhone may have a more significant potential to transform local cultures than radio and television broadcasts because they are user-driven. In other words, the users create and manage the content and disseminate what they want, which gives them more control than radio and television that typically feeds them with information. Through a sampling of dialogues, researchers have found social media to change the behavioral patterns and perspectives of young people toward certain health practices. In a

Table 3.5   Internet usage and population in South America compared to the world, 2018 stats

Internet users and population statistics for South America—produced in 2018

Region	Population[a] (2018 est.)	% Pop. of world	Internet users, 31-Dec-2017	Penetration (% population)	Internet[b] % users	Facebook, 31-Dec-2017
South America	428,240,515	5.6	306,349,946	71.5	7.4	266,583,100
Rest of world	7,206,517,913	94.4	3,850,582,194	53.4	92.6	1,852,477,052
World total	7,634,758,428	100.0	4,156,932,140	54.4	100.0	2,119,060,152

[a]Population figures are based on stats from the United Nations Population Data Division
[b]The internet data were pulled from figures published online by Nielson and the ITU
Source Internet World Stats, https://www.internetworldstats.com/stats15.htm. Table has been mildly modified

Table 3.6 Population penetration: internet users and Facebook subscribers per country vs the world

Country	Population (2018 est.)	Internet users 31-Dec-2000	Internet users 31-Dec-2017	Penetration (% population) (%)	Internet growth % 2000–2017	Facebook subscribers 31-Dec-2017
Algeria	42,008,054	50,000	18,580,000	44.2	37,060	19,000,000
Angola	30,774,205	30,000	5,951,453	19.3	19,738	3,800,000
Benin	11,458,674	15,000	3,801,758	33.1	25,245	920,000
Botswana	2,333,201	15,000	923,528	39.6	6057	830,000
Burkina Faso	19,751,651	10,000	3,704,265	18.8	36,942	840,000
Burundi	11,216,450	3000	617,116	5.5	20,470	450,000
Cabo Verde	553,335	8000	265,972	48.1	3225	240,000
Cameroon	24,678,234	20,000	6,128,422	24.8	30,542	2,700,000
Central African Rep.	4,737,423	1500	256,432	5.4	16,995	96,000
Chad	15,353,184	1000	768,274	5.0	76,727	260,000
Comoros	832,347	1500	130,578	15.7	8605	120,000
Congo	5,399,895	500	650,000	12.0	129,900	600,000
Congo, Dem. Rep.	84,004,989	500	5,137,271	6.1	1,027,354	2,100,000
Cote d'Ivoire	24,905,843	40,000	6,318,355	26.3	16,246	3,800,000
Djibouti	971,408	1400	180,000	18.5	12,757	180,000
Egypt	99,375,741	450,000	49,231,493	49.5	10,840	35,000,000
Equatorial Guinea	1,313,894	500	312,704	23.8	62,441	67,000
Eritrea	5,187,948	5000	71,000	1.4	1320	63,000
Ethiopia	107,534,882	10,000	16,437,811	15.3	164,278	4,500,000
Gabon	2,067,561	15,000	985,492	47.7	6470	620,000
Gambia	2,163,765	4000	392,277	18.1	9707	310,000
Ghana	29,463,643	30,000	10,110,000	34.3	33,600	4,900,000
Guinea	13,052,608	8000	1,602,485	12.3	19,931	1,500,000

(continued)

Table 3.6 (continued)

Country	Population (2018 est.)	Internet users 31-Dec-2000	Internet users 31-Dec-2017	Penetration (% population) (%)	Internet growth % 2000-2017	Facebook subscribers 31-Dec-2017
Guinea-Bissau	1,907,268	1500	120,000	6.3	7900	110,000
Kenya	50,950,879	200,000	43,329,434	85.0	21,564	7,000,000
Lesotho	2,263,010	4000	627,860	27.7	15,596	310,000
Liberia	4,853,516	500	395,063	8.1	78,912	330,000
Libya	6,470,956	10,000	3,800,000	58.7	37,900	3,500,000
Madagascar	26,262,810	30,000	1,900,000	7.2	6233	1,700,000
Malawi	19,164,728	15,000	1,828,503	9.5	12,090	720,000
Mali	19,107,706	18,800	12,480,176	65.3	66,283	1,500,000
Mauritania	4,540,068	5000	810,000	17.8	16,100	770,000
Mauritius	1,268,315	87,000	803,896	63.4	824	700,000
Mayotte (FR)	259,682	n/a	107,940	41.6	n/a	71,000
Morocco	36,191,805	100,000	22,567,154	62.4	22,467	15,000,000
Mozambique	30,528,673	30,000	5,279,135	17.3	17,497	1,800,000
Namibia	2,587,801	30,000	797,027	30.8	2557	570,000
Niger	22,311,375	5000	951,548	4.3	18,931	440,000
Nigeria	195,875,237	200,000	98,391,456	50.2	49,096	17,000,000
Reunion (FR)	883,247	130,000	480,000	54.3	269	420,000
Rwanda	12,501,156	5000	3,724,678	29.8	74,393	490,000
Saint Helena (UK)	4049	n/a	2200	54.3	n/a	1700
Sao Tome and Principe	208,818	6500	57,875	27.7	790	52,000
Senegal	16,294,270	40,000	9,749,527	59.8	24,274	2,900,000
Seychelles	95,235	6000	67,119	70.5	1018	61,000
Sierra Leone	7,719,729	5000	902,462	11.7	17,949	450,000

(continued)

Table 3.6 (continued)

Country	Population (2018 est.)	Internet users 31-Dec-2000	Internet users 31-Dec-2017	Penetration (% population) (%)	Internet growth % 2000–2017	Facebook subscribers 31-Dec-2017
Somalia	15,181,925	200	1,200,000	7.9	599,900	1,100,000
South Africa	57,398,421	2,400,000	30,815,634	53.7	1184	16,000,000
South Sudan	12,919,053	n/a	2,229,963	17.3	n/a	180,000
Sudan	41,511,526	30,000	11,816,570	28.5	39,288	2,600,000
Swaziland	1,391,385	10,000	446,051	32.1	4360	170,000
Tanzania	59,091,392	115,000	23,000,000	38.9	19,900	6,100,000
Togo	7,990,926	100,000	899,956	11.3	800	560,000
Tunisia	11,659,174	100,000	7,898,534	67.7	7798	6,400,000
Uganda	44,270,563	40,000	19,000,000	42.9	47,400	2,600,000
Western Sahara	561,257	n/a	28,000	5.0	n/a	24,000
Zambia	17,609,178	20,000	7,248,773	41.2	36,144	1,600,000
Zimbabwe	16,913,261	50,000	6,796,314	40.2	13,492	880,000
Total Africa	1,287,914,329	4,514,400	453,329,534	35.2	9942	177,005,700
Rest of world	6,346,844,099	83.1%	3,703,602,606	58.4	89.1	1,942,054,452
World total	7,634,758,428	100.0%	4,156,932,140	54.4	100.0	2,119,060,152

Source Internet World Statistics, https://www.internetworldstats.com/stats1.htm. Retrieved October 2018

Table 3.7   General statistics on active social media users in regions in Africa (October 2018)

Facebook: 13 million in Africa
LinkedIn: Users create a network of people they know and trust professionally
Instagram: 2.7 million users in Africa
Google+: Hosts Facebook and Twitter users
Video sharing: Most engaging way of sharing video content
YouTube: 8.28 million. 1.5 billion viewers watch 6 billion videos per day
Vimeo: Offered 4k video data in 2016, according to a post by Katy Takaoka. Vimeo's community is mainly video professionals and indie filmmakers
Live Streaming: Type of video sharing. Platforms for users to broadcast and watch live video from their computers and smartphones
Periscope: Good for a replay of videos. Was Launched in 2015
Blab: Allows 4 people on air and others to interact
Twitter: 7.5 million users in Africa (only allows 140 characters per tweet)
Tumblr: Similar to Twitter. Allows re-blogging
Blogging;
Photo sharing
WordPress
Live Journal:
Reddit

Source http://www.pcmag.com

case study of love Life, and South Africa's largest HIV-prevention initiative, youth were engaged in vivid dialogues on Facebook about societal grievances, and results confirmed that there are elements of a dialogue for change inherent in the analyzed dialogue sample and emphasize the potential of social media dialogues to drive social change (Benzinger 2014). However, other studies that focus on HIV/AIDS among the older adults in Africa found that participants use email and social media to maintain contact with family and friends outside of, and sometimes even within the neighborhood (Bosch and Currin 2015).

Research has also interrogated the role of the media in helping or deterring voting engagement and perceptions among young people (quote Morocco), and have found that local media fail to engage young people with content that advances their political identities. In a study of the young people's role in voting, Vanessa Malila, a researcher at the Journalism and Media Studies department, Rhodes University, found that despite high levels of media consumption, youths are engaging with formal politics because of pressure from family or due to socioeconomic limitations, rather than a desire to add value to their citizenship (2016). Other factors such as strong family values, the high cost of maintaining and using the gadgets, and ongoing political climate may also affect the longevity or extinction of local cultures. Overall, there is a multidirectional approach for understanding the role of media in constructing cultural identities in a newly globalized media environment (Gentz and Kramer 2006), and the media has implications for understanding how globalization works and how cultures are affected.

Contextualizing Local Culture and Globalization

This study sees *local culture* as the values, practices, and knowledge a group continuously exposed and which subsequently drive its collective actions. It assumes the cultural convergence approach—which people are capable of being whatever they want to be when exposed to knowledge, and the things people learn and differentiate them from other people. The more cultures interact, the more their values, ideologies, behaviors, and customs will begin to reflect each other. In addition, because they have natural reasoning skills, individuals can mix all of the cultures with those tools to create a variety of meaning. A group's exposure to globally accessible information technology (e.g., iPhone and internet) determines whether its quality of life is improving, deteriorating or stagnant. Thus, this author applied the stance that the ideas, meanings, beliefs, and values people learn as members of a given community can be applied in the global information marketplace (GIM) with expectant clashes.

Given that each cultural group its unique way of thinking and acting based on own beliefs and values, this study sought to know whether young African men and women would be swept into the whirlwind of globalization and become world citizens, whether the younger ones would inculcate some of the foreign values present on social media which they found to be relevant to their immediate educational-economic circumstances, or they merely utilize the gadgets for entertainment. It invokes Castells' (1996) position that networked communities have changed to such an extent that one can talk of a new society fundamentally different because there has been a massive use of communication technology. Indeed, the mind can engage with other cultures. It is open to various experiences. Cultural identities erode, and new identities are created through exposure to communication as the political activist and sociologist, Stuart Hall (1992) has earlier indicated. Of course, it is possible that there can be a coexistence, harmony, and synchronization of cultures in one space, whether it is oral, written, printed, mass, or cyber mediated. The fact that electronic media have created new social situations that are no longer shaped by where we are reveals that with our continued use of electronic media we can lose our natural relation to culture and our legal claim to space (geographic location) we occupy (Kraidy 2002, 2005) globalization (Ngwainmbi 2000).

That cyber or networked community is indeed a new society within a more extensive network—the global society—because its members interact cannot be undermined, if we know that people in a given community have tools that are capable of creating, disseminating, and retrieving, storing and sharing knowledge and building communities and relationships.

Organizations are helping young people develop relationships by sponsoring events around emerging media and digital culture. Another study has found Facebook useful in helping college students develop positive relationships with their peers on campus (Ellison et al. 2007); another study tackled digital divides concerning youth participation in SNS—whether adolescent participation in SNS influence their personal development in terms of self-esteem and psychological wellbeing (Ahn 2011). In a survey conducted in South Africa to determine how dialogue could be used to effect social change on Facebook, Benzinger (2014) found that dialogues among the youth trigger thought processes and create mutual understanding about the societal situation. In a study conducted in 2017, Martin Ndlela and Abraham Mulwo determined that young people in Kenya create spaces on social media to connect, interact, communicate and engage others on different issues. Elsewhere, email and social media have been found useful in maintaining contact with family and friends within and outside the neighborhood. Another study found that older adults in Cape Town, South Africa get gratification from computers—participants felt connected with society through their communication with and observation of people. It kept them informed about news and current interest topics (Bosch and Currin 2015). Such efforts aimed at gauging the positive values of social media communication in active communities.

A PSEUDO-SCIENTIFIC PERSPECTIVE OF THE AFRICAN CULTURAL MILIEU

The value of a thing, be it an object or a belief, is generally defined as its worth. Just as an object is seen to be of a high value that is treasured, our beliefs about what is right or wrong that are worth being held are equally treasured (Idang 2015). Per that view, a value can be considered a point of view or conviction by with or for we can live or even die. Our social, moral, political, religious, aesthetic, and economic values are bound by our determination to perform and replicate our actions around what we represent. Thus, by declaring our actions, objects, situations, feelings or thoughts as wrong or right, beautiful or hideous, useful or useless only explains why to carry out related activities and spend time dealing with them. Culture is a way of life freely selected and accepted by a group of people in time and space; it is not a science.

Anthropologists, socio-linguists, sociologists have theorized about the practical importance of values and customs in keeping African communities together, but development communication scholars, particularly those involved with the economics of globalization and communication such as Ngwainmbi (2014a, b, c), Kraidy (2005). The presence of the first Europeans on African inside shores since the fifteenth-century influenced customs, resulting in a set of hybrid values and customs across that continent, some of which have forced the African born youth to practice a mélange of Afro-Western culture and be perceived as a stranger in own community. This one of the reasons why young Africans are taking steps to change global perceptions about African culture and initiating policy reform in their own countries. The wave of public demonstrations in Northern Africa that started in 2010, led by college graduates and other youth saw a change in government policies and replacement of dictators across Tunisia, Egypt, and Libya (Ngwainmbi 2017). In addition, the Official Custodian of South African Nation Brand, a web-based national initiative that encourages all South Africans to contribute to positive change presents 21-year-old Zingisa Socikwa (a film student) and an 11th Grade student who have taken measures to redefine and model how people in the world view their African identity and move away from harmful, preconceived, colonial mindset. The social movement, Blackboard Africa aims to change the perceptions of black youth to a positive narrative.

However, there may be a more significant concern that African cultures are in danger of being practiced by those young people spending much time on iPhones or the internet. Looking at local practices that foster group interactions and community cohesiveness such as marital rites, childbirth and death ceremonies, installment of local leaders, court proceedings, and town criers who deliver essential announcements for community well-being there is reason to wonder whether those customs may be compromised or they may be forced to compete for the young people's attention.

Among the most appropriate African cultural values that foreigners should know before they travel to Africa, it should be noted that actions speak louder than words, especially if there is a barrier between languages. In addition, among Africans close kinship relations are held at a high premium (Idang 2015). To the extent that social media is the pastime of African youth and middle-aged, educated ones, we can consider the technology a new form of colonization of the African mind. Instead of spending much of their time reading about a world they are economically prepared to face, the youth ought to focus on developing concepts and thoughts with their roots in Africa. This position is consistent with others that an African-centered thought process is an act of decolonizing the African mind (Chinweizu 1987; Asante and Abarry 1996) and that the development of concepts rooted in the African tradition has the prospect of working towards the decolonization of the African intellectual landscape and eventually the Africa-centered mind or "Africanity." For the Africa-centered mind to grow, each group is expected to apply existing resources best known to its milieu. For the African youth and the working class of the twenty-first century, social media and its gadgets are the primary resources.

There is more evidence that activities carried out on social media enhance communication, social connection, and even technical skills (Ito et al. 2010). New social media configurations such as Facebook, Myspace, and Twitter; gaming sites and virtual worlds such as Club Penguin, Second Life, and video sites such as YouTube; and blogs invariably offer young people and working adults' alternative spaces for communicating and mediating with their caste. In various countries, more young people rely heavily on handheld gadgets and online platforms to share news and information or entertain themselves. A growing number of clinical practitioners is examining youth participation on social network sites and their potentially harmful effects on the emotional fitness of the youngsters. Gwenn Schurgin O'Keeffe and Kathleen

Clarke-Pearson of the Council on Communications and Media citing widespread bullying on social media networks have urged parents to monitor for potential problems with cyberbullying, pointing out that pediatricians are in a unique position to help families understand these sites (2011).

Drawing from the rich experiences that researchers and marketing teams have recorded about the intimate uses and gratifications social media platforms offer their consumers, and that some young people in several African countries identified other socioeconomic benefits in a pilot study in 2017, media and communication analysts should be curious to find out if there has been a shift in the trend. An inquisition into how IT consumers in the developing world, particularly young people and employed persons in a country, are investing their time and spending their money on social media networks could give decision-makers and businesses a clue to alternative strategies they need to chart sustainable futures for their respective countries.

Study Background

This study seeks to know which cyber-mediated devices were more likely to deepen their understanding of and participation in the globalization process—iPhones or the internet (gadgets). It examined whether the "internal socialization," "inter—extra personal socialization" or "personal advancement" is the primary reason why they own those devices. In comparing their age group and education level with profession and length of the exposure to those gadgets, the study wanted to know whether those factors had any impact on the frequency with which the two groups their local customs. It assumed that increased reliance on foreign information channels such as the iPhone and internet could destabilize their sense of commonality and a context for detaching themselves from their traditional values—the things that culturally identify them as Africans.

Respondents were reached online in cities and rural areas in Cameroon, Nigeria, Gambia, Kenya, and South Africa using open and close-ended questions. Some respondents were reached on the streets. The study was expected to show the more substantial use of iPhones and reliance on "foreign news and entertainment content" by rural residents compared to urban populations. The study expected that results might help non-profit organizations involved in strengthening indigenous communities and foreign businesses in packaging and disseminating messages tailored to the targeted group.

The results could also help leaders in the selected countries to design governance policies aimed at promoting nationalism and limiting circumstances that bring divisions among the cyber-informed educated ones and the local leaders, and subsequently fragile state institutions.

CONTEXTUAL FRAMEWORKS

The expectation in this study is that, given the heavy social presence by younger adults around the world, younger Africans aged 18–29 would be more likely to draw entertainment gratifications from social media than the older ones (aged 30–44, or 45 and above). Their education level, profession, length of time using the iPhone or internet and the purpose of its use could shed some light on the extent of their global acculturation. Further, this study could confirm emerging research studies that youth spend a considerable portion of their daily life interacting through social media, which pointed out the power of online dialogues in change processes by making topics being present in the minds of people and making them discussed.

DESIGN AND PROCEDURE

The research design of this study was experimental as it wanted to know the extent to which iPhone use brought gratification among students, teachers, lecturers, nurses, journalists and economists aged between 18 and older. In the questionnaire preamble, the researcher informed participants that answers would be published and asked them not to include their identity, but to freely express their views on how they felt iPhones has fostered or can foster participation of the African continent in the globalization process on a project to be published, and to email them back to the researcher. The study asked participants to state whether the internet or iPhone had a negative or positive impact on their communication skills.

The following widely shared beliefs guided the study:

• that social life, as a rule, is governed by patterns of joint action;
• that the individual cannot function without a relationship (Gergen's 1997, p. 124);

- that the vast part of human action grows out of interchange and leads to further interchange;
- that digital media facilitates social interaction and empowers people; and
- that social media can help to deepen relationships and facilitate the formation of support networks—68% of teen social media users have received support on these platforms during tough times (World Economic Forum 2016).

The study asked them to explain how they typically use the iPhone/internet for and whether they believe, the quality of their life improved or worsened since they started using the gadget, and how their country could utilize those gadgets to make Africa's contributions to the GIM. The questions were the following (Table 3.8).

Table 3.8 Questionnaire for the youth and working class in Africa

Name your country _____

a. Please highlight or underline the correct answer. Your age range is
   1. 18–29
   2. 30–44
   3. 45–54
   4. 55 and above

b. Your level of education is
   1. High school Graduate
   2. Bachelor's degree
   3. Masters, doctorate
   4. Vocation

c. What is your profession?
   1. Student
   2. Teacher/Lecturer
   3. Medical (nurse, researcher)
   4. Journalist

d. For how long have you been using the internet and how much time do you spend per day on the gadget?
   1. less than one year
   2. One year
   3. 5 years
   4. 10 years

(continued)

Table 3.8   (continued)

e. For how long have you been using the iPhone and how much time do you spend per day on the gadget?

  1. Less than one year
  2. 1 year
  3. 5 years
  4. 10 years

f. What do you typically use the internet for?

  1. To read the news in order to know what is happening in other regions/countries
  2. To understand the cultures and entertainment styles in other countries/regions
  3. To receive and send emails
  4. For business

g. What do you typically use your iPhone for?

  1. To read the news in order to know what's happening in other regions/countries
  2. To understand the cultures and entertainment styles in other countries/regions
  3. To receive and send emails
  4. For business

h. Overall, do you believe the quality of your life has improved or it has worsened since you started using the gadget?

  1. It's good
  2. It's better
  3. It's bad
  4. It's worse

i. Give your reasons. Please be brief

j. What should your country/region do to contribute to the global information marketplace?

  1. Invent its own technology (internet, iPhones)
  2. Invent its own technology (internet, iPhones) and distribute it to other countries
  3. Only design the programs/software/language to be used on the internet and iPhone
  4. Continue using the gadgets. I'm happy with my iPhone/internet
  5. Change some items on the iPhone such as _____
  6. Reduce the cost of using the internet or iPhone
  7. All of the above

k. How has your use of the internet or your iPhone negatively affected your communication skills? Has your use of the internet/iPhone improved your social and cultural habits, or it has been a setback? Please explain

l. If you were asked to recommend specific developing traditional/local communication and knowledge-sharing methods that could help the people in your country to develop their economy (e.g. enable more people to get jobs, improve the infrastructures, improve people's health and other living standards), which communication/knowledge-sharing skills would you recommend?

CODING

The ten questions asked requested basic demographics such as age, education, and profession, to questions asking about the length of time spent per day, monthly or yearly using the iPhone and/or internet; purpose of use; its impact on the individual's life; and how the gadget could improve the quality of lives of people in their respective nations.

Each question had six possible answers. Item 6 in questions b, c, f, and g was coded based on the specific response provided by the participant. Questions f and g allowed respondents to select more than one answer while questions k and l purposely wanted them to elaborate their knowledge and understanding of the usefulness of the gadgets to their socioeconomic circumstances.

PARTICIPANTS

The study sampled persons aged between 18 years old to at least 55 years old. Although the youth make up the majority of the African population per census recently conducted by the United Nations Population Fund, this study purposely included persons above 35 years to measure not only the degree to which social media penetration in Africa had affected the values of young people compared to older people, but also whether their exposure to iPhone and internet had enhanced knowledge of their readiness for economic empowerment vis-à-vis the international community. This is why participants were asked to recommend developing local communication and knowledge-sharing methods that could help the people in their respective countries to develop their economy (e.g., enable more people to get jobs, improve the infrastructures, improve people's health and other living standards), which knowledge-sharing skills they could recommend to state policymakers.

Participants were based in South Africa, Malawi, Nigeria, Cameroon, Kenya, and the Gambia.

METHOD

The researcher pulled emails from a roster of development experts published by NEPAD member countries with an email provided to receive completed questions. The roster contains questions about users' demographic information (age, profession, country of current residence), how long they had used the iPhone and internet, their objectives for using the gadget, and what they thought their country or region do to contribute to the GIM. The majority of respondents took the survey from android platforms and desktop computers.

The researcher also selected contacts from the following personal sources gathered during 20 years' professional consultations with international development organizations sponsored by the Nations organization: (1) United Nations agencies; (2) the New Partnership for African Development (NEPAD); (3) the African Capacity Building Foundation (ACBF) with a mission to build strategic partnerships, offer technical support, and provide access to relevant knowledge related to capacity building in Africa; (4) Africa Infrastructure Development Foundation; and (5) African Development Bank—a regional finance and development institution with various experts.

The questions were emailed between October 1, 2017 and January 10, 2018, to sixty potential participants. The researcher asked potential respondents to share the questionnaire with other African (potential respondents) in their email accounts.

ANALYSIS

Demographics

Participants were high school and middle school, high school, college students, teachers, economics, journalists, as well as people in business, lawyer, and biomedical researchers. One hundred ten (110) persons in South Africa, Malawi, Nigeria, Cameroon, Kenya, and the Gambia completed the survey.

RQ4 (d). For how long have you been using the internet and how much time do you spend per day on the gadget?

The question sought to determine whether the length of time spent surfing the internet and individual financial investment in that technology was only for personal gratification (such as sending and receiving emails, enjoying sports and music on YouTube or gaining knowledge about the world through online newsfeeds and news articles). The study assumed that users who spent just one hour per day for a few years were more likely to communicate with friends and loved ones less likely to search and read the news or learn about cultures and traditions in other counties. However, those who spent more time online daily and had been using the platform for five or more years were more likely to see it as a significant resource for their socioeconomic growth. For as this author has argued elsewhere (Ngwainmbi 2000, 2005, 2007), longevity in the use of information technology will not only make the African mind more dependent on its use, it could provide a context for the user to develop creative skills—talent, intellectual capital—needed for individual and/or team advancement.

Participants were also asked how long they had used the internet. The reason for this was to see whether the iPhone had a more significant influence on their worldviews, assuming that such a portable communication tool typically gives users instant access to information and news happening anywhere, subsequently allowing them to broaden their knowledge and outreach.

To know whether the targeted population in Africa used those relatively new channels for social interaction in Africa only for instant gratification or constructively, the study used the following phrasing: **RQ6 (f)**: What do you typically do on the internet? Select one or more answers that apply.

a. To read the news in order to know what is happening in other regions/countries.
b. To understand the cultures/way of life in other countries/regions.
c. To understand the political climate in other countries and how the youth deal with policies.
d. To receive and send emails.
e. For entertainment such as watching football, access music on YouTube.
f. Describe other reasons.

The study asked them to explain why they used their iPhone as well.

RQ8 (h). Overall, do you believe the quality of your life has improved, or it has worsened since you started using the gadget?

The question allowed participants to describe in their own words the socioeconomic and cultural impact of the iPhone and the internet on them.

RQ10 (j). How has your use of the internet or your iPhone affected your communication skills? Has your use of the internet/iPhone improved your social and cultural habits, or it has been a setback? Please explain.

RQ11. If you were asked to recommend specific developing local communication and knowledge-sharing methods that could help the people in your country to develop their economy (e.g., enable more people to get jobs, improve the infrastructures, improve people's health and other living standards), which communication/knowledge-sharing skills would you recommend?

All participants indicated they had noticed a significant improvement in the quality of life since they started using the iPhone and internet. Among them, 61% were journalists, economists, and businesspersons; 30% of students; and 9% were teachers and science researchers. 53% had a Masters or doctorate; 15% vocational; 15% high school students; and 15% with a BS degree.

There was a correlation between the level of education and profession and longevity of iPhone and internet use. 68% of those with advanced degrees (BS, MS, Doctorate) had spent over ten years using the iPhone and internet with only 15% of vocational people, and only 10% of high school students have spent less than one year on the internet. Per the chart, there is a correlation between being well-educated and spending more time on the internet and iPhone use. Further, 84% of all persons who had used both gadgets for more than ten years were well-educated (had at least the BS degree) and were professionals (journalists, economists, biomedical researchers, and people in business). Only 16% were high school students.

Asked why they used it, 38% of all respondents said they used the internet to get news and information, with 76% indicating they used the iPhone for the same purpose. 61% accessed the internet to send and receive emails while only 15% used the iPhone for the same purpose. 23% of all respondents used the iPhone for entertainment and to learn about foreign cultures or entertainment themselves, while 46% were businesspersons. 61% respondents stated that they used the internet to communicate; 15% used it for the same purpose. Based on the overall use of both gadgets we may extrapolate that veteran users (business people, journalists, economists, and biomedical researchers) found the gadgets credible tools for gaining knowledge or entertainment. Moreover, the fact that a whopping 96% relied heavily on both gadgets to harvest knowledge about foreign cultures or get news about happenings around the world (a cumulative 110%) shows the extent to which social media networks can serve as a conduit for defining the African youth and working population's place in the ongoing globalization process. Clearly, the internet is seen as a significant source of news and information while the iPhone is a very important tool for communicating personal thoughts as Figs. 3.3 and 3.5 show (Fig. 3.4).

Further, the study shows that the longer the time users spent on the gadget, they seemed to acquire and pursue more information about things happening around the world (see Fig. 3.5).

The internet is the largest data distributor in the world; it has the overwhelming power in influencing modern pop-culture and is capable

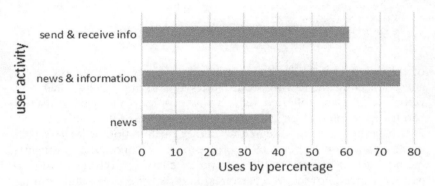

Fig. 3.3 Distribution of internet use by all groups

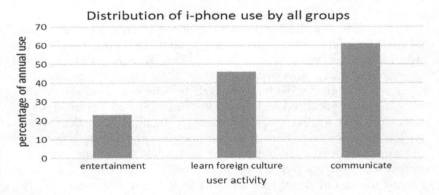

Fig. 3.4 Distribution of iPhones by all groups

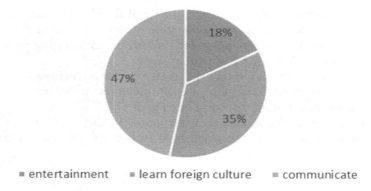

Fig. 3.5 Longevity of iPhone use

of enlightening well-educated youth and professionals about the world, and connecting them with social fabrics abroad and honing their non-verbal skills. Data collected reflects this position. All participants who had used the internet for ten years or more expressed its positive impact, 78% had the Bachelor's degree or higher qualification as well as technicians (vocational), and 69% professionals (economists, journalists, biomedical researchers). Although no teachers or lecturers, who are par excellence knowledge repertoires, knowledge-seekers, and communicators, took part in the survey, we cannot extrapolate from the overwhelming response the well-educated persons and the working class group that teachers would have found the internet a useful resource as well.

The key question how has your use of the internet or your iPhone affected your communication skills? Sought to know whether the hypothesis of previous studies by the Pew Research Center would apply to the group interviewed, whether their exposure to communication activity on the World Wide Web fraught with multivariate content (including good and bad images and texts) as well diverse linguistic expressions and writing styles had advanced or diminished their morality. The locus for that verbiage in that question was that unfettered and un-tutored exposure to information received could trump one's ability to express real thoughts and feelings or compromise one's values, as distinguished scholars in global media studies such as Jan Nederveen Pieterse, Jonathan Friedman, Manuel Castells, Homi Bhabha, Mikhail Bakhtin, Arjun Appadurai, or Hamid Mowlana have invariably noted.

The study juxtaposed the responses of the economists and biomedical researchers with those of persons representing the education community—teachers, students, and journalists—and found no negative impact of communicating online. Only the journalists were critical of the platform and they warned that the internet is a distraction. Unless controlled, these technological advances are a severe intrusion to one's life and tranquility (Table 3.9).

The results summarized in Table 3.10 show that the internet and iPhone had a positive impact on youth and working adults.

Table 3.9 Summary of participant statements: internet use and its impact

Profession	Education	Purpose	Length of internet use	Overall impact
	High school Bachelor	– Read news – Receive/send emails	Five years and above	– Keeps contact with friends worldwide – Helped me learn
Businessmen	Master's	– Receive/send emails	10 years and above	– Taught me how to correct mistakes and treat people better in my community
Lab researcher	Doctorate	– Receive/send emails – Work correspondence, banking, bills	10 years and above	– Spellings are more incorrect – Eases face to face discussion – Interaction has reduced, social interactions have been limited – Gossip has increased with unverified facts
Journalist	Doctorate Master's	– Receive/send emails	Over 10 years and above	– The internet is a distraction – Unless controlled, these technological advances are a severe intrusion to one's life and tranquility
Economist	Master's	– Read news	Over 10 years	– Internet keeps contact with friends worldwide
Lawyer	Master's	– Correspondence, banking, bills	Over 10 years	– Keeps contact with friends worldwide

Table 3.10 iPhone per profession, education level, and the gadget's overall impact

Profession	Education	Purpose	Length of iPhone use	Overall impact
Student	High school Bachelor	– Read news – Receive/send emails	Less than 5 years	– Can research at own pace – Can communicate with different people online – It has improved my social skills
Businessmen	Master's	– Receive/send emails	Less than 5 years	– Can search for information for personal growth
Lab researcher	Doctorate	– Receive/send emails	Over 10 years	– Gossip has increased with unverified facts
Journalist	Doctorate Master's	– Receive/send emails	Over 10 years	– The internet is a distraction – Unless controlled, these technological advances are a severe intrusion to one's life and tranquility
Economist	Master's	– Read news	Less than 1 year	– Phone keeps in contact with friends around the world
Lawyer	Master's	– Correspondence, banking, bills	Over 10 years	– Keeps contact with friends worldwide

Given that the majority of respondents were quite familiar with the two products and had continuously used them for more than ten years, the study wanted to know how they felt about their country's standing in the GIM, whether the technology they were using could give their country some form of recognition vis-à-vis the world. The question "In what ways should your country utilize the internet and iPhone to contribute to the global information marketplace?" invoked resourcefulness

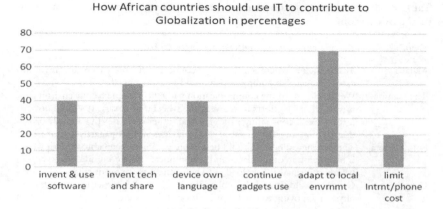

Fig. 3.6 Respondent views on how African countries should use IT to contribute to globalization

among African youth—a sense that African countries should become the vanguard of their destiny by creating information technology and controlling its content, instead or relying on existing tools. Results show that an overwhelming majority of respondents want their country to invent their own IT gadgets or at least adapt internet and iPhone content to local realities—language and content as shown in the graph (Fig. 3.6).

Q11 that respondents to recommend specific local communication and knowledge-sharing methods that could help the people in their respective country to develop strategic areas in their economy to enable more people to get jobs, improve the infrastructures, improve people's health and other living standards, which communication/knowledge-sharing skills, the participants in this study made the following recommendations (Table 3.11).

Commentary

Responses are consistent with the concept that African youth and working populations, whether they are offspring of the independence era in their respective countries or social media generation (today's youth aged 18–34) are victims of Euro-Western intellectually incarcerated, that the

Table 3.11 Participant recommendations for future socioeconomic and cultural participation

Country	Recommendations for contribution to the GIM
Malawi	Telemedicine/whereby experts are connected remotely to review medical cases (images, lab findings) with local less experienced staff
The Gambia	We should adopt the communication gadgets in vogue to our environment and make efforts to reinvent the wheel if necessary. It should not just be about consuming products from other countries but actually producing our gadgets that speak our languages and propagate our cultures
South Africa	The internet, iPhones should help more people to keep abreast with what is happening in other places and communicate with communities, everywhere, information overload; also make them more productive
Cameroon	Capacity building and skill enhancement through internet learning unlike physically moving to particular locations for refresher training
Kenya	It is hard to find any country that has been able to develop without domesticating its culture and language. Thus, internet content should have aspects of local cultures
Zambia	Persons expect rapid almost instantaneous responses to their cellphone communications, which is a real disruption to my pattern and pace of life. Unless controlled, these technological advances are a severe intrusion to one's life and tranquility

African's psychology is still skewed, and still dependent on external processes. This position reminds us of the prevailing notion that the state of African intellectual imprisonment in European value and belief systems occasioned by ignorance of African philosophical, cultural and historical truths. CI is the goal of miseducation, the result of de-acculturalization, and the major obstacle to innovative, creative and liberal African thought and practice (Nobles 1986).

The respondents recommend developing traditional, local communication and knowledge-sharing methods that could help the people in their country to develop their economies, such as enabling more people to get jobs, improve the infrastructures, improve people's health and other living standards, which communication/knowledge-sharing skills.

STUDY LIMITATIONS AND RECOMMENDATIONS FOR FURTHER INVESTIGATION

The primary purpose of the study was to know the extent to which the use of the internet and iPhone by the youth and working class in Africa had advanced their knowledge of things happening outside Africa, subsequently worsening or improving their socioeconomic condition. Although we may know how the youth and working class population use the iPhone and internet for social and cultural activities, we cannot comfortably make specific conclusions about whether they are more or less disconnected from their own cultures nor can we confidently state that they have become global citizens. The broad-based nature of recommendations initiated by the open-ended questions suggests that iPhone and internet users have not spent ample time on the gadgets to inform their leaders and lawmakers on appropriate measures for preparing national social policies. Nor have their general answers given local company executives the research data to help them prepare business plans targeting youth and working class.

Second, the study did not identify the income levels of the working class population, explain the contexts of "culture" or probe the close-ended questions to determine clear perspectives of iPhone and internet use. Factors such as electricity shortage, access to communication products, internet censorship, or financial ability were not mentioned.

The sample size was small, and not representative of the broader spectrum of the social media population.

Next, the respondents' age range is rather broad and may not reflect each group's longevity in using the gadget. Similarly, there may have been the sporadic use of a given gadget over some years because of the limited presence of electricity, job loss, financial hardship, and a government crackdown on users or other factors.

Further, the opinions of the participants may not represent all "African youth" and "working class."

Lastly, the countries do not represent Africa, which is a place with varying religious, cultural beliefs, and varying economic circumstances that can affect people's attitude toward communication and information sharing as well as their purchasing power. Further studies should address those limitations. For example, in-depth interviews might be conducted to understand the topic further.

SUGGESTIONS FOR SOCIAL AND ECONOMIC CHANGE

Since teachers and lecturers customarily recognized as knowledge generators and distributors did not participate in this study, it would be important for research to focus on that group, mainly because in developing regions like Africa educators' opinions are highly respected. Lastly, given the high costs of airtime, massive unemployment, censorship of political content, the lack of durable ICT infrastructure, and the absence of social media policies in some countries it is hard to get a clear picture of the social impact of the social media use among the youth and working class in Africa.

QUESTIONS FOR DISCUSSION

1. Social media is an accurate test of our personality. Do you agree? Give concrete reasons.
2. Which data published about internet penetration, particularly Facebook use in your country are you most likely to trust? Would you trust data from a statistics division in your government, the UN, Nielson, Internet World Stats or all of them? Give your reasons.
3. In his book titled *Too Much of a Good Thing: Are You Addicted to Your Smartphone?*

Dr. James Roberts, marketing professor at Baylor University's Hankamer School of Business identifies conditions that show smartphone addiction. Identify and explain them and indicate whether you agree with the research.

4. If you were a psychologist, which methods would you use to test for social media addiction?
5. Should every country on this planet give its citizens unfettered access to the internet?

REFERENCES

Adegoke, Y. (2017, March 6). Why Social Media Is the Only Media in Africa. *Quartz*.
Ahn, J. (2011). The Effect of Social Network Sites on Adolescents' Social and Academic Development: Current Theories and Controversies. *Journal of the Association for Information Science, 62*(8), 1435–1445.
Arvidson, A. (2006). *Brands: Meaning and Value in the Media Culture*. Abingdon, Oxon: Routledge.
Asante, M., & Abarry, A. S. (1996). *African Intellectual Heritage: A Book of Sources*. Philadelphia, PA: Temple University Press.

Baran, J. S. (2017). *Introduction to Mass Communication: Media Literacy and Culture* (10th ed.). New York: McGraw Hill.

Benzinger, B. (2014). A Dialogue for Social Change on Facebook: A South African Case Study. *Global Media Journal: African Edition, 8*(2), 275–300, 26pp.

Bosch, T., & Currin, B. (2015). Uses and Gratifications of Computers in South African Elderly People. *Communicate, 23*(45), 9–17, 9pp.

Castells, M. (1996). *The Rise of the Networked Society*. Malden, MA: Blackwell.

Chinweizu, O. J. (1987). *Decolonizing the African Mind*. Lagos, Nigeria: Pero Publishers.

Ellison, N. B., Steinfield, C., & Lampe, C. (2007). The benefits of Facebook "Friends": Social Capital and College Students' Use of Online Social Network Sites. *Journal of Computer-Mediated Communication, 12*(4), article 1. http://jcmc.indiana.edu/vol12/issue4/ellison.html.

Furedi, F. (2015, February 16). *How the Internet and Social Media Are Changing the Culture*. The Aspen Institute.

Galarneau, L. (2017, July 21). The Revolutionary Role of Social Media. In *Planetary Liberation Force—The Resistance*. https://medium.com/planetary-liberation-front. Retrieved September 6, 2019.

Garlick, B. (2015, March 18). *Advantages and Disadvantages of Social Media as a News Channel*. https://www.linkedin.com/pulse/advantages-disadvantages-social-media-news-channel-bob-garlick/. Accessed February 5, 2018.

Genrwot, J. (2013, March). Main Uses of the Internet in Kenya a Cause for Concern. *PCTech Magazine*.

Gentz, N., & Kramer, S. (2006). *Globalization, Cultural Identities, and Media Representations*. Albany: State University of New York Press.

Gergen, K. (1997). Social Psychology as Social Construction: The Emerging Vision. In C. McCarty & A. S. Haslam (Eds.), *The Message of Social Psychology: Perspectives of Mind in Society* (pp. 113–128). Oxford, UK: Blackwell.

Gobe, M. (2001). *Emotional Branding: The New Paradigm for Connecting Brands to People*. New York: Allworth Press.

Greico, E. (2017, November 2). *More Americans Are Turning to Multiple Social Media Sites for News*. The Pew Research Center. http://www.pewresearch.org/fact-tank/2017/11/02/more-americans-are-turning-to-multiple-social-media-sites-for-news/. Retrieved September 15, 2018.

Gündüz, U. (2017). The Effect of Social Media on Identity Construction. *Mediterranean Journal of Social Sciences, 8*(5), 85–92.

Hall, S. (1992). New Ethnicities. In S. Thornham, C. Bassett, & P. Harris (Eds.), *Media Studies: A Reader* (pp. 269–276). Washington Square, NY: New York University Press.

Human Implications of Digital Media. (2016). *A Report Published in 2016 by the World Economic Forum*. http://reports.weforum.org. Retrieved September 5, 2018.

Idang, E. G. (2015). African Culture and Values. *Phronimon, 16*(2), 97–111.

Ito, M., Horst, H., Brittany, M., et al. (2010). *Living and Learning with New Media: Summary of Findings from the Digital Youth Project.* Chicago, IL: John D. and Catherine T. MacArthur Foundation Reports on Digital Media and Learning; 2008. Available at http://digitalyouth.ischool.berkeley.edu/files/report/digitalyouth-TwoPageSummary.pdf. Accessed January 9, 2018.

Kraidy, M. (2002). Hybridity in Cultural Globalization. *Communication Theory, 12*(3), 316–339. https://doi.org/10.1111/j.1468-2885.2002.tb00272.x.

Kraidy, M. (2005). *Hybridity, or the Cultural Logic of Globalization.* Philadelphia: Temple University Press.

Malila, V. (2016, June). Voting Void? Young South Africans, Elections, and the Media. *Communication: South African Journal for Communication Theory & Research, 42*(2), 170–190, 21pp.

McLuhan, M. ([1964] 1994). *Understanding Media: The Extensions of Man.* Boston, MA: MIT Press.

Merolli, M., Gray, K., & Martin-Sanchez, F. (2013, August 8). Developing a Framework to Generate Evidence of Health Outcomes from Social Media Use in Chronic Disease Management. *Medicine 2.0, 2*(2), e3. https://doi.org/10.2196/med20.2717.

Ndlela, M. N., & Mulwo, A. (2017). Social Media, Youth and Everyday Life in Kenya. *Journal of African Media Studies, 9*(2), 277–290.

Ngwainmbi, E. K. (2000). Africa in the Global Info Supermarket: Perspectives and Prospects. *Journal of Black Studies, 30*(4), 534–552.

Ngwainmbi, E. K. (2005). Globalization, and Nepad's Development Perspective: Bridging the Digital Divide with Good Governance. *Journal of Black Studies, 5,* 3.

Ngwainmbi, E. K. (2007). NEPAD and the Politics of Globalization: Redefining Local Space, Group Dynamics, and Economic Development. In A. Mazama & M. K. Asante (Eds.), *African in the 21st Century: Toward a New Future.* Thousand Oaks, CA: Sage.

Ngwainmbi, E. K. (2014a). The Mediatization of Violence: A Model for Utilizing Public Discourse and Networking to Counter Global Terrorism. *Journal of Mass Communication & Journalism.* https://doi.org/10.4172/2165-7912.1000302.

Ngwainmbi, E. K. (2014b, July). Media and Translation—An Interdisciplinary Approach. *International Journal of Communication,* Vol. 8. A Review.

Ngwainmbi, E. K. (Ed.). (2014c). *Healthcare Management Strategy, Communication and Development Challenges and Solutions in Developing Countries.* Lanham, MD: Lexington Book.

Ngwainmbi, E. K. (2017). *Social Media Use Among African Youth and Implications for Cultural Globalization.* Paper presented to the 16th Annual

Africana Studies Symposium, University of North Carolina, Charlotte, February 22–23, 2018.

Nobles, W. (1986). *African Psychology: Toward Its Reclamation, Revitalization, and Recession*. Oakland, CA: Black Family Institute.

O'Keeffe, S. G., & Clarke-Pearson, K. (2011, April). The Impact of Social Media on Children, Adolescents, and Families. *Pediatrics, 127*(4), 800–804.

Petras, J. (2000). *Cultural Imperialism in the Late 20th Century*. https://www.globalpolicy.org/component/content/article/154/25597.html.

Pew Research Center: Attitudes and Trends. (2015, April). https://www.pewresearch.org/global/2015/04/15/cell-phones-in-africa-communication-lifeline/africa-phones-6/. Retrieved September 7, 2019.

Poushter, J., Bishop, C., & Chwe, H. (2018, June 19). *Social Media Use Continues to Rise in Developing Countries but Plateaus Across Developed Ones*. Pew Research Center.

Sin, S. (2016). Social Media and Problematic Everyday Life Information-Seeking Outcomes: Differences Across Use Frequency, Gender, and Problem-Solving Styles. *Journal of the Association for Information Science & Technology, 67*(8), 1793–1807, 15pp.

The Global Situation of Young People: The World Youth Report 2003. (2004). New York: United Nations Department of Economic and Social Affairs.

The Guardian. (2018). *Internet Use on Mobile Phones in Africa Predicted to Increase 20-Fold*. https://www.theguardian.com/world/2014/jun/05/internet-use-mobile-phones-africa-predicted-increase-20-fold.   Retrieved October 21, 2018.

The Mobile Economy. (2018). https://www.gsmaintelligence.com/research. Retrieved September 7, 2019.

Wong, C., Tan, G., Loke, S., & Ooi, K. (2015). Adoption of Mobile Social Networking Sites for Learning? *Online Information Review, 39*(6), 762–778. https://doi.org/10.1108/OIR-05-2015-0152.

Additional Resources

Castells, M., et al. (2009). *Mobile Communication and Society: A Global Perspective*. Cambridge, MA: MIT Press.

Castells, M. (2015). *Networks of Outrage and Hope: Social Movements in the Internet Age*. Cambridge, UK: Policy Press.

Ngwainmbi, E. K. (Ed.). (2017). *Citizenship, Democracies, and Media Engagement Among Emerging Economies and Marginalized Communities*. New York: Palgrave Macmillan.

CHAPTER 4

Fake News Reporting on Social Media Platforms and Implications for Nation-State Building

Emmanuel K. Ngwainmbi

INTRODUCTION

Easy access to social media platforms has created a *tsunami* of news and information flows to eager and unwitting audiences and markets alike around the world, with significant implications on users' consumption patterns and attitudes toward the topics shared. Social media has become a major driver in determining political outcomes, including in politically fragile nations, emerging communities, and industrialized regions. In recent years, social media platforms have become the new *vox populi* pushing away dictatorial regimes and fostering misinformation, fake news and related forms of free speech. Studies show social media use as both a post-truth engine and a hate-monger. Take the case of the 2017 Jakarta Gubernatorial Election in Indonesia—the world's most populous Muslim nation—where social media, while encouraging freedom of expression misleads ordinary citizens, emboldens people to hate and contributes to increasing polarization among citizens (Lim 2017). In addition, during the 2016 US presidential elections, fake news articles

E. K. Ngwainmbi (✉)
Charlotte, NC, USA

© The Author(s) 2019
E. K. Ngwainmbi (ed.), *Media in the Global Context*,
https://doi.org/10.1007/978-3-030-26450-5_4

published on social media and widely distributed by mainstream media about the candidates' social life ushers in social media as a vital source of news. That style of communication suggests the democratic process itself is under threat. Through a nationwide survey, Allcott and Gentzkow (2017) have found that of the false news stories appearing in online platforms three months before the election, those favoring then Presidential Candidate Trump have shared a total of 30 million times on Facebook, while those supporting his opponent Hilary Clinton were shared eight million times. That form of messaging suggests the democratic process itself may be under a new threat.

The threat to democracy is per se not the primary concern of the growing number of young people in developing countries who are being radicalized by the news and information delivered primarily through WhatsApp and YouTube internet and influence decisions about the sociopolitical direction of their community. There is the desire by young people to access and utilize content transmitted through social media platforms, rather than rely on the news sources from the private press and state-run media outlets.

CONTEXTUAL DEFINITION

Fake news is a type of yellow journalism or propaganda that consists of deliberate misinformation or hoaxes spread via traditional print and broadcast news media or online social media (Leonhardt and Thompson 2017). Fake news is written and published with the intent to mislead the public and damage an agency, entity, or person, and gain financially or politically (Hunt 2016; Schlesinger 2017). News creators use sensationalist, misleading, or fabricated headlines to increase readership, sharing, and generate revenue.

"Nation-building" refers to the process of putting together a socially cohesive and mass-mediated process to shape and share knowledge and bring positive, tangible change within that defined space. Here, the term "building" typically associated with advancement—positive change—should not be construed as the norm. Rather, we argue that the notion of "building" as a form of "change" may eventually take a positive and productive or negative and destructive turn based on the values and beliefs of the majority. We also refer to three interrelated concepts of "nation" advanced by Nadel (1996, p. 6). Nadal describes "nation" as a set of common images and narratives that people share when they think of their nation and see themselves as citizens of that nation. For Deery (2012, p. 69), "nation" is a sense people have of people of themselves, a territory with identified boundaries, an entity with its own governing body and communication mechanisms used within that space.

Invoking the Social Interaction Uses and Gratifications Theories

Media content has a silver bullet shot from a media gun to penetrate a hapless audience (Anderson 1988). Rather than the objects and events surrounding the actor being the thing that interprets the meaning of the scene, it is the actor that gives sense to the facts and artifacts, taking matters into any context the producer wishes to portray.[1] In this case, the receiver (content consumer) is neither hapless nor passive but is controlled by the fake news creator whose actions are not governed by any structured cultural or social order but by personal worldviews. Consistent with this notion of mediated information generation and flow or what we merely perceive as hidden messages that influence the content receivers is Manuel Castell's (2004, 2010) views of social interaction. Castells has advanced the following worthwhile positions: media audiences participate actively in mediated communication; they construct meanings from the content they perceive. He further states that communication interaction involves actors' intent, receivers' interpretations, and message content. The purpose is not delivered during the communication process; instead, it is constructed within, and each communication act generates separate and potentially different sides of this construction.

Therefore, the social interaction theory determines the intentions of the media creator (e.g., producer, director, actor, and writer), examines the media content (visual, verbal, musical, etc.), identify possible receiver interpretations, and assesses the potential effects on receivers. It provides a contrast with the selective exposure hypothesis of cognitive dissonance, reaffirming the power of the press while maintaining individual freedom; it is consistent with a "use and gratification" approach to television viewers' motives. Uses and gratifications theory (UGT) is an approach to understanding why and how people actively seek out specific media to

[1] John Rey Abad, Social Action Theory. https://www.scribd.com/document/171827740/Social-Action-Theory.

satisfy particular needs. UGT is an audience-centered approach to understanding mass communication,[2] and different positions on media impact on people and what people do with media.[3] Given that scenario, we can visualize the potential impact of fake news on social media platforms on networked communities by revisiting Melvin De Fleur and Sandra Ball-Rokeach (1989). The scholars contended that audiences depend on media information to meet needs and reach goals and that media systems interact with audiences to create obligations, interests, and motives in the person.

SOME ESSENTIAL CHARACTERISTICS OF FAKE NEWS

Fake news is a significant fabric in our society so much that essential world figures are publicly discussing its impact on the community. In the news media world today, media personnel are using communication technology to gather text, video, and images from around the globe with unprecedented speed and different levels of editorial control. Technology allows news media to disseminate this information to audiences to spread around the world. Because it is so easy to create a social platform, news monitoring agents cannot control the spread of inaccurate information. According to a report sponsored by the Shorenstein Center on Media, Politics and Public Policy and the Ash Center for Democratic Governance and Innovation at Harvard University, numerous information sources online leads people to rely heavily on heuristics and social cues. The reliance helps them determine the credibility of information and to shape their beliefs, which are in turn extremely difficult to correct or change. With a relatively small, but continuously changing number of sources that produce misinformation on social media, the task of applying real-time detection algorithms or delivering targeted socio-technical interventions is now more daunting than ever.

Fake stories can reach more people more quickly through social media than what old-fashioned reporting and bulk emails have accomplished accomplish in recent years. Unlike bulk emails that request services and

---

[2] Katz, Elihu (1959). "Mass Communications Research and the Study of Popular Culture: An Editorial Note on a Possible Future for This Journal." *Departmental Papers (ASC)*: 1–6.

[3] Severin, Werner and Tankard, James (1997). *Communication Theories: Origins, Methods, and Uses in the Mass Media*. Longman. ISBN 0801317037.

mobilization or financial resources by the content (news) recipient, fake news typically aims to entertain the receiver. For example, digital publishing platforms like Facebook and Google have built ecosystems that reward clicks on website links and one of the most effective ways to drive traffic to a website is to entice readers[4] with exciting content.

False news shocks and entertains, is worth sharing among the masses, and in some cases, it yields rewards. Macedonian teenagers became infamous after the press revealed they were behind several fake stories shared during the US election, mostly in support of Mr. Trump, earned thousands of dollars by getting thousands of clicks on articles they shared on Facebook (Olewe 2017).

Fake news reporting also has a double-edged nature. While it provides people the luxury of receiving news items within a short amount of time, they are inundated with many tidbits and unable to process or assess its content. Moreover, not all the news shared on social media platforms can be verified. Aggression, intimidation and even death threats are among factors that can cause false news reporting in specific communities. Print journalists and writers in fascist regimes support the need to publish fake news for the public, particularly to caress the kind sentiments of the leaders of authoritarian regimes because the journalists' lives are continually under threat when they tell the truth. Even in some fragile states where the militia operates, journalists are forced to sugarcoat or "un-report" facts to avoid persecution. Velasco (2017, pp. 232–233) describes how drug trafficking organizations and government forces in Mexico masterminded the assassination or disappearance of 127 journalists from 2000 to 2015. Hence, press censorship and self-censorship exist in those states thereby taking democracy hostage. Such crude actions toward journalists obstruct press freedom and consequently endanger democratic reform.

Conversely, in open societies, false news reporting is much-needed entertainment. After having a stressful day at work or with other strenuous chores, people need something to help them unwind. Typically, however, it is assumed that individuals with lower (versus higher) levels of cognitive ability are less equipped to adjust to existing schemes and initial judgments when confronted with new, more reliable information. Information that is later proven to be incorrect has a more perseverant influence on social impressions for those individuals with lower (versus

---

[4]https://www.bbc.com/news/world-africa-38883347.

higher) levels of cognitive ability (De Keersmaecker and Roets 2017, p. 107).

It is more challenging to correct fake news because it is mass-produced and spreads fast within a short time, and people do not take the time to verify its content. Most readers do not find it necessary to cross-check the entire source or review the posted opinions after they learn that such information was inaccurate, which leads to the abundance of fake news on social media platforms.

The false news gives the reader a sense of detachment from everyday reality or routine, a shirking of responsibilities, and a lack of concern for the values generally associated with "getting on" in the world (Collier 2013). As a social construct, fake news has a profound effect on interpersonal and third-person relationships and implications for counterfeit media literacy. Fake news has elements of fiction and deception. Publications with an anonymous author; excessive exclamation points, capital letters, and misspellings; captions that begin with "This is NOT a hoax!", "Breaking News," "Shared as received," or "forwarded as received" are among the alarming signs the content could be fake. In addition, news published on dot.com sites without a URL and editorial staff and their contacts might not be trusted. Typically, readers and viewers lend themselves to psychological frailty. Next, fake news is capable of entertaining its users because it contains at least one of the following elements: gossip, hearsay, rumor, tittle-tattle, scandal.

FRAMEWORKS FOR DETECTING FAKE NEWS ON SOCIAL MEDIA PLATFORMS

The main reason for supporting phony news sharing culls from the notion that not all facts are useful for people and not all-false information is inadequate for progress, including nation-building. We learn from human relationships by predicting, understanding, or changing behaviors, and the knowledge to either improve our lives or create more challenges. Within this framework, fake news is a form of misinformation that has the trappings of traditional broadcast and presumed to follow the editorial process and other standards associated with news reporting. It is nonpartisan, but a biased imposter content—a misleading and disingenuous use of information to frame an issue or an individual. Fake news is detected when official sources are impersonated with false, made-up sources (Wardle 2017). As French philosopher Jean Baudrillard (1981) explained, simulation or fakery is determined when a copy exists without an original or when something exists with no relationship to reality. Satire or parody shared with no actual intention to harm has the potential to deceive. Indeed, the rapid growth of fake news has outpaced society's average level of media literacy or the ability to access, analyze, evaluate and create media. Moreover, in the field of journalism, there is a growing concern that new news broadcasters use information creation and dissemination tools indiscriminately to share messages to different groups. That process undermines the integrity of the noble profession, although any attempt at preventing fake news generation and dissemination is bound to collide with many democratic values like freedom of speech.

Having the ability to identify fake news on any social media platform should limit its mitigating its effects on users in particular and society in general. Social media users should avoid forwarding messages to others without a byline or author's name as doing so only promulgates the spread of fake news. Persons taking part in a movement for change should attempt to authenticate statements such as "My sources say," "My informant at the Presidency has just told me that," or "Breaking News" that bloggers share on Facebook, and other social media platforms before sharing them. Their primary goal for using such catchy statements is to spur excitement. Social media groups with a common agenda should closely monitor bloggers, especially the popular ones who frequently share "pertinent" information; and note how many times the bloggers get their information right.

YouTube audiences should also examine the footage and headlines of any videos they receive to see if the information explains or complements the photo.

Recently, *The Telegraph*, a UK-based online newspaper, put together ways of detecting fake news from Facebook's tips for spotting false news. The reporters provide the following details:

- Be skeptical of headlines. The headlines of false news stories are often catchy and contain lots of capital letters and exclamation marks. If claims in the headline sound unbelievable, they may well be.
- Look closely at the URL. Many false news stories mimic authentic news sources by making small changes to the URL. You can go to the site to compare the URL to established sources.

- Check the source. Ensure the story comes from a source with a reputation for accuracy. If the story comes from a site you have not heard of, check their "About" section to learn more.
- Watch for special formatting. Many false news stories often contain spelling and grammar errors, as well as an awkward-looking layout.
- Check the photos. Fake news stories often include manipulated images or videos. Sometimes the picture may be authentic but taken out of context. You can do an internet search for the model to find out its origin.
- Check the dates. Fake news stories may contain timelines that make no sense or event dates which are wrong or have been altered.
- Check the evidence. Check the author's sources to confirm they are accurate. Lack of evidence or reliance on unnamed experts may indicate false news.
- Look at other reports. If no other news source is reporting the same story, it could suggest that it is false.
- Sometimes false news stories can be hard to distinguish from humorous articles. Check whether the source is known for parody and whether the story's details and tone suggest it may be just for fun.
- Some stories are intentionally false. Think critically about the stories that you read, and only share articles that you know to be credible. (Facebook's tips for spotting fake news[5] [*Telegraph Reporters* 2018].)

WHY FAKE NEWS REPORTING IS CONVENTIONAL IN THE MEDIA

Lies and inaccurate information are as old as humanity, but never before have they been so easily spread than through social media platforms.[6]Branded initially as "disinformation" during World War I and World War II "freak journalism" when influential US newspaper publishers turned up the heat to promote war with its adversaries. In his book, City Editor, published in 1934, Stanley Walker, City Editor of the New York Herald Tribune, asserted that newspapers had presented great fake stories. Fake news has since gained popularity in all communities

---

[5]http://www.newsweek.com/facebook-campaign-against-fake-news-print-newspaper-uk-e.

[6]Maggie Fox (March 8, 2018). Fake News: Lies spread faster on social media than truth does. https://www.nbcnews.com/health/health-news/fake-news-liesspread-faster-social-media-truth-does-n854896.

around the world because it is shared across some social media platforms and through traditional broadcast media networks. The false news even is discussed and dissected on real TV news shows. Editors of the mind-opening book titled *Misinformation and Mass Audiences* (2018) have explained that people do not share information just because it is false; they share it because it is exciting and receivers want it. Tweeting, retweeting, discussions in chatrooms about "hot" issues of the day, e-blasts, and forwarding content received have made fake news the most popular form of infotainment. When there is, breaking news develops; people rely on social media for the latest updates. The use of social media in such situations comes with the caveat that new information released piecemeal may encourage rumors, many of which remain unverified long after their point of release (Zubiaga et al. 2016). We may recall a broadcast aired on March 26, 2017, on CBS, one the three largest networks in America. Scott Pelley was the *Evening News* correspondent and Michael Radetzky, Guy Campanile and Andrew Bast, producers. The report stated that con artists had inserted fraudulent software that scans a user's social media account, resulting in millions of viewers getting fake stories (https://www.cbsnews.com/news/how-fake-news-find-your-social-media-feeds. Retrieved January 7, 2018).

Peer to peer sharing, especially on Facebook and WhatsApp, allows users to pass around stories like gossip while improving algorithms build filter bubbles that probably favor the spread of false, even outrageous stories. In a blog posted on January 20, 2017, Ashley Rose Atkinson, a Marketing and Social Media Coordinator at White-Wilson Medical Center observed that the creators of fake news produce domain names similar to those on credible news sites, which surfers know and trust such as ABCNews.com.co versus ABCNew.go.com. Atkinson penned these thoughts:

> Creators of fake news… utilize outlandish headlines to draw readers to immediately sharing without investigating further and create fake authors with fake accolades that would put Robert Frost to shame. Moreover, these are a few of the multiple techniques they employ to trick readers, reputable news organizations like CNN and Fox News, even international governments.

Mainstream news organizations validate the phenomenon of false news when they cite false news sources published elsewhere. For example, during the 2016 US presidential election when inaccurate stories were published online aimed at denigrating the image of the Democratic Presidential candidate, Hilary Clinton. According to CNN, Fox News and other American news networks, the stories were reportedly sponsored by the Republican candidate, Donald Trump. Tabloids in North America such as *National Examiner, Globe,* and *The National Inquirer* started in 1926 have been publishing false stories under the guise of "news" and selling their papers in supermarkets and online. Those tabloids have been in circulation for so many decades, which suggests that readers benefit from their content. The topics covered include sensational crime stories, astrology, celebrity gossip, and unverified television news. People who believe fake news tend to trust the channels used to disseminate the news. Aggressive social media campaign teams post hyper-partisan news on sites regarded as sources of information. Besides, there is no filtering mechanism can verify material published online.

PSYCHOLOGICAL FACTORS: MISINFORMATION AS A SUPPORTIVE INGREDIENT

History has shown a distraction to be an integral part of our being. Most psychologists rightly argue that sometimes the mind needs to get lost in a book of fiction, get distracted in a game, or let itself wander. Alan Brinkley, the author of *Culture and Politics in the Great Depression,* describes how escapism became the new, acceptable trend for dealing with the hardships created by the US stock market crash in 1929. Brinkley (1999) examines the genesis of the American dream, explaining how American people used persistence, empathy, rebellion, and community helped to cope with the Great Depression. Brinkley rightly points out that magazines, radio, and movies were aimed to help people mentally escape from the mass poverty and economic downturn, according to open access online sources. We have a genuine need to laugh at others and ourselves—we cherish moments, incidents, situations or dialogue that relieve us of our psychological burdens. Thus, satire, lampoon, and language that ridicule a public figure are more likely to be accepted by the masses than facts. The increasing public interest in fake news is the latest sign of the evolution of our consciousness, given that we are facing more problems than ever in history. By most accounts, people in industrialized and developing nations, particularly politically fragile states might experience the most problems if they avoid self-gratifying incentives. Psychologists have found that eating, sleeping, exercise, and sexual intercourse can become avenues of escapism when taken to extremes or out of proper context.

The excitement of reading fake news is not only a desirable, but it is also a necessity, a need that complements our modus operandi. Our tendency to seek distraction from things we must endure validates fantasy as a necessary element in our lives. For those reasons, we biasedly argue that false information shared with more people creates a potentially harmful or positive impact on both the originator and the recipient and that it has a massive influence on their day-to-day dealings if shared on a long-term basis. What matters is that we depend on or need false information to stay connected with friends in the networked society and hence prolong relationships.

FAKE NEWS PROLIFERATION ON SOCIAL MEDIA PLATFORMS

Social media is essential to storytelling, and news sharing in that content reaches the more people quicker an in a "friendly" atmosphere. Social media tools are utilized across all traditional news outlets and on online resources alike to reach various audiences. Introduced in 1997, social media has not only allowed users to upload profiles, develop friendships with other users and create blogging sites as well as Facebook, tweeter accounts, it has succeeded in getting communities to participate in generating communication news and information locally and across national borders. Anyone with a small amount of money and iPhone can now create and share content online as long as he/she accepts the terms of use, making it easy to disseminate unfiltered information. Depending on its nature and purpose, such information may be entertaining, distracting or may have devastating consequences for the sender and receiver(s).

Ultimately, information sharing no matter what its origins, size, and purpose are intrinsic to understanding our nature. To exist, resist, or advance ourselves, we have to give, receive, retrieve, store and analyze information. As social animals, we have always relied on communication to strengthen, reconsider, or reject our relationships with others. As part of the data, new things are by physiological and psychological accounts more desirable than obvious things. The premise for such a view is that behavior patterns and simple rules govern human interactions.

People remember negative things more strongly and in more detail than positive things, meaning the brain handles positive and negative information in different hemispheres. Scientifically grounded research has found flattery, for example, is an emotion that human beings want and appreciate, not criticism, which is stressful, negative (Nass and Yen 2010). *The New York Times,* Nass stated that human beings tend to see people who share negative information as smarter than those who share positive information (Tugend 2012).

That is probably one of the reasons why fake news has leapfrogged into prominence among information consumers. Indian media mogul Rahul Roushan, founder of *Faking News,* a website that publishes satirical phony news on Indian politics and society can be credited for bringing this type of information to the limelight. The site occasionally publishes critiques of news from television stations.

Civil society has also weighed in on the moral value of fake news. Pope Francis has lamented the spread of false news, calling it "evil" and saying it leads to "arrogance and hatred." Based on other online press reports published between January and May 2018, the Pope has called on journalists and social media users to shun and unmask manipulative that foment division to serve political and economic interests, calling it "satanic." In a posting by Reuters, on Yahoo News January 31, 2018, the Pontiff said, "Fake news is a sign of intolerant and hypersensitive attitudes, and leads only to the spread of arrogance and hatred. That is the result of untruth."[7] Then on February 26, 2018, CNN reporter Rosa Flores said that Pope Francis had likened fake news to 'crafty serpent' in the Book of Genesis. Media companies, community activists, influential local authorities, and country leaders should reexamine their conscience concerning the spread of fake news following the strong remarks of the most influential person in the world, the Pope.

How Academia Fosters False Information

Hermeneutics is not immune to the blame associated with packaging and disseminating half-truths and information aimed at convincing a targeted audience. Text interpretation, especially the description of philosophical

---

[7] https://www.nationalreview.com/2018/01/pope-francis-asks-kinder-communication/.

texts is not based on science but the reader's imagination and his/her understanding of related documents. In literature, for example, an analysis of a text is perceived as the truth and information from secondary sources known as literary critics that are by their right removed from the fact is used to support a perception or perceptions. The critic of a literary genre (e.g., fiction, poetry, prose) creates his/her own story from the original author's imagination-fantasy world. In that respect, writers and literary critics can be considered creators of fake news. Mostly, the social sciences are involved in creating and sharing what we can find as "false information," because researchers pursue and use data to support their thesis, which is often regarded by other researchers as faulty. The fact that researchers focus on their own belief and collect data to help that belief opens the door for different views to be shared.

Even the hard sciences are not transparent when it comes to producing reliable data; they contribute their quota to the politicization of distorted information. Science is politicized when a company sponsors a scientist or research center to conduct research and produce data on its product to be shared with the company's potential audience. Scientists, science reporters, and politicians have warned that some individual scientists hold eccentric, subjective views. Dr. Victor Grech of the Department of Pediatrics at the Mater Dei Hospital in Malta has explained how science should be transparent in the advent of fake news. He states that the politicization of science for personal purposes, with the peddling of false news composed of the careful selection of facts that politicians wish to pursue and the data they are willing to promote or denigrate (2017). A Boston-based Science Correspondent for the *Independent* paper pens that science and its industry can make "dangerous use of fake news and alternative facts" and warns people to become aware of "fake news" or "alternative facts" from big corporations and "eccentric" scientists—not just politicians and the media. For his part, Professor Kevin Elliott, philosopher specializing in the ethics of science advises people to trust the opinion of a major scientific organization, rather than read too much into a single piece of research. During a presentation at the American Association for the Advancement of Science's annual meeting in Boston in February 2017, Elliott said the public should find out if someone had a "significant vested interest that could skew their judgment" when reading about the latest supposedly stunning breakthrough (Johnston 2017). We posit that sponsored research and programs often produce and disseminate results to other media audiences based on the objectives of the sponsor that may be biased and open to different interpretations.

International organizations that promote public and private enterprise have found misinformation on social media platforms as something that has positive and negative implications for their output. For example, the World Economic Forum in 2013 identified the spread of misinformation online as a significant risk in its Global Risks Report, but it was unable to determine steps to fix the problem.

Fake News, Politics, and Social Mobilization

Some media think tank groups are making efforts to enlighten minority populations about the adverse effects of relying heavily on online news sources to obtain advice on businesses opportunities or learn about the world. Keeping it real, a think tank group in Durham, NC, regularly has been explaining the impact of US government policy decisions and activities of major companies from online publications for over a decade. In a web posting in 2010 titled, BP "Oil Masters and the Art of masterful Deception," dealing with the oil spill in the Gulf of Mexico, the US Congress and US President reportedly failed to hold British Petroleum (BP) responsible. The writer warned Americans that the oil company BP functions as a sovereign government, contrary to the widespread view that it respects American laws (http://fahimknightsworld. blogspot.com). By pointing out the lawmakers' laxity in sanctioning the petroleum company, the blogger suggested that minorities and people of good should have developed alternatives in dealing with dominant global political and economic players such as the US government and the British Petroleum company.

Hostile government actors have also been involved in generating and propagating fake news, particularly during elections (Merlo 2017). Messages shared on some social networks about the ongoing Anglophone crises in Cameroon reveal that social media activists have been fanning the campaign against Presidential elections set to hold in October 2018, in retaliation, the government has planned to block internet supply to prevent citizens in favor of independence from being brainwashed by communications from the Diaspora. According to various YouTube postings and text messages on their iPhones, pro-independence activists have accused the government of Cameroon of maiming and killing unarmed independence seekers (civilians) while the government-owned television network, CRTV, has branded that the pro-independence groups as separatists and terrorists. This sort of propaganda by both sides makes it challenging to fact-check or persuade the entire public to determine the truth. However, the BBC and Al Jazeera and other external news media are beginning to fact check the stories. It is difficult to assess the integrity of the message, however many people who received it believe it based on a straw poll conducted by this author.

Reports, particularly those broadcast through globally recognized cable news sources such as CNN, BBC, French, Chinese, and Russian news agencies and other media in significant economies, show the potential consequences of the proliferation of cyber-mediated false news stories on global politics and partisanship. They also give users insight into how any information can easily persuade us to take action without remorse as long such information is delivered in a way that makes believe. Replication and repetition help give a perception of reality. Thus, re-publishing stories posted on unreliable networks such as Facebook and websites with no URLs, or sharing messages received from other networked communities contributes to the spread and believability of fake news.

There is scientific evidence of the influence of fake news sharing on social media on political outcomes. Viewers' access to fake news broadcasts can influence their decision-making and their attitudes of inefficacy, alienation, and cynicism toward the subjects covered. It can also serve as a moderator of the association of viewing hard news, fake news with their perceived realism as studies recently conducted in Israel and the United States have shown. Using survey data from the 2006 Israeli election campaign, Balmas (2014) has found evidence of an indirect positive effect of fake news viewing in fostering feelings of inefficacy, alienation, and cynicism, through the mediator variable of perceived realism of fake news (pp. 430–454). Other recent studies show that traditional activities understood to be in the domain of online privacy—sharing social media updates, commercial transactions, news gathering—can be reframed through the economic conceptions of labor and currency (Soto-Vásquez 2017). Further, online survey responses from national samples in the United States on voters' decision-making indicate that partisan identity and external political efficacy are not only positive predictors of third-person perception, but such perception leads to different ways of combating fake news online (Jang and Kim 2008). However, the actual effect of fake news on voters' decisions is still unknown, and concerns over the perceived effect of fake news online prevail in the United States and other countries.

Take the case of Southern Cameroonians that caught the world's attention in October 2016 when lawyers and teachers took to the streets to decry perceived economic injustice as well as cultural and linguistic discrimination. A year later, activists later created an interim government headed by a certain Julius Ayuk Tabe that started making plans to ensure total independence from the so-called Republic of Cameroon. A YouTube video posting with the headline, "Ayuk Tabe is not a terrorist," referring to the leader falsely accused of sponsoring militia groups to fight against the troops of the government of the Republic of Cameroon. Anti-separation groups in the French-speaking region in Cameroon have interpreted the same video content as fake. Further, there have been numerous postings on YouTube and other social media platforms from or about the "interim government of the Federal Republic of Ambazonia" since the latter declared its independence from the Republic of Cameroun on October 1, 2017. The authenticity of the postings written and shared by pro-independence groups is hardly ever verified. A story posted at *Journal du Cameroon.com* on May 24, 2018, reads, "US Ambassador leaves Cameroon amidst diplomatic fracas." The story follows a flurry of reports on social media that the US Ambassador asked the Cameroon President to step down after media reports posted online showed the Cameroon military torturing and killing civilians in Ambazonia, the territory pro-activists claim to belong to them. It has become clear to most observers that interest in the burgeoning political crises has increased globally. Powerful countries, regional governing bodies (e.g., UNISA, African Union), international governing bodies (like the UN, UNHCR, Commonwealth of Nations); media agencies such as the BBC, France 24, VOA Africa, have called on both parties to dialogue and bring a lasting solution to the crises. It is also widely understood that messages, some unverified, provided to American lawmakers to seek answers and to media, agencies have come from social media platforms. Here, we see that news reporting on social media has significant implications for social mobilization, and that news content must not be truthful to persuade groups to take decisive action. It should also be noted that Cameroon is one of Al Jazeera's most robust communities online.

FAKE NEWS AND SOCIAL RESPONSIBILITY

We have to question whether communication scholars and media organizations were prepared for the different digital media would play in denigrating our ethos—a practice that is characterized by fake news, digital overload, disinformation, propaganda, and immorality. We wonder whether it is not too late for the networked society to engage in responsible social media use. That statement begs the question for almost every iPhone or YouTube user has knowingly or inadvertently shared unverified content laden with inflammatory messages. Media experts, particularly news journalists, admit that news that deals with conflicts, disasters, and deaths sell papers. However, if their news coverage journalists do not strike a balance between the positive and negative reporting, they risk alienating an important segment of the global audience. Journalists are required to be truthful in telling a story because they are considered as the first teachers in society, so they should avoid sourcing social media platforms to write stories. No matter the number of fake news consumers, traditional news organizations should note that their journalist integrity matters. Otherwise, any false information released that is promptly corrected could result in loss of respect, negatively affect public policy, and even lead an organization to make bad decisions, especially in developing nations where people get their news mainly from traditional media. Falsified information could cause some human casualties. The risks of believing fake news range from personal injury to national security. Thus, it is equally incumbent upon the media Facebook and I-pad owners to understand what constitutes false news if the risks of delivering and consuming such content outweigh the benefits.

Fake News Reporting in Underdeveloped Nations

Fake news reporting is an old phenomenon for African tabloid newspaper writers. The private press in financially strapped countries like Eritrea, Ghana, Cameroon, Nigeria, Chad, Niger, Mali, Cote d'Ivoire, and Tunisia usually pick up stories from newswires and social media platforms and republish them without verifying their source because it lacks the resources to investigate information. Private newspapers disseminate information critical of the way the government manages its institutions, giving the public a voice to comment on injustices in their country. In a bid to satisfy its readers and sustain its market, the private press ends up delivering misleading information to an unwitting national and international population. According to a press release posted by the *Global Press* journal on November 14, 2017, false rumors invaded social media several days before Zimbabwe's longtime President Robert Mugabe resigned. Bloggers had their version of the resignation. Headlines flooded social media platforms such as "The president is dead." "No, he was fired." "No, he resigned." "No, he is under house arrest." The truth remained murky to most social media audiences for days, due in part to tight-lipped officials, but mostly to doctored photographs and forged documents invading social media. On WhatsApp and Facebook, the most popular social media platforms in Zimbabwe, some bloggers mentioned the country was under siege. Doctored photos of tanks rolling into Harare, the capital city, spread like wildfires during a harmattan. The public in Zimbabwe was interested mostly in learning about the incident from private news sources, not state-run media or any other channel.

ANALYSIS OF LESSONS LEARNED

Fake news is an acceptable source of public discourse that engages people. When unmonitored activities on social media platforms undermine fact-based reporting, we must expect media researchers to respond. If false news reporting is unwarranted by the community, the question becomes one of content control—whether the media industry should be organized as a monopoly or a competition and who should have the right to monitor the information to be shared.

From another angle of our reading of the content above, we come away with the idea that fake news requires a more significant inquiry by media students and faculty, policymakers grappling with questions of regulation and prevention, and those concerned about this certain situation.

We also note that (1) exciting news content can engage people of all socioeconomic and backgrounds; (2) that potentially inflammatory news content creates new communities; and (3) that the goal of inflammatory news content creators is to spread rumors on social media by monitoring conversational threads. We understand that people accept news content before its authenticity status is resolved. Hence the fabricated story pretending to be real journalism is not likely to go away—the genre has rapidly become a means for writers to make money and potentially influence public discourse. Consequently, we find four emerging interlocking paradigms: fake news is per se the federal agency that brings people together, occupies their "productive" time, gives them something else to think about as a group and act upon, and helps massage their emotions. Most important, fake news sharing is capable of advocating measurable positive change within the communities that use social media. In short, fake news is a necessary ingredient in the stewpot in our collective social life. Fake news can counteract the efforts of the politically fragile nations in the world that want to continue controlling news flow to suppress information that can cause public uprisings because it is created by anyone and shared on personal media platforms.

IMPLICATIONS OF FALSE INFORMATION SHARING FOR NATION-BUILDING

Fake news is necessary for forecasting revenue and post-truth politics for media outlets because they spend much time commenting on its components, thereby attracting viewers to their websites, a great ploy to broaden participation, viewership, and discourse and generate broadcast and online advertising revenue. Research shows that easy access to online advertisement revenue increased political polarization, and the popularity of social media, primarily the Facebook News Feed are implicated in the spread of fake news (Hunt 2016; Woolf 2016). Publishing a story with malicious content on a commercial media platform that attracts readers and this eventually benefits advertisers and ratings. Thus, advertising has a real opportunity to state its case in a powerful, direct, and compelling way so there will be no doubt, what the product represents. However, as blogger Rance Crain (2017) has stated in a blog at AdAge, advertisers would lose the opportunity if they end up supporting fake news because they cannot control where their digital ads run. Fake news sites are using disinformation to pull in big audiences and significant ad revenue in turn.

We further contend that the act of believing in the news is a matter of custom or character, and each nation must see a fake story based on its perception, culture, or reality. This position is grounded on the premise that morals involve developing, defending, and recommending concepts of right and wrong behavior. However, these concepts do not change as one's desires, and motivations vary. Thus, a nation can utilize fake news reports to evaluate its population's interest or make plans for its educational, cultural and economic advancement. Fake news can help construct specific business sectors of the nation and still keep the universally approved journalistic standards that include the free exchange of information that is accurate, fair and thoroughly researched.

The ongoing demand for alternative facts has moved the yardstick for measuring the consumer-driven economy, and advertising seems to be leading the way. The ability for I-pads and iPhones to carry online content gives consumers more knowledge about market products and services, which helps them, make decisions. For their part, media advertising companies have succeeded in unearthing financial benefits of marketing inaccurate news to targeted audiences. For example, 71% of people in the United Kingdom connect advertising with fake news. Research commissioned by Rakuten Marketing reveals that Brits lead the way when it comes to campaign skepticism in comparison with Europe and the United States, where the comparative figures sit at 54 and 58% respectively. Some observers have even claimed that fake news makes advertising more believable. It appears that individual nations enjoy financial benefits when false stories disseminated. In the United States, for example, where without prior thorough investigation has become an important mechanism for generating revenue among media companies and has increased fierce competition for consumers' attention and their money. In an article posted at the *Daily Grill* January 29, 2018, at www.dailygrail.com, blogger Fahim A. Knight-El, wrote:

> The news networks, particularly television stations in the United States have lowered their newsgathering and packaging standards, and resorted to using primitive methods of reporting to attract viewers. Traditional media outlets that are warring to present breaking stories and capitalizing on national and global audiences before anyone else, but social media is covertly driving mainstream media to this end. (Knight-El 2018)

Worse, daily and weekday newspaper circulation has plummeted from 62 million to an estimated 35 million over 26 years, as 93% of adults in the U.S. have turned to get their news online through mobile devices or desktops (Loechner 2018). This trend may be leveraging tremendous pressure on journalists to work expeditiously to get to the reporting finish line first, using every means at their disposal.

Further to the fear that false news reporting could be diminishing journalistic standards and profit-focused based information sharing phenomenon in the media industry is the growing trend among state governments in shaping media policies to meet market demands, especially the information demand-supply chain. Faced with increasing information flows within their national borders, information ministers, senators, even heads-of-state are advocating the design or amendment of their information and communication policies to meet the demands of the growing IT market, at the expense of good journalistic ethics, and promoting the fake news reporting agenda. Concern about misinformation on social media has led Facebook and Google to announce plans to crack down on fake news sites, restricting their ability to garner ad revenue. Perhaps that could limit the amount of malarkey online even though news consumers themselves are the best defense against the spread of misinformation.

Another problem on social media is that people validate the information by forwarding it to others without vetting. Validation of false news propaganda occurs when influential public figures weigh in on the subject. For example, since he became the United States President, Donald Trump has lambasted US news outlets for reporting "fake news" on his tweeter account, thereby fostering speculation that Russia had meddled in the US presidential election from which he emerged the winner (https://www.dailygrail.com/blog/fake-news). Through various media outlets, political scientists and leaders of democratic nations have decried the misuse of media platforms by elected public officials to spread false information to the masses. In an eye-opening article written on how to Spot Fake News Eugene Kiely and Lori Robertson (2016) FactCheck.org, a project of The Annenberg Public Policy Center, argue that some the misinformation shared online is complete fiction.

ENGAGING SOCIALLY MEDIATED MESSAGES FOR NATION-BUILDING

Although more citizens in developing states are relying on the private press for news about social and economic matters than state-run media known for promoting government propaganda, this phenomenon is likely to change in next few years for a number reasons. First, from socioeconomic perspective handheld devices are affordable and are being used by more people. IPhones are being mass-produced, are cheaper and compatible with local telephone towers. Refurbished iPhone and affordable ones imported from China, the UAE, and Dubai are in demand in the towns and cities. Further, there is broad interest among the youth in using social media products, which make up over 75% of Africa's population.

The youth in fragile states depend on social media, and development institutions have found some success in engaging the youth with messages geared for social change (Fayoyin 2015).

Other reasons to engage social media in the advancement of nation-building are that (1) Reporters in fragile states do not have adequate resources to verify news sources. (2) There is fierce competition among the private newspapers to publish breaking news, so they rush to print the papers. (3) Specific zones are insecure and dangerous—too risky for journalists. (4) Government officials punish journalists who criticize the government. They shut the business, imprison journalists, or cut funding, so some papers resort to providing favorable coverage to escape from those repressive actions. (5) Some reporters do not have adequate training in storytelling, including data collection and interviewing techniques.

NATION-BUILDING TECHNIQUES: USING SOCIAL MEDIA AND TRADITIONAL MEDIA REPORTING AS SUPPLEMENTS

More citizens are getting news from the private press because they find news produced by government-run press fake, less worthy or limited regarding the quality. To estimate the value of news flow in shaping community wellbeing and decision-making in developing states, we must identify who indeed owns or controls the media. Three World Bank authors and the highly regarded Russian-American Harvard-based economist Andrei Shleifer have carefully examined patterns of media ownership. They have found that in most countries around the world, the most extensive media firms are owned by the government and property is more pervasive in broadcasting than in the printed media. Professor Shleifer, Simeon Djankov, Caralee McLeish and Tatiana Nenova (2003) found that media firms in 97 countries have ownership structures with shareholders who are families or governments countries that are poorer, more autocratic, with lower levels of primary school enrollment, and higher levels of state intervention in the economy (p. 373). As part of their development agenda, many new nation-states have been investing in public information management, mainly the programming and delivery of news across the nation after the United States began privatizing internet operations in 1995. While some governments purchased computers and related

IT tools to facilitate data storage and improve learning in schools, others used the technology to monitor free speech in the country.

The informed public observers have roundly condemned the way governments have applied modern information and communication technology in their respective nations to bring social change. Communication for change researchers invariably criticizes them for stunting freedom of expression in the media and slowing development at the national level (Ainslie 1966; Babatunde 1975; Bourgault 1996; Ngwainmbi 1994, 2014). As more social media platforms become available to the citizens, they will likely seek other avenues to exercise their right to free speech and the willingness to receive and share any information. It should be noted that the young people in the world's most press repressive regimes such as Eritrea, Syria, Iran, China, Cuba share information on Facebook and iPhones critical of their government. Some have been organizing rallies and advocating for immediate reform on those platforms, yet the government security forces have not succeeded in suppressing such activities, according to media reports.

In some cases, however, the advocates tend to report erroneous information about government operations forcing officials to issue press releases, or speak on television to correct the information. Those approaches are designed to ensure information control by the state-sponsored media, but they seem to backfire as social media influencers usually spread their version on social media before the news anchors air the story.

There exists a fair amount of moral panic in the professional African media and sociopolitical communities that have created a backdrop for debates about the real impact of fabricated news on national politics and governance in Africa. The problem seems so severe that some news agencies have taken steps to educate the public about the potential effects of fake consumption on democratization. In December 2017, Eye Witness News (EWN) a South African television news network published a manual for dealing with false news online amid allegations that the governing African National Congress (ANC) had planned to run a campaign to create and disseminate false information to discredit opponents ahead of the local election.[8] EWN placed a bold alert, FAKE! On stories posted online, whose content could not be verified. The news network also

[8] https://www.bbc.com/news/world-africa-38883347.

provided a link to another page with tips on how to spot fake news, and a list of websites it had identified as purveyors of false reports. The publication also invited readers to submit any false news they come across and stories they are unsure about (Olewe 2017). In another bid to control fake news proliferation online, the world-renowned British Broadcast Corporation (BBC) website republished an article warning readers not to read a story about Eritrean men posted on the BBC portal. The word fake (in red) superimposed over the body of the article (http://www.bbc.com/news/world-africa-38883347).

TECHNIQUES FOR USING FAKE NEWS PLATFORMS TO FOSTER NATIONAL DEVELOPMENT

The quest for a system to initiate the creation of false news often collides with basic principles of democratic values like freedom of expression. However, we can see the sharing of false information as a cohesive force—a means of keeping people engaged in a conversation, a discourse over its potential short- to medium-term value or uselessness. Global multimedia technology companies such as Yahoo, Google, Facebook, and Apple should take immediate stringent measures to slow the spread of fake news on social media platforms because it mostly misinforms and misdirects the innocent news consumers who lack appropriate tools to identify it and are overwhelmed by its constant presence. Google can be applauded for taking the fight against false news sharing to a new level by announcing initiatives aimed at combating the spread of misinformation on the internet. For instance, Google invested $300 million from 2018 to 2021 to support real journalistic news reporting and limit fake news (Anthony Ha 2018). By collaborating with the news industry to surface accurate information and sponsoring an International Fact Check Network to track and suppress misinformation when news breaks on Facebook, Google would be contributing hugely to good journalistic practice globally.

Sharing fake news can help reduce stress. In industrialized, mechanized open societies like the United States, Germany, France, Japan, and the UK where suicide rates are high, where people keep long work hours, and the cost of living continues to increase, fake news sharing on all media platforms should be encouraged. On the contrary, pure news reports bring sad feelings. Tragedies, conflicts, and health and economic crises get all the attention in the media, but such information has long-term adverse psychological effects on the audience. Thankfully, billions of people are using social media every day. With an estimated 2.44 billion people currently using social media platforms for personal relationships, entertainment, at work and in studies, there is a potential for messages to be distributed on this platform to package messages or even use the fake news audience to develop a new business model.

Infotainment, a characteristic of fake news, can be useful for democracy in that only a minority of news audiences follow the hard news. Conversely, social media platforms provide a forum free expression. For example, with a small amount of money, political activists can own a channel on YouTube where they post their views about the government, public figure or any other trending topic they may like or dislike.

Misinformation can influence our behaviors on a massive scale. Hence, lawmakers, social science researchers, behavior change experts and social welfare sectors in the government should invest resources in understanding how it works and what must be done to mitigate its harmful effects on the sociopolitical and economic advancement of the nation.

Finally, the lessons learned from mistakes such as heavy reliance on the fake news could in due course be assessed to find new ways of dealing with it in the future if the nation's lawmakers and their people jointly determine that fake news is detrimental to the nation's growth. Otherwise, variations of false news reporting should be encouraged by the people and their lawmakers if they find phony news useful in fostering a national spirit.

QUESTIONS FOR DISCUSSION

1. Is fake news good for the soul?
2. Name three main media networks in your country known for publishing fake news and give reasons why they are still in business.
3. How can fake news improve a business or government's chances to progress?
4. Describe the roles media organs play in fostering the dissemination of false information and how they might benefit from doing so.
5. You are the CEO in a big company such as Intel with employees and offices around the world. A major news network such as the

BBC has just broadcast false information about your company. Explain steps you would take to bring the situation under control.
6. When writing a research paper, how would you provide arguments that support misinformation?

WORKS CITED

Ainslie, R. (1966). *The Press in Africa*. London: Victor Gollancz Ltd.
Allcott, H., & Gentzkow, M. (2017). *Social Media and Fake News in the 2016 Election* (Working Paper for the National Bureau of Economic Research, No. 23089). See also http://rajatrepik.com/in-2017-tech-turned-dark/.
Anderson, A. J. (1988). *Mediated Communication: A Social Action Perspective*. Beverly Hills, CA: Sage.
Atkinson, R. (2017, January 20). *Fact or Fiction: How Fake News Became so Popular*. https://ashleyroseatkinson.wordpress.com. Retrieved February 18, 2018.
Babatunde, J. (1975). Press Freedom in Africa. *African Affairs, 74*, 255–262.
Balmas, M. (2014). When Fake News Becomes Real. *Communication Research, 41*(3), 430–454.
Baudrillard, J. (1981). *Simulacres et Simulation*. Paris: Éditions Galilée.
Bourgault, L. (1996). Press Freedom in Africa: A Cultural Analysis. *Journal of Communication Inquiry, 17*(2), 69–92.
Brinkley, A. (1999). *Culture and Politics in the Great Depression*. Waco, TX: Markham Press Fund. See also http://www.citethisforme.com/topic-ideas/history/The%20Great%20Depression-992320.
Castells, M. (2004). Informationalism, Networks, and the Network: A Theoretical Blueprint. In M. Castells (Ed.), *The Network Society: A Cross-Cultural Perspective*. Northampton, MA: Edward Elgar.
Castells, M. (2010, November). Globalization, Networking, Urbanization: Reflections on the Spatial Dynamics of the Information Age. *Urban Studies, 47*(13), 2737–2745.
Collier, G. (2013, April). Escapism, and Contemporary Life. *Psychology Today*. https://www.psychologytoday.com/blog/the-consciousness-question/201310/escapism-and-contemporary-life.
Combating Fake News: An Agenda for Research and Action. Shorenstein Center on Media, Politics and Public Policy. https://shorensteincenter.org/combating-fake-news-agenda-for-research/. Posted May 2, 2017.
Communication and Media Studies. (n.d.). Retrieved from http://oncommunicationmedia.com/journal/featured-articles.

Crain, R. (2017, February 6). *How Fake News Could Make Advertising More Believable*. http://adage.com. Retrieved May 22, 2018. http://adage.com/article/rance-crain/fake-news-make-advertising-believable/307836/.

De Fleur, M., & Ball-Rokeach, S. J. (1989). *Theories of Mass Communication*. New York: Longman.

De Keersmaecker, J., & Roets, A. (2017). 'Fake News': Incorrect, but Hard to Correct. The Role of Cognitive Ability on the Impact of False Information on Social Impressions. *Intelligence, 65*, 107–111. https://doi.org/10.1016/j.intell.2017.10.005.

Deery, J. (2012). *Consuming Reality: The Commercialization of Factual Entertainment*. New York: Palgrave Macmillan.

Djankov, S., McLeish, C., Nenova, T., & Shleifer, A. (2003, October). Who Owns the Media. *Journal of Law and Economics, 46*(2), 341–381. See also https://scholar.harvard.edu/shleifer/publications/who-owns-media.

Kiely, E., & Robertson, L. (2016, November 18). *How to Spot Fake News*. https://www.factcheck.org/2016/11/how-to-spot-fake-news.

"Fake News Busters." POLITICO. 2017-09-14. Retrieved September 15 2017.

Fake News—Wikipedia. (n.d.). Retrieved from https://en.wikipedia.org/wiki/Fake_news.

Fayoyin, A. (2015). Positioning Youth Development Agenda in Public Discourse in Nigeria: An Advocacy Imperative. *Open Access Library Journal, 2*, e1875.

Grech, V. (2017). Fake News and Post-truth Pronouncements in General and in Early Human Development. *Early Human Development, 115*, 118–120.

Ha, A. (2018, March 20). *Google Unveils Its $300M News*. https://techcrunch.com/2018/03/20/google-news-initiative/. Retrieved September 6, 2019.

How Fake News Becomes a Favorite, Trending Topic. CBS News. https://www.cbsnews.com/news/how-fake-news-find-your-social-media-feeds/. Retrieved February 6, 2018.

Hunt, E. (December 17, 2016). What Is Fake News? How to Spot It and What You Can Do to Stop It. *The Guardian*. Retrieved January 15, 2017.

Jang, S. M. & Kim, J. K. (2008) Third-Person Effects of Fake News: Fake News Regulation and Media Literacy Interventions. *Computers in Human Behavior, 80*, 295–302.

Johnston, I. (2017, February 19). Science Can Make Dangerous Use of Fake News and Alternative Facts. *Independent*. https://www.independent.co.uk. Retrieved May 17, 2017.

Knight-El, F. (2018, January 29). *Fake News, What Is the Global Implication; What Is the Price?* https://www.dailygrail.com/blog. Accessed February 12, 2018.

Leonhardt, D., & Thompson, S. A. (2017, June 23). Trump's Lies. *The New York Times*. Retrieved February 18, 2018.

Lim, M. (2017). Freedom to Hate: Social Media, Algorithmic Enclaves, and the Rise of Tribal Nationalism in Indonesia. *Journal of Critical Asian Studies*, *3*(49), 411–427.

Loechner, J. (2018). *"Fake News" Possible Benefit.* https://www.mediapost.com. Retrieved February 13.

Merlo, C. (2017). *Millonario Negocio Fake News.* Univision Noticias.

Nadel, A. (1996). *Television in Black-and-White: Race and National Identity.* Lawrence, KS: University Press of Kansas.

Nass, C., & Yen, C. (2010). *The Man Who Lied to His Laptop: What Machines Teach Us About Human Relationships?* New York, NY: Penguin.

Ngwainmbi, K. E. (1994). *Communication Efficiency and Rural Development in Africa: The Case of Cameroon.* Lanham, MD: University Press of America.

Ngwainmbi, K. E. (2014, July). Media, and Translation—An Interdisciplinary Approach. *International Journal of Communication, 8.* Review.

Olewe, D. (2017, February 16). *Fake News: How Can African Media Deal with the Problem?* https://www.bbc.com/Africa. Retrieved February 6, 2018.

Schlesinger, R. (2017, April 14). Fake News in Reality. *U.S. News & World Report.*

Soto-Vásquez, A. D. (2017). Reconceptualizing Digital Privacy: Examining Two Alternatives in the 2016 Presidential Election. *The Journal of Communication and Media Studies, 2*(2), 33–45. https://doi.org/10.18848/2470-9247/cgp/v02i02/33-45.

The Coin Telegraph. *Big Brands Are Now Using Blockchain to Fight Ad Fraud and Fake Views.* https://thenextweb.com. Accessed February 16, 2018.

Tugend, A. (2012, March). Praise is Fleeting, but Brickbats we Recall. *The New York Times.* https://nytimes.com. Retrieved January 27, 2018.

Velasco, J. (2017). The Assassination of Journalists in Mexico: A Product of Criminal and Electoral Competition. In Emmanuel K. Ngwainmbi (Ed.), *Citizenship, Democracies, and Media Engagement among Emerging Economies and Marginalized Communities* (pp. 227–250). New York: Palgrave Macmillan.

Wardle, C. (2017). *Fake News. It's Complicated.* First Draft News. https://first-draftnews.com/fake-news-complicated/. Accessed August 25, 2017.

Who Owns the Media? | Andrei Shleifer—Harvard University. (n.d.). Retrieved from https://scholar.harvard.edu/shleifer/publications/who-owns-media.

Woolf, N. (2016, November 11). How to Solve Facebook's Fake News Problem: Experts Pitch Their Ideas. *The Guardian.* Retrieved January 15, 2017.

Zubiaga, A., et al. (2016). *Analyzing How People Orient and Spread Rumors in Social Media by Looking at Conversational Threads.* https://doi.org/10.1371/journal.pone.0150989.

Further Reading

Castells, M. (2013). *Communication Power*. London, UK: Oxford University Press.

Costanza-Chock, S. (2009). *Out of the Shadows, into the Streets! Transmedia Organizing and the Immigrant Rights Movement*. Cambridge, MA: The MIT Press.

Jabbar, J. (2013). Role of Media in National Development in the 21st Century. *Criterion Quarterly, 2*(2). http://www.criterion-quarterly.com/.

Kuusik, N. (August, 2018) The Role of the Media in Peace Building, Conflict Management, and Prevention. *E-International Relations*. https://www.e-ir. info/.

Singh, S. A. (Ed.). (2016). *Role of Media in Nation Building*. Newcastle, UK: Cambridge Scholars Publishing.

Trappel, J. (Ed.). (2019). *Digital Media Inequalities: Policies Against Divides, Distrust and Discrimination*. Göteborg, Sweden: Nordicom.

PART III

Media, Emerging Nations and Sociopolitical Change

Confronting the Lion with Bare Hands: Social Media and the Anglophone Cameroonian Protest

Kehbuma Langmia

INTRODUCTION

Most dictators in the Middle East and Africa have experienced a new form of civil unrest by the populace. This unrest is carried out on cyberspace and targeting long-term ruler ship of those with a firm grip on power. A case in point is the Arab Spring (Lotan et al. 2011; Stepan and Linz 2013; Acemoglu et al. 2017) riots that contributed in no small way to the fall of President Ben Ali of Tunisia, Hosni Mubarak of Egypt and Colonel Moammar Kaddafi of Libya. The people whose voices of descent had erstwhile been asphyxiated and stymied by these dictatorial regimes found a new outlet with social media. This time the revolution was no longer to be televised, but Facebooked, twitted, and Whatsapped. Young men and women, the elderly, politicians and peasants took to the streets spurred not by traditional media but by new media applications on their mobile phones for quick and easy interpersonal and mass

K. Langmia (✉)
Department of Strategic, Legal and Management Communication, Howard University, Washington, DC, USA
e-mail: Klangmia@howard.edu

© The Author(s) 2019
E. K. Ngwainmbi (ed.), *Media in the Global Context*,
https://doi.org/10.1007/978-3-030-26450-5_5

communication with the clarion call for a new dawn. They came out in droves in these countries above seeking long-awaited change. The internet revolution, has now, opened the floodgates for unrestricted freedom of speech for the downtrodden mostly in the developing economies of the world. Social media, this new digital public sphere have also become the means for Anglophone Cameroonians in Tropical Africa to seek freedom from oppression. This new mediated form of inter-human communication has, therefore, become the alternative outlet for publishing uncensored messages to the rest of the world using virtual private network (VPN) or the internet. The case of Anglophone Cameroonians in West Africa constitutes the focus of this study. In their attempt to protest long years of marginalization by the central government of Cameroon, the Anglophone Cameroonians of the southern part of the country are dishing out gory pictures of police brutality on them for daring to raise a voice of dissent to the 35 years old government of President Paul Biya. They have found the social media freedom, powered by the internet as the pathway to trumpet their 56 years old marginalization, inequalities, arrests, and detention to the rest of the world. Their stifled voices that have been silenced for years have been finally unleashed to the world. But the government has seen this as an attempt by the Anglophone speaking minorities of the country to secede from the union that they had agreed upon in the 1961 Referendum when President Amadou Ahidjo (representing East Cameroon) met with John Ngu Foncha (representing West Cameroon) decided to unite the two entities into what was called the United Republic of Cameroon. The political quack mire that both parties find themselves in now is because the activists see this issue of union differently from the government. To them, the union was a rape and not a mutual consensus, the reason why today it is no longer the United Republic of Cameroon but only the Republic of Cameroon. A change initiated in the 1980s by the current President Paul Biya. They now clamor for the restoration of their statehood.

Consequently, the action of the activists in the North West and South West region of the country that contain majority of the Anglophone population has created sociocultural and political uneasiness to the regime and they have responded with brutal crackdown by kidnapping/arresting their leaders, killing hundreds of protesters and pushing thousands to flee to neighboring Nigeria as refugees. As of today, the UNHCR reports that over 15,000 refugees are currently seeking refuge in Nigeria (Carsten 2018). This chapter analyzes two significant events of September 22 and October 1, 2017, respectively. September 22 saw thousands of activist Southern Cameroonians on the streets to demand the restoration of their UN-mandated statehood of October 1, 1961. Therefore, on October 1, 2017, they came out again but this time for symbolic Independence Day proclamation marked by street demonstrations and hosting of the Southern Cameroon flags. These two events will be analyzed using qualitative content analysis of texts from online newspapers like the Southern Cameroon Journal online news and two social media sites like Mark Baretta and Southern Cameroon Television (SCTV) Facebook pages. These selected sites are owned and operated by teams with news sources credited to the homeland. Mindful of the fact that fake news now engulfed the social mediascape, there is the need to examine mainly sites that are not often populated by unreliable information from the homeland. Another reason for choosing these sites to analyze is the number of followers and subscribers that have chosen to rely on these sites for credible, uncensored news from the homeland that is devoid of government interference.

Brief Historical Background

Two official linguistic and cultural entities characterize the Cameroonian citizenry. They were orchestrated by the imposed British and French colonial legacies. Since language is the vehicle of culture, these two entities are alive and well in the Southern and Eastern part of the country. Because of colonialism, the citizens were forced to inculcate and develop Western cultural traits because their first administrators before independence in the 60s were from these two countries, Britain and France.

Consequently, they have been trained—educationally speaking—to act and behave in ways analogous to that of these imperial nations. That is why with over 200 ethnic languages in the country with tribal leanings who acted during the pre-colonial era as one Bantu group of people, the colonial experience split them between French-fried and Anglophone Cameroonians. All citizens belonging to the territories seized by France during the scramble for Cameroon when the Germans (the second colonial masters) were driven after the first all European war of 1914. They do speak, act and imitate French tastes, fashion and culture and the same is true of the British territories south-west of the country. When most African countries finally gained independence in the 1960s, these two entities in Cameroon had to agree on what form of statehood they were to adopt. They had to come to a compromise on how they were to be self-governed. The British Southern Cameroons were given the option by a UN Trusteeship to choose between joining Nigeria or the Republic of Cameroon. According to Anyefru (2010), they decided to join La Republic du Cameroon on the terms that they are treated on an equal basis like their Frenchified counterparts. However, that agreement was never adhered to for 56 years, the reason why they want restoration of their statehood according to the UN-mandated Trusteeship agreement. Eyoh's (1998), article "Conflicting narratives of Anglophone Cameroonian protest and politics of identity in Cameroon," summarizes the terms of agreement by stating that the actual tally of votes in 1961 plebiscite was 233,579 for and 97,741 against and in October of that very year a two state-federal system of governance with La Republique du Cameroun was reached giving birth to the then Federal Republic of East and West Cameroon. This is the backdrop to the clamor for the restoration of the Southern Cameroonian statehood that the English-speaking people of the North West and South West regions have been seeking since October 2016.

LITERATURE ASSESSMENT

Cameroon, the Africa in miniature nation, boasting of bilingual hereditary from two powerful European colonial nations of Britain and France has now surprisingly become another failed state on the continent of Africa (Eyoh 1998, 2004; Takougang and Krieger 1998; Mbembe 2001; Konings and Njamnjoh 2003; Amin 2008; Baxter 2008). According to Amin (2008), the Cameroonian youths have become the forerunners of street protests in Cameroon that has exposed the dismal internal livelihood in that country. It began, according to Julius Amin in 2008 during the famous petroleum and small commodities price rise in the nation. The nations' youths took to the streets and the Head of State, President Paul reacted with brutal force and chastised them in a nationally televised speech in which he promised mayhem to all the culprits, and he did. This time for the youths it was not just the standard order of relying on a few die-hearts to march on the streets as was done in the 90s during the multiparty riots and the stolen election victory of Ni John Fru Ndi of the SDF, the primary challenger to President Paul Biya in 1992. They resorted to exploiting the power of the social media because:

> In 2008, the Cameroonian youth was more sophisticated and knowing. Many had cell phones, and some had two of them, one from MTN and the other from Orange phone companies. They knew how to upload images quickly onto computers. A generation effectively used social media. (Amin 2008, p. 34)

As a result, their images were seen worldwide. By 2017, more than eight years after, the youths have become more adept at social media, most especially WhatsApp, Facebook, Blogs, and Twitter.

Anyefru (2011) demonstrates the overwhelming role that foreign culture, especially America culture has had on the lives of people in Cameroon through the excessive consumption of Western traditional media outlets. The most influence is from traditional media outlets like Cable News (CNN), images from American movies that feature MTV stars in the hip-hop generation. Of course, the influence of social media was equally overwhelming by 2011, but this paper has dwelled mostly on the traditional Western media impact shaping the culture of the natives in Anglophone Cameroonians. Tazanu (2012) one year later uncovers the power of information communication technologies (ICTs) mostly by residents of Buea in the South West Anglophone region of Cameroon to interconnect with migrants (bushfallers) abroad (De Bruijn and Brinkman 2011). To Tazanu, most residents were using the call boxes for transnational social bonding. Today, call boxes have been turned into Cybercafés with internet access for social media transactions and other forms of voice over internet protocol (VOIP). The difference that five years can bring to the communicative systems for people in this part of the world would form the focus of this study. The influx of new media gadgets like cell/smartphones, tablets, laptops, nooks, iPods, and iPads have impacted intra/international communicative systems among Africans especially in Cameroon where cultural affinities seem to have taken a toll as a result. A study by Tita and Agbome (2017) exposes the rupture of the proper traditional hierarchical communicative protocol between "Fons" (kings) of North West regions of Cameroon and their subjects due to the influence of new media communications. One of the Fons in the interview for this study remarked that his phone acts like an "information highway just like the palace" (146) and so he keeps his phone open 24/7 so anyone can easily reach him. We emphasize that before the advent of new media incursion into the traditional communicative spaces in Africa, there were no "direct" communications between the citizens and the Fons of the North West or the Chiefs of the South West regions. An intermediary transmitted the in-person messages to the Chief or the Fon. Today, citizens at home and abroad can text, emojify, FaceTime, and skype these traditional dignitaries from any part of the world without any safeguards whatsoever. Most inhabitants of the country have smartphones with apps like WhatsApp, Facebook, and Twitter for quick and secure transmission of messages, images, and videos to the rest of the world. This study on the influence of social media and the Anglophone Cameroonian protest will examine how prominent platforms like WhatsApp and Facebook including online newspaper like The Southern Cameroon Journal and SCTV were able to be effective in rallying the people to the streets and broadcasting messages, audio, images, and videos to the rest of the world.

METHODOLOGY

A methodological approach for a study of this nature takes into consideration the ontological, epistemological, and axiological stances of the participants and context of data collection and analysis. Anglophone Cameroonians have minimal African-driven educational curricular in their primary, secondary, and tertiary education. They were trained in mostly British educational systems while the Frenchified are trained in the French systems. With more than 200 ethnic languages in the country, none is taught in schools. The same goes for cultural value systems. This is one of the reasons earlier mentioned why Western modes of life (British and French) and now American value systems have invaded the cultural and communicative cognitive spheres of both Anglophone and Frenchified Cameroonians. Thus, in order to examine the issues at stake concerning how social media have been instrumental in exposing the Anglophone Cameroonian protests, the researcher asked two questions, RQ1: To what extent have Bareta Facebook site and Southern Cameroonian Television (SCTV) been instrumental in furthering the cause of Anglophone Cameroonians? RQ2: How has The Southern Cameroon Journal online site through news postings promoted the Anglophone Cameroonian case? In order to respond adequately to these two research questions, a qualitative content analysis of Bareta Facebook site, SCTV online site and the Southern Cameroon Journal online news site of September 22 and October 1, 2017, were undertaken. As already mentioned these two days were significant because they marked the preparation and symbolic inauguration of the independence of Southern Cameroon. Images, Videos, and messages from these sites on such historical days will shed light on the magnitude of the march toward self-rule and determination of the marginalized Southern Cameroonians.

Hsieh and Shannon (2005) outline three approaches to conducting qualitative content analysis: Conventional, directed, and summative. In order to ascertain the predominant themes, present in the videos, images, and messages on Mark Bareta Facebook pages of September 22 and October 1; SCTV online line broadcasts on September 22 and October 1 and the Southern Cameroon Journal online (cameroonjournal.com) on those same dates, a summative technique has been utilized. According to Hsiu Hsieh and Sarah Shannon, "A summative content analysis involves counting and comparisons, usually of keywords or content, followed by the interpretation of the underlying context" (Hsieh and Shannon 2005, p. 1277).

DATA ANALYSIS

September 22 and October 1, 2017, will undoubtedly go down in the annals of history as the dates when Southern Cameroonians also were known as Ambazonia started the march toward self-rule. They started with pre-independence rally at home in the South West and North West regions of Cameroon and abroad on September 22 and the considerable success of this event took the administration by surprise because millions of old men and women, children and the entire youth population at home in South West and North West Regions of the country came out to demonstrate their support for self-rule and restoration of independence. As seen from the table above in Mark Bareta Facebook site, the videos that were posted received 447,000 views; 54,480 comments, 14,816 likes, loves and wows; 13,123 shares. It must be stressed that these are videos that Facebook provided using the search term Mark Bareta and Bareta News (Table 5.1).

The Theme of "Crowd Marching" in Buea on October 22 followed by the theme of "Battle with police and Tear gas" had the highest viewership of 60,000 and 61,000 respectively in his page. The images attracted comments of 1931 on those events. However, the event that recorded the largest amount of comment was the event of October 1 under the theme "May the Souls of Fallen heroes rest in peace."

Table 5.1   Access to Facebook by "Ground Zero" (local) population

Home and abroad

Location/date	Views	Subject/themes	Comments	LLW love, likes and (wows)	Shares
Video: Victoria(SW) Sept. 22	37,000	LRC Flag burning	92	669	780
Video: Ndu County (NW) Sept. 22	12,000	Ndu county marching on	22	472	368
Video: Buea (SW) Sept. 22	60,000	Crowd marching	131	1200	1800
Video: Bafia (SW) Sept. 22	N/A	Freedom now	241	2100	1600
Video: Lewoh (SW) Sept. 22	21,000	Marching	50	588	720
Video: Balangi(SW) Sept. 22	10,000	Balangi on the move	14	393	265
Video: Batibo (NW) Sept. 22	38,000	Hon. Mbah Ndam (SDF) declaration	113	1032	1079
Video: Menji (SW) Oct. 1	49,000	Singing Ambazonian Anthem	126	1175	1384
Image: Holland (Europe) Sept. 22	N/A	Takumbeng women in Whites	34	1100	457
Video: New York (USA) Sept. 22	44,724	Takumbeng/ Ambazonians Seeking UN intervention	99	957	768
Video: Bessi (NW) Oct. 1	55,000	Fon of Bessi and traditional homage	85	1000	1200
Video: Teke (SW) Oct. 1	50,000	Cutting a tree as weapon	82	715	613
Video: Mark Bareta (Europe) Oct. 1	50,000	May the Souls of Fallen heroes rest in peace	4320	2684	989
Video: Buea (SW) Oct. 1	61,000	Battle with police and tear gas	71	731	1100

Source Mark Bareta Facebook Page, September 22 and October 1, 2017

Commenting on the October 22 theme, one of the participants watching the march on the Streets of Buea said:

> Special thanks to God almighty. Finally, finally, Ambazonias oyeh. That's Independence for you. That's statehood restoration for you. That's your country Southern Cameroon Ambazonia given to you. That's God for you. Can somebody shout Amen [sic]? Victory comes from God. To God be the glory. (MB, September 22, 2017)

These are some of the pro-independence messages that filled the Mark Bareta Facebook pages. However, not all the messages were crafted to agree with the strategies employed by the activists on the ground and those on cyberspace. For instance, this message from another user code-named SY put the blame squarely on the feet of those activists on social media: "So this is how Southern Cameroonians are stupid. How are people gonna set [sit] abroad and make decisions for you people in Cameroon?" (SY, September 22, 2017). Those sentiments were expressed in the page but most of them blamed the autocratic government of La Republic du Cameroon. They could have engaged in meaningful dialogue with the leaders of the Consortium of Teachers and the Lawyers in both the North West and South West regions of the country that triggered this civil unrest. With respect to the second theme in Mark Bareta page that has to do with "May the Souls of Fallen heroes rest in peace," corpses of those killed with live bullets were carried on stretchers by the demonstrators and when internet users around the world saw that they were alarmed and wrote comments on the page comparing peaceful civilian demonstrations in the West and the violent ones in Cameroon. On this very day, Southern Cameroonians abroad also took to the streets. As seen under the theme "Takumbeng/Ambazonians seeking UN intervention," there were over 44,724 comments only on this gathering in New York. It was peaceful, and the forces of law and order to maintain peace rather than attack those protesting. This is how one of the Facebook comments indicated by a user named SK: "Those out of the country are manifesting in a civilized manner, and they are protected by the police. Why can't we do same here in Cameroon and avoid the killing" (SK, September 22, 2017)? They demonstrated in New York, during the UN National Assembly Meetings. The women were half-naked, holding blue and white Ambazonian flags and chanting, "Biya must go." Another viewer (NG) saw the unfolding of these events

Table 5.2   Access to SCTV News site on Facebook

Location/date	Subject/duration	Views	LLW	Comments	Shares
White House, Washington, DC (Oct. 1)	Independence Day Celebration (13:32 minutes)	7400	120	72	132
White House, Washington, DC (Oct. 1)	Independence Day Take 2 (1 hour, 47 minutes, 10 seconds)	40,000	1000	1000	1100

and wrote these statements directed to those protesting in New York: "Why don't you come back and do it here, [sic] you stay back and send sheep to die plus stop this and save lives" (NG, September 2017). This statement is in line with another one on October 1: "Ninety percent of those instigating open confrontation between the civilians and the military lives [sic] in the comfort of their air-conditioned apartment in the Diaspora. Let's not be stupid please to follow those type of people" (RM, October 1, 2017). These are the divergent viewpoints that were echoed on the Mark Bareta Facebook page on these two days of riots (Table 5.2).

The SCTV news site online covered the October 1 Independence Day parade at the steps of the United States White House. Southern Cameroonians from all over the United States and neighboring Canada chattered buses and launched an operation "meet at the White House" to send the message to President Donald Trump to recognize the independence of Southern Cameroonians. Apart from the huge crowd that turned out in their numbers as evidenced in the videos, viewership alone totaled 47,400 as well as 1072 comments on their pages.

The Southern Cameroon Journal

Chris Anu, the editorialist of the Southern Cameroon Journal central theme for the write-up on October 8, after the October 1 symbolic Independence proclamation centered on torture and killing of Anglophone Youths in Muea, Buea, and Mutengene in the South West Region. He quotes verbatim some reports from the field on the action of La Republique du

Cameroun soldiers breaking into homes and churches arresting civilians. This is one of the testimonies recorded by one of the victims:

> It's horrible here in Muea. Gendarmes are killing at random arresting youths for no crime committed! Today the 7th of October at 7 in the morning, La republic gendarmes arrested a friend of mine by name Tanga George. Crime? "he's an Anglophone." More than 70 other persons were arrested in Muea today. We are doom! Who put us in this shit? Where is UN Security and Britain? Please do something fast. (Chris Anu, Southern Cameroon Journal, October 8, 2017)

The thread of this theme populates this entire editorial in the newspaper. In the second editorial, he paints a picture of the atmosphere in the North West Fon's Palace in Ndu on September 22. The overarching theme of the editorial titled "In the North West, the protesters storm the palaces of Nso, Mankon, and Nkwen," is about Independence now! The population marched on the streets, met with their local leaders, and asked for their endorsement of the state of Ambazonia. They raised the blue and white flag of the new nation, but after a while, the military forces took them down. This was a show of defiance to the authorities in Yaoundé that they were no longer to be governed by them after 56 years. In the last editorial titled "Southern Cameroonians Defy Biya and LRC youth take to the streets in the thousands, Patrick Ekema's House Ransacked," the same theme of rebellion was echoed as the Head of State President Paul Biya was addressing the United Nations Assembly in New York. In the editorial, photographs of Takumbeng women wearing white robes and young men and women holding Ambazonian flags and tree leaves and dancing on the streets. This, concisely, is what Chris Anu wrote among many other observations:

> Despite the heavy presence of gov't forces in the streets of major towns, cities and in some rural areas, hundreds of thousands of Southern Cameroonians took to the streets chanting songs of freedom and demanding that they get their country back. Protest marches that started in the early hours today, Friday, September 22, were reported in towns and villages including Eyumojock, Ekona, Kumba, Ebonji, Buea, Muyuka, Fontem and many others in the South West region. The Northwest saw protests in Bamenda, Kumbo, Batibo, Widikum, Santa, Ndu and many others. (Chris Anu, Southern Cameroon Journal, September 22, 2017)

Discussion

Started in 2011 by the Arab Spring riot, social media can no longer be underestimated. They have now become the safety valves, the open window with fresh air flowing through the body of oppressed people mostly in North Africa and now in Tropical Africa. Since the state-owned traditional media outlets like Radio, Newspaper, and Television have become the talking drums that sing the praises of long-term dictators on the continent of Africa, social media have come to relay their downtrodden voices to the rest of the world. That is the case with the Anglophone Cameroonians using the social media platforms of Facebook, Twitter, WhatsApp and another online news site to trumpet their call for the restoration of independence. The various sites that have been examined by this study demonstrate the power of the North West and South West denizens seeking freedom from oppression, marginalization, and repression from the majority French speaking-led government of President Paul Biya.

This study posed two research questions: RQ1: To what extent have Bareta Facebook site and Southern Cameroonian Television (SCTV) been instrumental in furthering the cause of Anglophone Cameroonians? RQ2: How has the Southern Cameroon Journal online site through news postings promoted the Anglophone Cameroonian case? With respect to research question 1, Mark Bareta Facebook page has recorded the highest number of viewers of the September 22 and October 1, 2017, Anglophone Cameroonian Independence day celebration in the North West, South West regions of Cameroon and in the Diaspora. Presently, the two sites (Mark Bareta Facebook site and SCTV news online) continue to increase their membership as they report minute-by-minute events in the Northern and Southern regions of Cameroon. Since the events of the last year, the principal leaders of the Anglophone Cameroonian restoration Interim Government led by Sisiku Julius Ayuk Tabe including most of his Cabinet members have been abducted from their hide-outs in Nigeria and brought to Cameroon. Even though the Minister of Information, Issa Tchiroma Bakari said on National Television in February that they have been brought to Cameroon, the public has not seen them, nor have their lawyers had any contact with them.

Also, there has been an influx of Anglophone Cameroonian refugees in neighboring Nigeria as the government has increased its crackdown of what it terms secessionist armed activities in the North West and Southwest regions of the country. Now, Mark Bareta news site and SCTV news online continue to update subscribers on the conflict brewing between the Defense forces of Ambazonia (ADFs) and those of La Republique du Cameroon. Ghost towns are still being observed on certain days when called for by the Interim government that is acting in the place of the Sisiku government. The second research question was equally answered. Chris Anu, the voice behind the Southern Cameroon Journal has now become a member of the Interim government in charge of communications.

Conclusion

This chapter set out to answer two research questions related to the civil unrest in the Southern regions of Cameroon. The civil unrest is about the need to address issues by the marginalized and longtime oppressed English-speaking people of the North West and the South West regions of Cameroon. The unrest that was triggered by the teachers' and lawyer is sit-in strikes in 2016 to protest unjust laws in their regions plunged into open arm conflict with each side recording numerous casualties this year. The worldwide marches and local street protests as evidenced in the analysis aforementioned provided from the social media sites of Mark Bareta news, Chris Anu's Southern Cameroon Journal and the Southern Cameroon Television (SCTV) show the increasing weariness as to what lies ahead with no dialogue initiated by both sides to seek a lasting solution. The crisis should be resolved soon as more casualties have been identified and more refugees are streaming into Nigeria and other neighboring countries. The fact that leaders of the Southern Cameroon movement code-name Ambazonia have been abducted and no one seems to know their whereabouts only goes to support the thesis that this conflict is far from over. The fact that social media has been instrumental in publicizing this conflict to the rest of the world is an indication that the force of new media communication is overwhelming. In order to stop the broadcast of the gory images that are coming from those two regions, the government decided to shut down the internet and only allow limited access has not resolved matters; still, the people can use VPN and send information out to the rest of the world. Gone are the days when African government controlled state-owned traditional media outlets of radio, television, and newspapers. Today, the omnipotent force of the social media has exposed what is happening in Cameroon to the rest of the world. We hope leaders of both sides would come to their senses and initiate a meaningful dialogue to bring satisfactory solution and much-needed peace to the North West and South regions of the country.

QUESTIONS FOR DISCUSSION

1. How effective has social media influenced events in tropical Africa, especially in the Southern Cameroonian regions?
2. What are the advantages and disadvantages of relying on social media messages when examining social and political unrests in the tropical African regions?
3. To what extent can the government and the opposition forces in the tropical African regions like Cameroon use digital media to the advancement of their citizen's economic and political livelihood?

REFERENCES

Acemoglu, D., Hassan, T. A., & Tahoun, A. (2017). The Power of the Street: Evidence from Egypt's Arab Spring. *The Review of Financial Studies, 31*(1), 1–42.

Amin, J. (2008). Understanding the Protest of 2008 in Cameroon. *Africa Today, 58*(4), 22–42.

Anyefru, E. (2010). Paradoxes of Internationalization of the Anglophone Problem in Cameroon. *Journal of Contemporary African Studies, 28*(1), 85–101.

Anyefru, E. (2011). The Refusal to Belong: Limits of the Discourse on Anglophone Nationalism in Cameroon. *Journal of Third World Studies, 28*(2), 277–306.

Baxter, J. (2008). *Dust from Our Eyes: An Unblinkered Look at Africa*. Hamilton, ON: Wolsak and Wynn.

Carsten, P. (2018, January 11). *At Least 15,000 Cameroonian Refugees Flee to Nigeria Amid the Crackdown*. https://www.reuters.com/article/us-came-roon-separatists-nigeria/at-least-15000-cameroonian-refugees-flee-to-nige-ria-amid-crackdown-idUSKBN1F01Q6. Retrieved March 8, 2018.

De Bruijn, M., & Brinkman, I. (2011). "Communicating Africa." Researching Mobile Kin Communities Communication Technologies and Social Transformation in Angola and Cameroon. *Autrepart, 1*(57–58), 41–57.

Eyoh, D. (1998). Conflicting Narratives of Anglophone Protest and the Politics of Identity in Cameroon. *Journal of Contemporary African Studies, 16*(2), 249–276.

Eyoh, D. (2004). Contesting Local Citizenship: Liberalization and the Politics of Difference in Cameroon. In B. Berman, D. Eyoh, & W. Kymlicka (Eds.), *Ethnicity and Democracy in Africa*. Athens: Ohio University Press.

Hsieh, H., & Shannon, S. E. (2005). Three Approaches to Qualitative Content Analysis. *Qualitative Health Research, 15*(9), 1277–1288.

Konings, P., & Nyamnjoh, F. (2003). *Negotiating an Anglophone Identity: A Study of the Politics of Recognition and Representation in Cameroon*. Leiden and Boston: Brill.

Lotan, G., Graeff, E., Ananny, M., Gaffney, D., & Pearce, I. (2011). The Arab Spring | The Revolutions Were Tweeted: Information Flows During the 2011 Tunisian and Egyptian Revolutions. *International Journal of Communication, 5*, 31.

Mbembe, A. (2001). *On the Postcolony*. Berkeley: University of California Press.

Stepan, A., & Linz, J. J. (2013). Democratization Theory and the "Arab Spring". *Journal of Democracy, 24*(2), 15–30.

Takougang, J., & Krieger, M. (1998). *African State and Society in the 1990s: Cameroon's Political Crossroads*. Boulder, CO: Westview Press.

Tazanu, P. M. (2012). *Being Available and Reachable: New Media and Cameroonian Transnational Sociality*. Bamenda, Cameroon: Langa Research and Publishing.

Tita, J. C., & Agbome, S. (2017). ICTs and Power Relations in Traditional Settings in Cameroon: The Case of Bafut and Chomba Villages. In K. Langmia & T. Tyree (Eds.), *Social Media: Culture and Identity* (pp. 133–156). Lanham, MD: Lexington Books.

Further Reading

Amin, J. A. (2012). Understanding the Protest of February 2008 in Cameroon. *Africa Today, 58*(4), 21–43.

Kituyi, M., Langmia, K., Moya, M., Tsuma, C., & Mbarika, V. (2014). Towards a Framework for the Adoption of Social Media in Health in Sub-Saharan Africa. In *Proceedings of the 6th Annual International Conference on ICT for Africa 2014, 1–4th October, Yaoundé–Cameroon*.

Nyamnjoh, F. (2015). *New Media and Religious Transformations in Africa*. Bloomington, IN: Indiana University Press.

Social Media and Political Participation in Africa: Issues, Challenges, and Prospects. In *Communication and the New Media in Nigeria: Social Engagements, Political Development, and Public Discourse* (pp. 64–82). Nigeria: ACCE.

Tabe, C. A. (2016). Language and Humor in Cameroon Social Media. *Analyzing Language and Humor in Online Communication, 9*(8), 131–163.

CHAPTER 6

Young Women and Internet Cafés in China: Risks and Aspirations in a Contested Techno-social Space

Janice Hua Xu

INTRODUCTION

Digital Divide, Young People, and Gender

Scholars have observed that all information and communication technologies (ICTs) are accompanied by reactions and predictions regarding their impact on the existing social order (Thurlow 2006; Herring 2007). For young people, access to the internet could provide many of the resources for explorations of identity, emotion, and sexuality, for experimentation with self-disclosure and intimacy (Livingstone and Helsper 2007). It could affect their experiences of community life, planning of personal activities, or the way they organize their social relationships. In popular representations of technology users, young people tend to be portrayed as either innocent youth or youth at risk, vulnerable to the addictive power of the internet. Among scholars, there has been much effort to address how internet use affect young people regarding

J. H. Xu (✉)
Department of Communication, Holy Family University, Philadelphia, PA, USA
e-mail: jxu@holyfamily.edu

© The Author(s) 2019
E. K. Ngwainmbi (ed.), *Media in the Global Context*,
https://doi.org/10.1007/978-3-030-26450-5_6

academic achievements, delinquency behavior, and social relationships, and even their first romantic relationship and sexual activities (Attewell et al. 2003; Ito et al. 2009; Cheng et al. 2014).

Young women in China have been active in engaging in online activities for many purposes typical of social media users of both genders (Kent et al. 2017), from professional development, networking, shopping, to entertainment and fashion, although there is a higher percentage of females reposting than authoring (Li et al. 2013). They have used social media collectively to create new traditions to highlight their youthful female images and identities, to differentiate from female role models in official media that tend to be associated with state-sponsored feminism. For instance, many Chinese female students celebrate Girl's Day on March 7th, a campus festival invented in the 1990s and spread through social media to different universities, instead of International Women's Day on March 8th. As individuals, many young females have used online activities such as e-stores and video blogging to express their creativity, promote their e-commerce businesses or pursue their dreams of becoming celebrities (Sullivan and Kehoe 2018).

Young adults are the most highly connected age group in many societies, but that does not mean that they use the internet in the same ways or with the same consequence. Access to and use of ICT is considered an essential social equality issue for various geographic regions, social groups, and individuals in the information economy (Attewell 2001). Location, income, gender, education, age have been contributing factors in the digital divide. Selwyn (2004) argues that there is a lack of the distinction between "access" and "use" of ICT, as well as consideration of the consequences of engagement with ICT. Hargittai and Hinnart (2008) researched young adult internet users and found that those with higher levels of education and of a more resource-rich background use the web for more "capital enhancing" activities. Being a male and member of the higher socioeconomic class is associated with more variety of online activities and higher levels of web-use skill, and in countries like China, one's opportunity as an online opinion leader with higher visibility and credibility (Svensson 2014).

Recent scholarly findings have demonstrated the mediating role of economic, cultural, and social forms of capital in shaping individuals' engagements with ICT. Joiner et al. (2015) examined gender and digital divide and suggest the secondary gender digital divide between males and females is best explained by a combination of negative gendered stereotypes concerning technology and social expectations based on gender roles. Specifically, they found that although the number of female internet users was gradually catching up with male users, the online culture developed in the early days of internet reflected masculine norms of acceptable behavior and language use—tolerance of flaming and harassment—and made it less attractive to women.

In developing countries, the issues of poverty, social inequality, and uneven development of information infrastructure could further complicate the role of ICT in the lives of young people. A research report by Intel indicates that in developing countries, an average of 23% fewer women than men are online, putting them at a disadvantage regarding access to new ideas, resources, and opportunities (Weingarten 2013). Privately owned internet cafés in developing countries have played a useful role in narrowing the digital divide, in addition to publicly funded facilities such as libraries and school computers labs, as these businesses reflect local needs and market conditions. However, although internet cafés are one of the easiest ways for people to access the web in many developing countries, they are found to be impractical for those women who cannot leave their homes for religious and cultural reasons.

While the increasing smartphone ownership and use among less advantaged social groups in many countries have brought new hope to bridge the digital divide, researchers have proven that different devices do not lead to the same internet experience, particularly in non-Western countries such as South Africa (Donner et al. 2011). In a study among internet users in Armenia, a former Soviet republic categorized as a developing country, Pearce and Rice (2013, p. 721) find that the use of different devices affects the extent of usage and engagement in different internet activities. "Although the mobile Internet is available for those on the wrong side of the digital divide, those mobile Internet users do not engage as much in many online activities that could be capital-enhancing" as compared to PC users. Therefore, there is evidence that inequalities in society can be easily replicated online, although there are opportunities for narrowing digital divides by enhancing access, skills and meaningful connectivity (Katz and Gonzalez 2016).

People's perceptions and level of trust could determine their habit and choice in ICT adoption, as technology is never neutral. The use of public access venues could be shaped by safety concerns, the relevance of the information, the reputation of the institution, and users' perceptions of how "cool" these venues are (Gomez and Gould 2010). It could also be related to the confidence of the people in the technology regarding privacy or cybercrime. In a study of online gamer in Taiwan (Lin 2005), it is found that young people in metropolitan Taipei regard home as a space of domestic surveillance and discipline, characterized by adult supervision and interruptions of their online activities. In contrast, internet café is seen as a public leisure space, which is not suitable for girls, due to its stigmatized image associated with various internet-related crimes and deviant behaviors. The appeal and excitement of the internet café come mainly from the uninterrupted playing experience and group interactions, in addition to better equipment. At the same time, student dormitory is gender-segregated space where males engage in extensive group gaming activities, and females keep a low profile and play usually in isolation.

Internet café is seen as an escape from the moral judgments and parental restrictions and control at home. In communities with developed technology, it gives adolescents, predominantly males, a public space to maintain, negotiate, and establish relationships with friends and peers outside school (Jonsson 2010). The popularity of internet cafés among young people pose challenges to societies as this brings new questions of how public space, social network, and leisure time are organized. This is particularly relevant in Asian cities with large populations, dense urban space, and traditions of emphasizing education among middle-class families.

This chapter aims to study the dynamics of gender, class, and youth around private internet cafés in the context of China's rapid adoption of internet technology in urban areas. Specifically, it examines women's relationship with these urban spaces and addresses their concerns and preferences overuse of these facilities, as well as the community-based obstacles preventing them from taking advantage of the local technology resources.

INTERNET CAFÉS AND YOUNG PEOPLE IN CHINA

Initially only available in state-funded research institutions and universities, China's internet service started to get connected internationally in the late 1980s (CERNET 2001) and turned rapidly into commercial businesses. The dramatic growth of the internet industry in the last two decades has made profound impacts to various aspects of the society and people's daily routines, creating e-commerce multimillionaires such

Alibaba's Jack Ma, and has drawn full scholarly attention. The number of internet users in mainland China increased from 620,000 in 1997 to 731 million people at the end of 2016, accounting for 53.2% of the total population of the country, up 2.9 percentage points from the end of 2015 (CNNIC 2017).[1] Most users are aged between 10 and 39 years, using the internet for activities from social networking, business transaction, and online entertainment to public services. Although fixed-line and mobile phones have become more affordable than in the past, there are significant disparities in penetration rates among users in different provinces and between urban and rural settings.

Internet cafés in mainland China had a booming era in the 2000s when the demand for the internet was high, but private ownership of devices like mobile phones and computers was relatively low. By the end of 2009, 580,000 people were working at 138,000 cybercafés in China. Rooted in the local economy and powered by private entrepreneurs, the industry contributed to community renewal during the neoliberal reform of state-owned enterprises and urban, collective enterprises through job creation for laid-off workers and providing affordable entertainment, and provided local information services different from official media channels (Qiu 2013).

For young people in China who are generally the only child of the family, the cafés serve as a "third place" outside the daily routines and demands of home and school, offering relief in a society with sharp social stratification, competition, insecurity, and consumerism. They frequent the internet cafés for a sense of freedom, relaxation, community, and fun, which can hardly be found elsewhere in their lives, despite the official and parental "demonization" of the social space (Liu 2009). Internet café played an essential role as a site of leisure practice outside the confines of parental control and an often stressful and monotonous educational career. Many game players, including youth and adults, prefer internet cafés even

---

[1] The telecommunication industry was a priority industry in China's economic reform, and went through several rounds of large scale restructuring since the creation of the Ministry of Information Industry in 1998, tasked to serve the information needs of the nation and its 1.3 billion population. It has evolved from an inefficient monopoly to the current oligopoly dominated by state telecom giants, with foreign competitors gradually allowed in following China's entry to WTO in 2001. Chinese private enterprises, such as search engine Baidu, also played a huge role in the growth of online services.

though computer connections became available at home. Internet cafés provide incentives for teenagers to meet friends they know online and offline and thus adding a face-to-face component to internet use.

As the government views the development of internet technology vital to the nation's information revolution, internet cafés are seen with an ambivalent attitude, as it provides information and social spaces deemed not conducive to the social/political order (Golub and Lingley 2008). The growth and regulation of the public space involve critical players at various levels: national regulators, local state agencies, café operators, user groups such as students and migrant workers, and members of the urban elite from parents to teachers (Qiu and Zhou 2005). As the industry thrived, internet cafés in China have been subject to many governmental regulations, crackdowns and raids, especially after a midnight fire in Beijing's university district in 2002 that killed 25 young people and injured 13, many drawn there by the nighttime discount. Following the fire, the government moved the power of managing internet cafés to the Ministry of Culture, and launched a nationwide inspection of internet cafés and stopped approving licenses for new cafés. Internet cafés were not allowed to operate within a radius of 200 meters from middle and primary schools. A law was passed to prohibit those under the age of 18 from entering for-profit internet cafés and imposed restrictions on minimum space size and number of computers for issuing licenses.

However, the rules were not always strictly enforced by owners or local authorities, which did not have consistent patterns to monitor the daily activities of these spaces, and sometimes tolerating violations by charging a fine or "protection fees" and turning a blind eye to fake IDs. Occasionally the clashes between customers and café staff or local administrative personnel led to violent incidents, as shown in crime news about female staff assaulted by gangs without IDs trying to get in. To enforce the rules and appease worried parents, the administrative branches under the Ministry of Culture organized more than 100 thousand people to monitor the activities of internet cafés and customers (Tuo 2016). Thousands of senior citizens and neighborhood committees formed volunteer teams to patrol local venues. Telephone hotlines and government websites were set ups for citizens to report on café activities that violated the bans against admitting minors or overnight business hours. "Green internet cafés" that installed filtering software were promoted and recommended to youth and their parents. More recently, authorities in some areas have installed monitoring cameras and even face-recognition software to help enforce the rules and control activities in these spaces.

Internet cafés were criticized widely by the Chinese elite for exposing young people to pornography, violence, and addictive online gaming. Parents and school authorities have appealed to local governments to ban illegal internet cafés in the neighborhoods, which sometimes allow overnight customers to stay for weeks. Slogans banners like "Keep away from *Internet* Bars" or "Say No to *Internet* Bars" can be seen in some schools. China's National People's Congress has estimated that 10% of China's internet users under age 18 are addicted (AP 2009), defined by Chinese psychologists as showing symptoms such as being online more than six hours a day for activities other than studying or working, and getting angry when unable to get online. Meanwhile, educators also worry young people could become involved with dangerous individuals or groups online. China's Ministry of Public Security investigated more than 7400 Internet crimes and detained more than 15,000 criminal suspects, including those involved in hacking, data theft, and financial fraud, or "harming national security online" (RFA 2015).

The authorities targeted not only against "harmful" sites relating to pornography and gambling, but also individual posts about current events that are considered "rumor-mongering." However, a wide variety of exploitative activities exist online. In 2016, media reports reveal that hundreds of photos and videos of naked female students were used as collateral for loans on a Chinese online lending service, which threatened to use them for blackmail if repayments were not made on time (*Financial Times* 2016).

As many students skipped school and indulged in long hours of gaming, or conflicted with their parents about these behaviors, thousands of male and female adolescents were sent by their parents to costly boot camps to treat their addiction. Some camps used the military method and electric shock therapy until it was banned in 2009. Popular media rhetoric compared internet addition to the opium epidemic that destroyed China's Qing Empire in the early twentieth century. In Chinese media reports, women frequenting internet cafés were portrayed as internet addicts, delinquents, or victims of male predators, even though women constitute a significant amount of labor force working in these grassroots businesses. The primary concern over young people's technology habits has been discussed in the context of the general moral crisis faced by Chinese, in response to rapid consumerism, the medicalization of mental illness, and new forms of public and publicity (Golub and Lingley 2008). Scholars also suggest that China's one-child policy, the highly competitive learning environment and rising economic expectations create a lot of pressure for adolescents to excel in their academic work as the hope of the family (Szablewicz 2012).

The fast growth of family computer ownership, tight restrictions, and periodic crackdowns brought a dip in the number of internet cafés. In 2012, as smartphones and mobile games became increasingly popular in China, some 10,000 internet cafés closed down, leaving just 136,000 licensed cafés, according to a report by Chinese tech giant Tencent. Meanwhile, along with mobile phone, tablet PC and smart TV, and the wireless network had popularized rapidly in public areas. Inexpensive internet cafés, which once were the only spots for online access for young people, became less attractive to urban residents and less profitable than before as land price escalated. To cater to affluent customers, a fraction of café owners adopted the "Starbucks model" with upgraded food and beverage services as well as gaming equipment, banned smoking, and offered memberships. The national chains also organize public relations events such as gaming competitions and user meet-ups. With the emergence of upscale chain-store, "wangka" that provide full service and tastefully decorated rooms with comfortable furniture, the sites of internet access and choice of leisure activity are increasingly used as indicators of social status and class (Lindtner and Szablewicz 2010).

In 2014, to revitalize the industry, the government lifted limitations about the minimum physical size of a venue and number of computers, which analysts think might help job creation and bring more of China's rural population online. Other services, such as female gaming companions for customers were also allowed. After some years of consolidation under pressure from tight competition, the internet café industry saw an upward trend again, mainly due to the popularity of gaming. In 2015, China had 146,000-internet café s with 20 million daily users, with the primary central growth regions in second line or third line cities in the provinces. More than 30% of users were students, and around 90% of users were males (Shunwang 2016).

The following research questions guided the project: (1) what are the activities and habit of young women as internet café s customers. (2) What are their attitudes and perceptions of the internet cafés they typically visit? (3) How do socioeconomic or regional differences affect their activities and preferences as internet café customers?

Research Methods

The author conducted an online survey to collect data from female respondents about their internet café activities, in addition to background research through documentary and website materials. Also, several groups of young people from Henan province and Shanghai were interviewed in the process of designing and preparing for the survey, including students, recent graduates, a few instructors, and internet café staff.

The central part of the research is an online survey of young women from three different academic institutions in China—a community college in Kaifeng (Henan province) resembling a professional school, a large four-year university in Qingdao (Shandong province), and a four-year technology university in Shaoxing (Zhejiang province). In total 132 female respondents finished, the survey conducted in April 2017. 90% of them were between the ages of 18 and 25, 7.6% were between 26 and 30, and 52% were under 20. The survey was completed with the assistance of three college instructors who introduced the online survey site to their current and former students. They also provided helpful input to adjust the questionnaire, so it is relevant to the local conditions.

The questionnaire contains questions about users' demographic information, cybercafé facilities, personal objectives, attitudes, safety perception, social norms, and experience. The questionnaire also includes questions on other people such as café customers and attitudes of family members. The majority of respondents took the survey from android platforms.

Findings

Respondents' Socioeconomic Background

The respondents came from different socioeconomic backgrounds and had different professional prospects. Among the three cities survey respondents reside, the city of Kaifeng is situated on the southern bank of the Yellow River, in China's inland Henan province, which is relatively low in economic development level. Shaoxing and Qingdao are located in the economically advanced east coast and are more prosperous.

Regarding family backgrounds, those attending the community college in Kaifeng mostly came from rural areas, and few of them owned laptops or home PCs. While some classrooms have computers for instruction, the college does not have computer labs for students' personal use. The curriculum focuses on hands-on professional skills. For instance, the Education Department mainly trains students to become daycare workers or rural elementary school teachers. Students often had to pay to go to the three internet cafés near campus for checking emails, occasional homework, or applying for government financial assistance. The facilities there are elementary, and cannot be compared to chain stores like Wangyu Wangka. According to the instructors, a significant portion of the students is categorized as impoverished students receiving a tuition waiver and living stipends, and those who own PCs or iPhone would not qualify. Many students work part-time for extra income. Because of their background, some students lack knowledge in traffic safety, fraud protection, and sex education, and were occasionally victimized by accidents or online fraud. They had close relationships with the college staff who managed the dormitory students carefully "like their parents" and sometimes accompanied them to hospitals in ambulances. Each dorm room has up to 6–8 students.

Students from universities in Shaoxing and Qingdao mostly came from urban backgrounds, and many had laptops, Ipads, and iPhones,

Fig. 6.1 Internet cafe users' monthly income

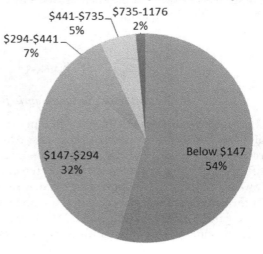

Respondents Monthly Income/Stipend

$441-$735
5%

$735-1176
2%

$294-$441
7%

$147-$294
32%

Below $147
54%

according to the instructors. Although all living in campus dormitories, they are less close to the staff as compared to the students in the community college. Compared to the community college, the universities were more difficult to get in, as their admission scores for students in the national entrance exam were higher.

Half (50%) of the respondents were from the community college in Kaifeng, and half are from the other two cities. Among all the respondents, 66.7% came from the rural family background. 53.8% of all respondents had a monthly income (including living stipends) of less than 1000 yuan (approximately US $147). 85.6% of all respondents had a monthly income of less than 2000 yuan. (The minimum monthly wage for full-time work in China is $333 in 2017) (Fig. 6.1).

Internet Café Usage, Attitudes, and Perceptions

All the respondents used internet cafés in the past, but only 38.6% of them used internet cafés within the past year, because the campuses had internet connections and many owned mobile devices. Respondents named a variety of reasons for going to internet cafés. "Gathering information" is the most important reason for going there, while "relaxation and entertainment" are second. Other reasons mentioned include "going with friends" "work," "gaming," and "space of freedom." Most of the venues they visit are open 24 hours a day and have 30–60 computers. A small portion of the venues has more than 100 computers.

Most respondents indicate that they go to internet cafés on a need basis, and did not have regular schedules. For each visit, 86.4% of them spend 1–2 hours there, and 9.8% spend 3–5 hours. There are 3.8% of the respondents who spend more than 5 hours per visit. 9.8% of respondents have memberships to the cafés they frequent, 11.4% visit different cafés where they have a membership for some of them. 78.8% do not have memberships. For internet café facilities, 19.7% feel they are well equipped and offer proper user functions. 11.4% feel the equipment were outdated or had slow internet speed, while 68.9% feel the facilities were average and acceptable.

Regarding the objectives and functions of using the internet cafés, 37.9% of respondents consider these spaces as helpful in acquiring new information and knowledge relevant to academic learning and professional skills. Precisely, about one-third of the entire respondent's name "computer knowledge" as the skill they could improve in internet cafés. Some identified "making charts" and "job search," "filling out forms," or "dance videos." A small fraction mention "gaming skills." 51.5% see these spaces as venues for relaxation and entertainment. 10.6% indicate that they intended to go there for work and study, but each time found that they spent time with various games and films.

One of the most important findings of the survey is that the majority of respondents do not have a favorable view of the level of safety at the internet cafés they go. 41.7% of respondents indicate they have a "low level" of a sense of being safe. 51.5% choose "average," and 6.8% choose "high level" of a sense of being safe.

Similarly, the majority of respondents do not have a favorable view of the level of comfort at the internet cafés they go. 33.3% of respondents indicate they have a "low level" of a sense of comfort. 56.8% choose "average," and 9.8% choose "high level" of a sense of comfort. For the question about the atmosphere of the internet cafés, only 3.8% indicate they like the atmosphere there. 41.7% select "dislike the poor atmosphere," while 54.5% select "acceptable/average." Among factors that the respondents saw as weird or unusual, they listed people screaming or cursing while playing games, smoking or sleeping, and long-term customers staying internet cafés for food and shelter. The respondents value their private space highly, and if affordable, they would prefer getting private rooms in the internet café with friends.

The majority of respondents consider the atmosphere of the internet cafés a critical factor in their decision to go there or not. 31.8% choose "highly important," and 30.3% chose "very important." Only 4.5% choose "not important," and 11.5% choose "not very important." 22% choose "average" regarding importance.

Relationship with Others

The respondents rarely try to get to know other customers. 93.2% do not believe it is possible to make friends with strangers there and refuse to have any connection with. Only 2.3% believe that if possible, those sharing the same interests could become friends or dates. 4.5% of the respondents believe that those who frequent the same places might become superficial "nodding acquaintances." 29.5% of the respondents visit the internet cafés only when accompanied by friends.

Most of the respondents indicate that their parents had negative attitudes about their use of internet cafés. Only one third report a neutral attitude. 37.1% of parents criticized these actions and did not allow them to go, while 29.5% expressed worry that their children might become addicted or get other bad influences. The potential bad influences cited range from "becoming friends with bad people in society" to "fantasizing too much and had a twisted view of reality." 21.2% of the parents took actual steps to prevent the children from going, while 59.8% used only verbal criticism and suggestions to caution them against going. Some women decided to frankly inform their parents about their internet café visits, while others chose to conceal these activities from their families.

The interview findings also reflect the significant disparities between young women and their parents over the norms of "proper" internet use and social expectations of pleasant dating experience in China. While a small portion of the young women considers online dating as acceptable, all of them feel that their parents would oppose this type of behavior.

From interviews with Wangyu Wangka chain store staff, it is found that the male and female staff all work 12-hour shifts per day, even though it is a membership-reliant store meeting the national standard in its operations regarding environment and equipment, and customer ID checking practice. The staff indicates the job is service natured and does not involve too much skill, and there is not much worry about security since the management measures became stricter. The interviewees explain that because male customers are the primary consumers of the internet cafés, the needs of females often are not taken into consideration. As a public social space, it became by default a male-dominated space. It is socially acceptable for females to frequent the internet cafés accompanied by their boyfriends, existing as the "silent partner" of the male. Thus, the few females who frequent the spaces would be considered "addicted girls" criticized in popular discourse or super gaming fans. A fraction of females using the space for work purpose usually stays very briefly.

In the survey there is a question about "whether you think working in internet cafés is a good job suitable for females." Most of the respondents answer that staff jobs at the internet cafés were not good for females, because of the long hours and night work, "chaotic" and poor environment, "too much variety" of people, and low pay and a low prospect. A few women say it is not safe, and one specifically expressed concern of violence—"might get beaten up." A couple of the respondents also cite health concerns over harmful computer radiation and lousy air quality. A small portion of respondents states this type of job is valuable and deserves respect, as it involves managing the space, keeps minors out, and maintain order.

The research also finds a small portion of women college graduates in their 20s has the resources to take advantage of internet cafés as a social and entertainment space, usually in urban environments they consider as "safe." However, they might encounter a different sort of risk. They are usually the only child of the family and center of their middle-class parents' attention, even after entering college or graduate schools. For these urban women who feel the pressure of academic expectations and have a relatively sheltered life, the appeal of online entertainment activities come from the freedom to escape the confines of reality and performing/playing various fantasy characters, or develop new relationships online and obtain emotional experiences that are not readily available in their immediate surroundings. However, it is found in the interviews that these women could sometimes feel hurt by behaviors of fellow players in a group game or males who have shared their romantic feelings. For instance, some women playing a group role-playing martial art game "Sword III" develop online "master-apprentice" or "couple" relationships with males online and even spend money to exchange game costumes and weapons with them. A few also participate in the meet-up gatherings dressed up as ancient, dynasty characters. While the chain-store internet cafés advertise the successful real-life romance of gamers who decided to meet offline, a few women unprepared for the fleeting nature of these engagements indicate they experienced shock and sorrow after being rejected or betrayed by their online partners, causing emotional distress, "days of crying," and absence from classes. The gendered social norms made it very hard for them to seek consolation from family and friends over these types of sense of loss or isolation, and the young women tend to blame themselves for lacking experience and knowledge of people in the real world. These young women find little resources available for guidance on handling irresponsible or abusive online behaviors.

DISCUSSION AND CONCLUSION

The issue of digital divide goes beyond unequal access to technology and involves quality, ease, and emotional associations of the experience. The paper finds that contrary to public concerns over the addictive power of internet cafés, many young women keep a distance from these male-dominated spaces based on considerations of personal security and atmosphere. However, a significant portion of young women chooses to use the space cautiously for a range of personal goals, despite criticism and admonitions from their families and popular discourse. In contrast to males, young women in public spaces are less likely to be fully immersed in the online world and are more aware of the surrounding environment. Women emphasize highly the atmosphere and the perceived level of personal safety in internet cafés, and make consumer decisions about whether to go to a venue based on these factors more frequently than the level of facilities. Their sense of self-protection and concern over strangers and the male-dominated environment in a basic level internet café make some women feel particular pride in declaring that they do not use internet café anymore as other online devices became available.

Not surprisingly, the research also finds that more expensive internet cafés are considered by women as safer and more comfortable, especially those charging more than 8 yuan an hour. However, this is beyond the consumption level of the majority of the students, and such venues are often located in affluent or urban commerce center areas, in contrast to those charging 2–3 yuan an hour for essential online access, where women might encounter male customers sitting next to them smoking, cursing, or screaming. Therefore, many women of average or low economic background chose not to go to internet cafés alone unless they need to get something done there, as the perceived safety risk or discomfort might outweigh the value of visiting the public space.

An overwhelming amount of women declares in the survey that they "don't talk to strangers" in internet cafés, or will only nod to those seen frequently, indicating that their trust stays within existing offline networks such as classmates and extended families, which they also include in their online "circles" on apps like WeChat. Young women in China face immense social pressure to marry before reaching 27 or 28, as there is deep prejudice of "leftover women" seen as too old to find desirable mates; therefore, they are very protective of their reputation and careful with contact with unknown males.

The existence of a digital divide among the women respondents from the different socioeconomic background is also shown in the perceived function of internet cafés as information source vs. entertainment/social space. The rural–urban gap regarding family income level and technology familiarity is evident among the young women, even though they have left their hometowns and reside on college campuses in urban areas. For female college students from a rural background, there is a higher rate of respondents seeing internet cafés as a vital information source, due to their relative lower ownership of personal online devices compared to those from urban backgrounds. They tend to view the experience of accessing the internet in public places as task related, to be accomplished briefly with 1–2 hours, with the benefits of improving their familiarity with computer operation or professional knowledge, but not something enjoyable or relaxing, or an occasion to talk to strangers. Women from middle-class family background, however, are more used to public entertainment venues and are less hesitant in spending money on leisure activities, which might include gaming alone or with friends and relatives. Their higher rate of PC ownership also makes it less necessary to go to internet cafés for information search.

The public stereotypes of internet café users are more evident among the parents of the young women, as there are misconceptions and parent–daughter gaps about the perceived risks of this public space. While many urban parents consider the ownership of personal PCs as a protection, a view probably shared by their daughters, some young women's consideration of friendship and social circles might make them view the internet cafés differently. Their aspirations to grow socially and professionally in the urban economy might embolden some of them to cautiously step in a male-dominated space against the warnings of their parents, to achieve personal objectives from filling out an online application form to meeting new friends. The generation gap is not always easy to overcome through communication, especially for first-generation college students from rural areas.

As an urban technology space involving the mingling of different social groups, internet cafés could bring potential benefits as well as risks for young women. The cautions over the urban techno-social space are related to the anxieties of young people and their parents over the paths for their future, as they navigate among shifting gender norms, job market, social network, and family expectations in the changing urban landscape. The unevenness in infrastructure development and community culture in various Chinese neighborhoods created different ecosystems for women seeking information nourishment for their personal growth, which surpass the issue of ICT access.

International scholarship on China's internet has often prioritized issues such as telecommunications industry growth, censorship, and social control, and there is an insufficient amount of study on the consequences it has for families, communities, and social relationships. The gender component of young people's internet experience in the public space could be addressed with more in-depth inquiries for future research. For educators, scholars, urban administrators, and businesses, there is a lot to be done in studying women's technology consumption activities to engage them fully in the increasingly tech-driven world.

QUESTIONS FOR DISCUSSION

1. Digital divide often refers to the gap between the "haves" and "have-nots" in terms of their access to information technology such as the internet. What factors could affect people's access to the internet?
2. Do you think parents have good reasons to worry about the technology use of their adult children in college?
3. Do you agree that those under 18 should be banned from using privately owned internet cafes? Why is the rule difficult to enforce?
4. What kind of religious or cultural factor could affect women's presence in public space in some developing countries?
5. What strategies could the internet cafes take to attract female customers?
6. Do you think PC ownership is more beneficial for online activities than just smartphone ownership?

REFERENCES

AP. (2009, July 14). *China Stops Shock Therapy for Internet Addicts*. http://www.nbcnews.com/id/31905111/ns/tech_and_science-tech_and_gadgets/t/china-stops-shock-therapy-internet-addicts/#.WkMa80trzOQ.

Attewell, P. (2001). The First and Second Digital Divides. *Sociology of Education, 74*(3), 252–259.

Attewell, P., Suazo-Garcia, B., & Battle, J. (2003). Computers and Young Children: Social Benefit or Social Problem? *Social Forces, 82,* 277–296.

Cheng, S., Ma, J., & Missari, S. (2014). The Effects of Internet Use on Adolescents' First Romantic and Sexual Relationships in Taiwan. *International Sociology, 29,* 324–347.

China Education and Research Network. (2001). *Evolution of Internet in China*. http://www.edu.cn/introduction_1378/20060323/t20060323_4285.shtml.

CNNIC (China Internet Network Report Center) Annual Report. (2017). https://cnnic.com.cn/IDR/ReportDownloads/201706/P0201706 08523740585924.pdf.

Donner, J., Gitau, S., & Marsden, G. (2011). Exploring Mobile-only Internet Use: Results of a Training Study in Urban South Africa. *International Journal of Communication, 5,* 574–597.

Financial Times. (2016, June 15). *Chinese Borrowers Told to Post Nude Photos as Collateral.* https://www.ft.com/content/cce6d400-32c6-11e6-ad39-3fee 5ffe5b5b.

Golub, A., & Lingley, K. (2008). "Just Like the Qing Empire": Internet Addiction, MMOGs, and Moral Crisis in Contemporary China. *Games and Culture, 3*(1), 59–75.

Gomez, R., & Gould, E. (2010). The "Cool Factor" of Public Access to ICT. *Information Technology & People, 23*(3), 247–264.

Hargittai, E., & Hinnart, A. (2008). Digital Inequality: Differences in Young Adults Use of the Internet. *Communication Research, 35*(5), 602–621.

Herring, S. C. (2007). Questioning the Generational Divide: Technological Exoticism and Adult Construction of Online Youth Identity. In D. Buckingham (Ed.), *Youth, Identity, and Digital Media* (pp. 71–94). Cambridge, MA: MIT Press.

Ito, M., Mahendran, D., Martinez, K. Z., et al. (2009). *Hanging Out, Messing Around, and Geeking Out: Kids Living and Learning with New Media.* Cambridge, MA: MIT Press.

Joiner, R., Stewart, C., & Beaney, C. (2015). The Gender Digital Divide: Does It Exist and What Are the Explanations? In D. R. Larry, N. Cheever, & M. Carrier (Eds.), *The Wiley Handbook of Psychology, Technology, and Society.* Wiley-Blackwell: Hoboken, NJ.

Jonsson, F. (2010). A Public Place of Their Own: A Field Study of a Game Café as a Third Place. In *Proceedings of DiGRA Nordic 2010.* Stockholm.

Katz, V. S., & Gonzalez, C. (2016). Toward Meaningful Connectivity: Using Multilevel Communication Research to Reframe Digital Inequality. *Journal of Communication, 66,* 236–249.

Kent, M., Ellis, K., & Xu, J. (2017). *Chinese Social Media: Social, Cultural, and Political Implications.* New York: Routledge.

Li, Y., Gao, H., Yang, M., Guan, W., Ma, H., Qian, W., et al. (2013). What Are Chinese Talking About in Hot Weibos? *Physica A: Statistical Mechanics and Its Applications, 419,* 546–557.

Lin, H. (2005). Gendered Gaming Experience in Social Space: From Home to Internet Café. In *Proceedings of DiGRA Conference.* Vancouver.

Lindtner, S., & Szablewicz, M. (2010, June 29–30). *In Between Wangba and Elite Entertainment: China's Many Internets.* Paper Presented at the 8th Annual Chinese Internet Research Conference. Beijing.

Liu, F. (2009). It Is Not Merely About Life on the Screen: Urban Chinese Youth and the Internet Café. *Journal of Youth Studies, 12*(2), 167–184.

Livingstone, S., & Helsper, E. (2007). Gradations in Digital Inclusion: Children, Young People, and the Digital Divide. *New Media and Society, 9,* 671–696.

Pearce, K. E., & Rice, R. E. (2013). Digital Divides from Access to Activities: Comparing Mobile and Personal Computer Internet Users. *Journal of Communication, 63,* 721–744.

Qiu, J. L. (2013). Cybercafés in China: Community Access Beyond Gaming and Tight Government Control. *Library Trends, 62*(1), 121–139.

Qiu, J. L., & Zhou, L. (2005). Through the Prism of the Internet Café: Managing Access in an Ecology of Games. *China Information, 19*(2), 261–297.

RFA. (2015). *China Holds More Than 15,000 for Alleged Cyber Crime: Police.* http://www.rfa.org/english/news/china/china-holds-more-than-15000-for-alleged-cyber-crime-police-08192015102607.html.

Selwyn, N. (2004). Reconsidering Political and Popular Understandings of the Digital Divide. *New Media & Society, 6,* 341–362.

Shunwang Network. (2016). *China Internet Bar Industry Big Data Blue Book.* http://www.imxdata.com/archives/11875.

Sullivan, J., & Kehoe, S. (2018). Truth, Good, and Beauty: The Politics of Celebrity in China. *China Quarterly.* http://eprints.nottingham.ac.uk/48653/1/The%20Politics%20of%20Celebrity%20in%20China%20Jonathan.pdf.

Svensson, M. (2014). Voice, Power and Connectivity in China's Microblogosphere: Digital Divides on Sina Weibo. *China Information, 28*(2), 169–189.

Szablewicz, M. (2012). From Addicts to Athletes: Youth Mobilities and the Politics of Digital Gaming in Urban China. Ph.D. diss., Rensselaer Polytechnic Institute.

Thurlow, C. (2006). From Statistical Panic to Moral Panic: The Metadiscursive Construction and Popular Exaggeration of New Media Language in the Print Media. *Journal of Computer-Mediated Communication, 11*(3), 667–670.

Tuo, Z. H. (2016) *When Culture Meets Internet Plus: Chronicles and Observation* (in Chinese). Beijing: Beijing University of Posts and Telecommunication Press.

Weingarten, E. (2013). The Developing World Needs More Female Internet Users: A New Report Outlines Some Ways to Make It Happen. *Slate.* http://www.slate.com/articles/technology/technology/2013/01/a_new_report_on_female_internet_users_from_the_developing_world.html.

Further Readings

Bourdieu, P. (1986). The Forms of Capital. In J. Richardson (Ed.), *Handbook of Theory and Research for the Sociology of Education* (pp. 241–258). New York: Greenwood.

Büchi, M., Just, N., & Latzer, M. (2016). Modeling the Second-Level Digital Divide: A Five-Country Study of Social Differences in Internet Use. *New Media & Society, 18*(11), 2703–2722.

Evans, H. (2002). Past, Perfect or Imperfect: Changing Images of the Ideal Wife. In B. Susan & J. N. Wasserstrom (Eds.), *Chinese Femininities, Chinese Masculinities: A Reader* (pp. 335–360). Berkeley: University of California Press.

Rofel, L. (2007). *Desiring China: Experiments in Neoliberalism, Sexuality, and Public Culture.* Durham, NC: Duke University Press.

Sun, W., & Guo, Y. (Eds.). (2013). *Unequal China: The Political Economy and Cultural Politics of Inequality.* New York: Routledge.

Zhang, L. (2010). *In Search of Paradise: Middle-Class Living in a Chinese Metropolis.* Ithaca, NY: Cornell University Press.

CHAPTER 7

A Textual Analysis of Chinese Netizens' Reactions to Counter-Terrorism Reports on *The People's Daily* from 2010 to 2017

Wei Sun

BACKGROUND

The September 11, 2001 terrorist attacks against the United States shocked the world and stimulated the establishment or reestablishment of counter-terrorism policies and laws in many countries. Led by the United States and its ally countries, global counter-terrorism efforts and operations have achieved numerous successes in the past decade. However, global counter-terrorism presents complex challenges (Keane and Kenneth 2014; Shoemake and Reese 2014) as the terrorist organizations have no uniform characteristics or ideologies and their targeted areas and populations are random. Catching terrorists or preventing acts of terrorism presents challenges.

Additionally, political, religious, and historical variations in each region have made counter-terrorism local and regional. Studies show that compared to their American counterparts, Chinese authorities and media have less interest in global terrorist groups (Wayne 2009). Instead, the Chinese government uses global counter-terrorism as an

W. Sun (✉)
Department of Communication, Culture and Media Studies,
Howard University, Washington, DC, USA

© The Author(s) 2019
E. K. Ngwainmbi (ed.), *Media in the Global Context*,
https://doi.org/10.1007/978-3-030-26450-5_7

ideology to strike on Muslim separates in Xinjiang, an autonomy bordering Afghanistan, where the majority of residents are Uyghur ethnicity (Cunningham 2012).

China experienced several terrorist attacks on its territory since the 1990s. It is believed that some militant members of the Turkestan Islamic Movement (ETIM) received training and support from radical Islamists (Buckely 2015; Byman 2015; Gill and Murphy 2005; Smith 2009; Sun 2010). It has taken years for the Chinese government to relate global counter-terrorism efforts to its national counter-separatism strategies finally national. On December 27, 2015, the 18th Session of the Standing Committee of the 12th National People's Congress passed the Anti-Terrorism Law of the People's Republic of China. Major western media outlets such as Reuters, Washington Post, and The New York Times immediately covered the news. Many critics feared that China was "overreacting" and the law was deemed "controversial" (Denyer 2015; Wong 2015). It is well acknowledged that the relations between the United States and China have improved over the years and that both governments have intentions to build positive and cooperative relationships in many areas of disagreement. Differences exist between countries' counter-terrorism tactics; there is no "one fits all" policies in international cooperation (IIbiz and Churtis 2015). China's roles in counter-terrorism and efforts in maintaining peace with neighboring countries should be given more focus.

Problem Statement

Studies on counter-terrorism have focused on US-led, military-oriented strategies. Wechsler (2017) stresses that a military strategy on counter-terrorism needs both military action and indirect actions. Indirect actions require the combined tactics of many governmental agencies. International cooperation in fighting terrorism is both necessary and urgent for world peace and regional stability (Cheng 2006). Educating citizens to be alert and reactive to government counter-terrorism strategies and policies broaden public surveillance and engagement.

Media coverage and netizens' reactions to counter-terrorism policies help government agencies understand citizens' levels of interest in international and domestic counter-terrorism operations. This aids government in tailoring diplomatic strategies to strengthen international cooperation on counter-terrorism.

This research is a textual analysis of Chinese netizens' reactions to *The People's Daily Newspaper* coverage from its largest online forum, "A Prosperous Nation." Of the three major government-owned media outlets, *The People's Daily* newspaper is China's most influential and well-subscribed newspaper. Regular readership of this newspaper is 3 million daily. Readership has increased 200% since the paper was digitized and offered free online in 2010. To increase its influence, the newspaper created official accounts on social media sites such as Weibo, Facebook, and Twitter.

"A Prosperous Nation," *The People's Daily Newspaper*'s most prominent online forum, was established in 1999 after the NATO bombing of the Chinese Embassy in Belgrade, Yugoslavia. The attack killed three Chinese journalists and outraged the Chinese (Sun and Starosta 2001). The forum has since become one of the largest Chinese online political forums.

LITERATURE REVIEW

The literature review covers Chinese media policies in the internet age, the supervised and controlled online political discourse, and Chinese people's perceptions of counter-terrorism ideology.

It is clear that China's media policies were influenced by Soviet-style policies from the early establishment of the state-owned media in the 1950s. Chinese media practiced "thought work" to promote the Communist Party's ideological hegemony and affirmed loyalty to the sitting leaders (Wong and Zhang 2016; Sun and Starosta 2008; Kalathil 2003; Lynch 1999; Lee 1990). State-owned media outlets were called "the throat of the Party." Radio, television, newspapers, magazines, and internet were each represented by a different official bureaucracy. There was a big leap in the late 1970s when China started its "Open Door Policy" to the Western world. Rapid economic development, an information revolution, commercialization, and globalization exerted tremendous pressure on China's media policy. Since 2003, under the "Marketing Economy" initiative, Chinese media reformed its media policies to increase competitive power. For example, except for the "Five Big Publications" of the Party—*People's Daily, Guangming Daily, Economic Daily, Liberation Daily*, and the magazine *Seeking the Truth*—all other media in the press industry no longer received direct financial support from the government and thus began to respond to market demand

(Sun and Starosta 2008; Lin 2004; Ren and Barry 2003). This "throat of the Party" ideology has been reinforced by President Xi Jinping since he came to office in 2012. He claims to be a Maoist, one who follows Mao's ideological framework in ruling the country, and he demands the loyalty of the journalists and news organizations to him and his party. Xi sends a clear signal that news organizations and journalists should serve as "the throat of the Party" to advance the Party's interests (Economy 2014; Wong and Zhang 2016). By the first quarter of 2018, Xi has changed the Constitution to ensure his remaining in power for unlimited terms, and he is believed to have full control of the modern Chinese society (Buckley and Bradsher 2018).

In the late 1990s, China entered the internet era; millions of citizens began to use PCs to connect to the internet. In less than ten years, China has grown to become the second largest online population with approximately 10% of China's population online (Baran 2017). By 2010, Chinese netizens grew in size to 30% of the population, or 460 million members. By 2016, 730 million people, or roughly half of the population, were internet users (Rapoza 2014; China Network Information Center 2017). In 2007, 24% of internet users went online via mobile phones. As of 2017, there are 601.8 million smartphone users in China, most of whom are also internet users. Internet and its increased availability of access through smartphones led to the creation of new forums for the dispersal of information and entertainment that challenge the control of the internet by the Chinese authority. The rapid spread of information on the internet can thwart the regulations set in place by the ruling party in China and creates a more democratic atmosphere for the public. Advocates for Chinese journalistic freedom have included journalists both in China and the Western world. Since no government has absolute censorship in a digital age, they are forced to be more open in specific areas of public interest (Sun and Starosta 2008; Heymann and Rodier 2004). A well-cited example would be the SARS outbreak in 2003, in which information was leaked through cellphone text messages and over the internet to overseas sources. When SARS became a public secret, the United Nation got involved, which made it, became painful and unwise not to cover the crisis (Sun and Starosta 2008). It was then that the Chinese government chose an open policy, reporting and revealing daily updates on possible SARS cases, actual death numbers, and proposed ways to address the disease. Such rationale has been stronger for international issues than for domestic ones to cover events according to established journalistic canons (1923). China always maintained "no interference" with foreign countries' domestic affairs and always hoped that international society would reciprocate this courtesy for China. The Chinese media has developed a dual attitude toward international events and domestic events, being objective and critical while reporting the former, but cautiously walking a thin line while reporting the latter. There is an implicit preference for news which the Chinese government is more willing to accept the status quo and it is expected that media has the responsibility for the "correct guidance of public opinion" by promoting the ideology of the central government (Sun and Starosta 2008, 2001; Lin 2004).

As reported by Economy (2014), President Xi Jinping proposed new internet regulations. When someone posts "rumors" to disturb the social stability, he or she could be arrested and sentenced. The more netizens read and spread the "rumor," the more severe punishment the originator would receive. As a result of "rumor spreading" on the topic of the disappearance of Malaysia Airlines Flight 370, there was a 70% drop in posts on Weibo (a famous Chinese mini blog social network platform) when over 100,000 Weibo accounts were sanctioned between March 2012 and December 2013. The censorship extended to WeChat (the most popular social network in China that is mostly used for instant messaging) by forcing netizens to use their real names when registering. Chinese leaders have publicly criticized and humiliated several well-known online celebrities who violated the regulations. China has been criticized for restricting free access to the internet by strengthening the website Firewall system (Wong 2015). Only certain ideological, financial, and intellectual elites enjoy limited freedom of speech. This does not apply to ordinary citizens (Rubio and Smith 2015).

Shen and Liu (2009) conducted quantitative research on Chinese college students' perceptions of anti-terrorism topics. It found that students were unlikely to broach the topic of counter-terrorism in interpersonal communication exchanges because of years of exposure to government media reports. When asked whether there was a relationship between Muslims and terrorist, 40% responded "I do not know" and 14.6% believed there was a secure connection. 52.2% regarded terrorism as an act of religious extremists. Shen and Liu (2009) concluded that overall perceptions of Muslims in China fall in line with stereotypes about Muslims produced by the official propaganda of Xinjiang Muslim Separatists since the 9/11 terrorist attacks. Chinese authorities ruled that terrorism, ethnic separatism, and religious extremism as three evil forces.

Surprisingly, more than 30% of Chinese students perceive Al-Qaeda members as heroes and have sympathy toward them. Some students even consider 9/11 to be a result of Western hegemony. China's anti-terrorism campaign started in 2001 at the United Nations and from the beginning; it was linked to East Turkestan Islam Movement (ETIM) to international terrorist groups, and asked the US-led campaign to incorporate this localized problem in China (Denyer 2015).

The Chinese government's strategy in blurring the differences of terrorism, separatism, and human rights advocacy has angered the international community, which deems "[China] has exploited a genuine terrorist threat to further empower its repressive state-security apparatus. It is, they say, invoking the dangers of violent extremism to justify and expand already harsh crackdown on civil rights and to punish foreign information technology companies that refuse to play by its rules" (Denyer 2015).

RESEARCH QUESTIONS

To make sense of Chinese netizens' responses to counter-terrorism reporting on the People's Daily Newspaper, this study investigates the following questions:

RQ1: What are the recurring themes in *The People's Daily* newspaper coverage on international and domestic anti-terrorism events and reports from 2010 to 2017?
RQ2: How do Chinese netizens make sense of and what are their responses to the international and domestic counter-terrorism media coverage?
RQ3: What are the implications of China's media coverage and audience responses to global counter-terrorism and domestic terrorism?
RQ4: What are the implications of using an online forum to promote counter-terrorism ideology?

THEORETICAL FRAMEWORK

The theoretical framework for this study is the Agenda Setting Theory (McCombs and Shaw 1972) and Social Influence Model Theory (Dholakia et al. 2004). Agenda Setting Theory is a mass media theory which looks at how issues covered by media news shape and influence public perceptions about social and political realities. Social Influence Model Theory emphasizes and enhances individual and social motives for participation and engagement in online communities. These two theories will be used to analyze narratives and interactions in *The People's Daily* online archives and its "A Prosperous Nation" forum.

RESEARCH METHODS, PROCEDURES, AND SIGNIFICANCE OF THE STUDY

This research employs a qualitative textual analysis method. Qualitative research methods examine the meanings associated with messages rather than the frequencies in which message variables occur. The textual analysis focuses on stories and storytelling in a specific context (Gatson 2011). Thematic content and narrative structure are intertwined with online participation (Riessman 2002). This research looks at *The People's Daily's* coverage on counter-terrorism events and reporting and how the netizens of "A Prosperous Nation" react to it. Themes will be identified from both approaches.

The research is conducted on *The People's Daily Newspaper* online archive from 1946 to 2017 (http://58.68.146.102/rmrb). It uses Chinese keywords such as "anti-terrorism," "Xinjiang Separatism," "ISIS," "China Antiterrorism", and "International Anti-terrorism" to search and select newspaper coverage and netizens' comments and posts on counter-terrorism between 2010 and 2017. This study looks at newspaper reporting on global and domestic terrorism news and analyzes how online citizens respond to such coverage. Categories of newspaper reporting and themes of netizens' reactions and comments are drawn for compare and contrast purposes.

This study aims to increase the understanding of Chinese media coverage and netizens' reactions to counter-terrorism. The findings help government agencies understand citizens' levels of interest in international and domestic counter-terrorism operations. In the future, this will aid the government in tailoring diplomatic strategies to strengthen international cooperation on topics of counter-terrorism.

DATA ANALYSIS AND DISCUSSION

There are two parts to the data analysis conducted: first, the author examines the categories of *The People's Daily* on anti-terrorism topics. Then, the author examines the themes of audience responses toward the published articles on an internet forum "A Prosperous Nation."

Phase I: Identify the categories of *The People's Daily's* anti-terrorism coverage

Keywords search on People's Daily Archival 2010 to June 2017 generated seven pages including more than 300 articles. After carefully examining the article titles and the brief contents, the following four categories of newspaper reporting emerged:

Category 1: News reports on International events and coverage have chronicled the international terrorist attacks and anti-terrorism action

Under this category, the newspaper articles took a relatively objective manner. The titles and the opening paragraphs usually reflect the tone of the articles:

#1: May 19, 2017: "Iraq's War on Terrorism Made Important Progress"

"The war between Iraqi government forces and the 'Islamic State' militants against Mosul continues. The future of the Iraqi situation is hard to say optimistic. The old city center of Mosul is of strategic importance in Iraq..."

#2: July 24, 2015: "Turkey Enhances Anti-terrorism Force at the Weak of the Attack"

"This is the second day after the two police officers were killed in Turkey after another attack on the police. ISIS has posed a threat to the security of the Middle East, and Turkey is not immune to the terrorist attacks. Turkey's policy mistakes particularly evident in the Syrian border city Cobani..."

#3: November 2013: "Putin Signed a New Law on Counter-terrorism"

"Russian President Vladimir Putin's "New Measures for Combating Terrorism" stipulates that if terrorists' relatives and friends are proved to receive funds from the terrorists, they need to pay the compensation of the loss caused by the terrorists..."

#4: January 12, 2010: "Yemen: large-scale encirclement of 'base' organizations"

"The United States has no intention to send troops to the large-scale encirclement of Yemen's terrorist "base" organizations. The Yemeni parliament announces that the universal assembly will cover all sectors of Yemeni society. Some analysts believe that the Yemeni government worried that the involvement of the United States and Britain in Yemen against Al Qaeda would lead to anti-American forces in Yemen as a place to implement jihad and Yiyuan, leading to the emergence of "Afghanistan" trend in Yemen..."

Category 2: Commentary and criticism of western ideologies on anti-terrorism

Chinese government's mixed use of anti-terrorism and silence dissidents under the name of "anti-terrorism" has garnered criticism from the Western world. Some of the *People's Daily* Commentary responded with counter-criticism. One article entitled "Beware of Western Countries' Misunderstandings about Counter-terrorism" published on April 11, 2016 represents this sentiment:

#5: *The 9-11 Terrorist Attacks in the United States shocked the world. Led by the United States, the Western countries launched a so-called "war on terror" against extremists on a global scale. However, during this "war", the scale of extremist organizations has been expanding, and the means of attack have been escalating, bringing great losses to the lives and property of many people. The Western "war on terror" did not bring the dawn of peace...*

In the aforementioned article, the author criticized the "War on Terror" as a failure. The author then proposed a few strategies which echoed the Chinese government's anti-terrorism principles: anti-terrorism policies should uphold the respect for other country's sovereignty; anti-terrorism policies should not have double standards; when national security conflicts with individual freedom, national security should be the top priority in the name of counter-terrorism; all countries should work together for counter-terrorism policies to be effective.

On March 22, 2016, a commentary entitled "Promote the Strategic Transformation of the International Counterterrorism" was published. The author highly valued the new published Anti-terrorism Law, and listed five characteristics of current terrorism: (1) Religious extremism has become the spiritual core of international terrorist organizations; (2) The structure of terrorist organizations is transforming from pyramid to network; (3) The generalized political pleas have become the goal of international terrorist attacks; (4) The activities of the international terrorist organizations have spread to many regions in the world; (5) There is an increase of terrorist attacks. Under these complexities, the author further explained:

#6: *Taking down Osama bin Laden in 2009 as a symbol of global anti-terrorism reached a high point. However, international terrorism has not been eliminated; on the contrary, it is getting worse. Thus, the model "putting power on one country over other countries' interests" would not solve the problem. It is necessary to establish an equal coordination with all countries.*

In another Commentary entitled "Challenges: Global Counter - terrorism Cooperation Needs to be Strengthened," dated January 20, 2015, it reads:

#7: *At present, ISIS and Al-Qaeda have become the world's two major terrorist networks that the international community needs to deal with urgently. To promote regional stability and to prevent the spread of the poison, the international community needs to focus on the eradication of local threats from the root, by encouraging of local governmental governance, easing national and sectarian conflicts... strengthening international cooperation...moreover, promoting the harmonious coexistence among different civilizations. Therefore, it is urgent to advocate for civilized dialogue and inclusive development among different nationalities and religions and to ease the antagonism between different religions...*

Category 3: Blaming the U.S. for being a hypocrite, and applying double standards toward China's counter-terrorism

Disappointed with each other on many issues, the United States and China blame each other for not taking responsibility in Counterterrorism movements. China is not taking the blame. On August 15, 2014, in a piece entitled "Recognize Extremes in Anti-terrorism," the author reviewed several terrorist organizations first initiated and supported by the United States:

#8: *The United States' biased intervention in the Middle East affairs and leaves a mess for others to clean up. Some of the quick mendings was unable to help those struggling in turmoil, poverty, and confusion. People in the*

Middle East are eager for peace and prosperity. If the problem is unsolved, it will leave room for the extremists for future terrorist activities.

On March 4, 2014, entitled "Absolute Hypocrisy and Cruelty," the Commentary reported that on March 1, 2014, in Kunming City's Train Station, a group of Uyghur terrorists killed 29 and wounded more than 100 civilians. When Western media criticized China for overreacting and mislabeled a "terrorist attack" for a domestic crime, China government was furious, in this article, the author called names of each US media outlet, accused them "invoking China's ethnic relations":

#9: *In the face of such a clear picture, the performance of these [Western] media has not only been hypocrisy, but also prejudice-driven with cold hearts. Don't you say "human rights"? Do you see innocent lives that fall in a pool of blood? Do your words reflect a little bit of concern for the human rights of the victims? If such a thing happens in the United States, even if the number of deaths is much smaller, will you judge the nature of the incident, will you be so mean to use the word "terrorists" hesitantly?*

On November 23, 2015, the Commentary entitled "US Anti-terrorism is Facing a Strategic Dilemma" criticized the US counter-terrorism policy:

#10: *The U.S counter-terrorism is facing a strategic dilemma. According to the latest poll, 63% of Americans worry about a similar terrorist attack as in Paris... The Obama administration has embarked on strategic adjustments, but the United States seems to be reluctant to be dragged back again to the quagmire of war and falls into a strategic dilemma in the anti-terrorism coalition.*

Harsh criticism on the US failure on international counter-terrorism military action appeared on May 2, 2017: "The United States Admits that the Counter-terrorism in the Middle East had 'Wounded the Innocent'"

#11: *It has been pointed out that extremiste cruelty is not a fig leaf of American's air strikes that result in a large number of casualties. "In order to get rid of a car or several snipers of the ISIS, the U.S'-led international alliance would rather kill dozens of innocent civilians," an anonymous source said... "Now the number of the U.S. troops in Iraq is more than any time after the withdrawal of the troops from Iraq in 2011. Although these actions are always under the guise of 'helping' or 'rescuing' the Iraqi people, the truth is that many innocent people died in the bombing. In this sense, it is better to say that the involvement of the U.S. military has hindered the progress of regional counter-terrorism, and has brought more disasters to the people of the Middle East."*

Category 4: Promote strategies and ideologies of Chinese characteristics on anti-terrorism

Many articles praise the Chinese government, soldiers, police officers, ordinary citizens and local governments in their combined efforts to counter-terrorism. In the same article entitled "Beware of Western Countries' Misunderstandings about Anti-terrorism," the author compares the US failure in anti-terrorism actions to the success of Chinese ways of reconstruction of the post-terrorism areas:

#12: *Unlike the Western countries, after the turmoil of the terrorist attacks, the Chinese government stresses the active fight against terrorists, analyzes the social causes of terrorist attacks, takes various measures to improve the educational level of ethnic areas, expands free education to more beneficiaries, and improves the living conditions of people in ethnic areas. Al aims to block the breeding of terrorist thinking from its origin.*

In one article published on April 14, 2017, entitled "For an Absolute Win of a People's War on Counter-terrorism," the article pointed out, to carry out President Xi's important direction on anti-terrorism, China must:

#13: *To unswervingly strike against terrorists, to strengthen the intelligence information channel, to eliminate the [terrorism] sprout in the bud stage. We will do everything to protect national security and to maintain social stability…we must mobilize the masses to participate in the anti-terrorism movement.*

On August 9, 2015, a commentary entitled "The People's Army can not Afford a Loss to Terrorists," tells the story of how one certain anti-terrorism army practice on the action in a hypothetical terrorist attack situation:

#14: *In the case of the ever-changing circumstances, there is no standard solution for counter-terrorism. The military commanders must pay attention to intelligence information, analyze the situation and make the right decisions... We must understand the hypothetical "terrorists" are more potent than the ones in real cases... so that the anti-terrorism unit could combat effectively.*

Other articles praise ordinary citizens, soldiers, combatting units, lower and high ranked officers on their volunteering, motivations, skill training, and dedications to China's anti-terrorism cause. The Chinese Communist Party has always believed a "Masses Movement" on various political and ideological campaigns. Mao was the originator and a master of the "Masses Revolution" in his ideological wars both n the battlefields (the 1940s) and the political struggles (1960s). As Mao's follower, President Xi managed to use this strategy in crackdown corrupted officers, and as well as in counter-terrorism. Civilian surveillance is encouraged and awarded in observing and reporting of suspicious activities. On August 4, 2014, entitled "Masses' War Against Terrorism Reflects People's heartfelt Feelings," the article recalled one terrorism incidence in Xinjiang:

#15: *Recently, Police in Hetian District of Xinjiang relied on masses' information to target a violent terrorist group. More than 30,000 people help the police. The success mobilization of the citizens led to a successful counter-terrorism action: 9 terrorists were killed, and one terrorist was arrested. The action of Xinjiang police to crackdown terrorists is amazing. Terrorists are monstrous and dangerous to the people and the society. The fact that more than 30,000 people volunteered to stand up with the police not only shows the determination of the people of Xinjiang against the terrorists, but also fully demonstrated the power of collective action. With the support of the masses, what kind of enemy we cannot defeat?*

Frequently, *The People's Daily* will publish local campaigns on educating and preparing citizens for terrorist attacks. In this article dated June 24, 2016, "Beijing Initiation Counter-terrorism Week Activities":

#16: *With the theme, "Everyone gets involved in Counter-terrorism, and build a peaceful capital city," Beijing's Counter-Terrorism Week started on June 23. Armed police "Counter-Strike Team", the police unmanned aerial vehicles and other advanced equipment exhibited in the event. According to the person in charge of the Beijing Municipal Public Security Bureau, the campaign week aims to help the public better understand the current counter-terrorism situation, understand their rights and responsibility in counter-terrorism, and enhance awareness and hand-on experience of fighting terrorist attacks.*

Phase II: Identify anti-terrorism themes of *The People's Daily's* online "A Prosperous Nation Forum"

Using the same sets of keywords to search on "A Prosperous Nation" forum of *The People's Daily* online, "counter-terrorism" alone would generate 300 pages with more than 15,000 posts. The author carefully read five pages of posts every 50 pages, and then randomly choose several pages in between to sort out new themes. Themes of Chinese netizens' reactions toward counter-terrorism reports emerged:

Theme 1: Debates about the US's role in international counter-terrorism, mixed feelings toward the U.S.'s hegemony in Asia

This kind of posts usually followed the Commentary Articles criticized the US intervention. Chinese netizens expressed the nationalist sentiments toward such commentaries. The following posts showed several examples of netizens' thoughts. Netizens were uneasy about Chinese "internal affairs" such as territories of Taiwan, Xinjiang, Tibet, and other places, all had been shadowed by separatism. In many Chinese citizens' understanding, separatism is equivalent to terrorism. Some even regard the United States is the biggest threat:

Post 1: Are you fool or intentional? Everyone on earth knows that the U.S. is the biggest threat to our country. It is a troublemaker. Taiwan, Tibet, Xinjiang, the Eastern Sea, the Southern Sea, and the so-called human rights problems. Their big boss in America. That is so bold. —July 16, 2014.

Post 2: I do not fully deny America's role in anti-terrorism. American culture, technology and political system are advanced. However, what annoyed me is, the U.S. always supports Separatism, attempts to separate China, I am appalled by this. —July 29, 2014.

Post 3: It is America who sanctioned technology, supported Xinjiang Separatism and Tibet Separatism. America made chaos in the Southern Sea. It is America who invoked Color Revolution, it is America who kept escaped corrupted officers... if anyone says America is not an enemy, and he is blind! —May 30, 2015.

Post 4: The main issue about Xinjiang is an issue with America. If this issue with America is not solved, nothing will happen for Xinjiang. —August 15, 2016.

Post 5: Who is supporting Taiwan Separatism, Xinjiang Separatism, Tibet Separatism, and Hong Kong Separatism? Isn't it America? —June 11, 2017.

Theme 2: China should be tougher toward domestic terrorists. Strengthen supervision over troubled areas and personnel

Many netizens support China's severe punishment and surveillance over troubled areas. Aggressive strategies toward separatism are suggested:

Post 6: We often say to take precautions – no matter it is about Tibet independence or Xinjiang independence, or problems with cults, or underworlds. I want to ask: all levels of governments and police force are you doing your job. —June 1, 2014.

Post 7: In the suspicious villages of southern Xinjiang, the government should implement 3-5 households supervision link. If one person commits a crime, the linked households should all be punished. If one leaves the residence, he needs to ask the authority for an excuse. We should become tough to those Xinjiang Separatists! Those who work in ethnic areas, they should be motivated with higher salaries and benefits. —July 14, 2014.

Post 8: If terrorism is a religious problem, the government should rely on its religious believers. We should avoid making things more complex. Anyway, there are few extremists. We should unite the majority. It is effective to distinguishing Xinjiang Separatists into three groups, we should advocate the locals to look out and watch over. —November 20, 2015.

Post 9: Several years ago, violent Xinjiang separatists and terrorists sneaked into Beijing to do evil things. This memory is not fading. For those stained the neighboring areas by taking in those trouble makers, law enforcement agencies should strengthen their inspections. —July 2, 2016.

Post 10: we are told 56 of Chinese ethnicities should unite as one. But look at Tibet, Xinjiang, Taiwan, Hong Kong, everywhere demands for independence. Before we care about outside intruders, we need to mend our backyard. —July 13, 2016.

Theme 3: Anyone who supported the separatists/terrorists is an enemy of China

Netizens use a "war rhetoric" to distinguish China's enemies from allies. Because China has disputes with several countries regarding national ownership, netizens have been disappointed that the Chinese government is not taking military strikes toward other countries, or arrest more dissents:

Post 11: In the past, the U.S. had bombed a China embassy by mistake; it had a plane collision with Chinese Air Force by mistake. Moreover, now it entered the Eastern Sea, Southern Sea by mistakes. It had wrongfully supported Japan, Philippine, Vietnam; by mistakes, it supported Xinjiang and Tibet separatists. So you fools say those invokes were all unintentional? Give me a break! —September 13, 2014.

Post 12: the Chinese government is too soft and too weak toward Hong Kong Occupants. They should be punished as Separatists in Xinjiang and Tibet! —October 26, 2014.

Post 13: Through its representatives, the U.S. is always against China. Isn't it a truth? It is so obvious. The U.S. representatives are not only the countries such as Japan, Vietnam, Philippine, Taiwan, the Separatists, Xinjiang Separatists, Hong Kong Separatists, but also those "public intellectuals" who echoed those oversea dissidents. —June 23, 2016.

Theme 4: Criticize the ineffectiveness of international counter-terrorism cooperation and suggest that China should take more responsibilities enhancing its national image

It is common knowledge that counter-terrorism requires the cooperation of many countries. Chinese netizens are disappointed at the lack of effective coordination among countries and call for China to play its role.

Post 14: Terrorist attacks, we say NO to you! There are so many areas around the world suffered the threats of terrorist attacks. Facing this serious challenge, the best way is to strengthen the communication about international counter-terrorism strategies and share intelligence information. —November 19, 2014.

Post 15: Terrorists are enemies of the world, public enemies of all human beings. As a great country, China should take responsibility, and China is able and obligated to participate in the international affairs on counter-terrorism. From the cooperation with the Turkish government, we can see it i is the 1 + 1 > 2 effect! —November 20, 2014.

Post 16: The United States, Russia, France and other countries already take actions toward anti-terrorism. What about China? China should go with the trend, participate in the international counter-terrorism actions, display our modern weapons, and demonstrate we are a stable country. — November 21, 2015.

Post 17: Don't you worry about anything! China already expressed, China's counter-terrorism at home is the best support of globe al counter-terrorism! Moreover, economic development is the priority of China, we can't be distracted! —November 25, 2015.

Post 18: Best wishes to the Shanghai Cooperation Organization! Especially wish SCO gradually developed military cooperation so that those countries can cooperate on counter-terrorism. It is essential for nations to have military cooperation nowadays. —June 10, 2017.

DISCUSSIONS

The previous section has displayed data drawn from *The People's Daily's* newspaper archival and its online forum "A Prosperous Nation." This section will discuss how to make sense of the data and to answer the research questions.

RQ1: What are the recurring themes in *The People's Daily* newspaper coverage on international and domestic anti-terrorism events and reports from 2010 to 2017?

As displayed in previous sections, between 2010 and 2017, *The People's Daily* newspaper coverage on international and domestic counter-terrorism has been centered on four categories/themes: (1) News reports on international events and coverage which chronicled international terrorist attacks and anti-terrorism actions, (2) Commentary and criticism of Western ideologies on anti-terrorism, (3) Blaming the United States for being a hypocrite, and applying double standards toward China's counter-terrorism, and (4) Promote strategies and ideologies of Chinese characteristics on anti-terrorism. The identified recurring themes on *The People's Daily* are the Chinese government's attitudes and policies toward international and national counter-terrorism. In many circumstances, China and the US-led international alliances each look at the terrorism from a different angle, especially on China's internal affairs. Chinese definition of terrorism, according to the newest Anti-terrorism Law, the Article III states: (China's People's Congress 2015):

> The term "terrorism" as used in this Law refers to the idea of creating social panic, endangering public safety, violating personal property, or intimidating state organs and international organizations through the means of violence, destruction and intimidation to achieve their political and ideological ends. (China's People's Congress 2015)

As discussed earlier, Western media condemned the Chinese government abuse of power regarding defining what the terrorism is and who are considered terrorists. Overall, the definition of terrorism is specific to each country. On the FBI's website, the term is broadly defined

We continue to identify individuals who seek to join the ranks of foreign fighters traveling in support of the Islamic State of Iraq and the Levant (ISIL), and homegrown violent extremists who may aspire to attack the United States from within.

(https://www.fbi.gov/investigate/terrorism)

Under the US Criminal Law, terrorism is defined as follows:

1. The term "international terrorism" means activities that—
   (A) involve violent acts or acts dangerous to human life that is a violation of the criminal laws of the United States or any State, or that would be a criminal violation if committed within the jurisdiction of the United States or any State;
   (B) Appear to be intended.

(uscode.house.gov)

Counter-terrorism is of national interests, it is difficult to persuade another nation to accept a definition made by the counterpart. The major dispute of the definition of terrorism shows that the United States and China each operate under very different juridical and political systems (Chesney 2013; Chinascope 2015; Duchatel 2011). There is a long way to go in achieving a common understanding and uncompromised coordination. Politicians, diplomats, and military commanders should increase sensitiveness in international communication contexts.

RQ2: How do Chinese netizens make sense of and what are their responses to the international and domestic counter-terrorism media coverage?

Most of the available comments and posts on "A Prosperous Nation Forum" echoed the Chinese government's ideologies on terrorism and international relations (Fu et al. 2015; Janbek and Wiliams 2014; Plümper and Neumayer 2014; Richard 2015; Wayne 2007). Four themes reflect Chinese netizens' attitudes from a nationalist/patriot perspective: (1) Debates on the US's role in international anti-terrorism, mixed feelings toward US's hegemony in Asia. (2) China should be more robust toward domestic terrorists and strengthen supervision over troubled areas and personnel. (3) Anyone who supported the separatists/ terrorists is an enemy of China. (4) Criticize the ineffectiveness of international anti-terrorism cooperation and suggest that China should take more responsibilities for its national image.

As China's economic power increased in the past several decades, so has Chinese citizens' national pride. Nationalism and patriotism are often displayed in many countries after terrorist attacks. It is a way for people to handle a tragedy, show courage, and lift spirits to show that they are not beaten by the terrorist attacks.

Dunn and her associates (2005) have conducted four studies on newspaper reporting on the Iraq war and found out the readers' perceptions and attitudes about the war changed when they received different media messages. Words choice in the newspaper could lead the audience to perceive the war differently, such as terrorism, violence, or patriotism. It demonstrates the power of national media in influencing people. That is how agenda setting theory apply. *The People's Daily* newspaper has a long history stood for State voice and setting the tone for the events. Netizens could be easily provoked and direct harsh words toward other strangers and other countries, since it seems such patriotic actions sometimes generate applause from unseen watchers. In the past decade, Chinese mobs have been watched for conducting violent boycotts, protests, and demonstration over South Korea, Japan, and the United States. Such demonstration and protests against the Chinese government usually guarantee an arrest. However, it is believed that the Chinese government may have implicitly allowed protests over foreign businesses or embassies as very few protesters would be arrested or punished. Some even have won the title of "heroes." Western media has called it irrational and chauvinistic and believe such demonstrations were conceived and were manipulated by the Chinese government (Liu 2006). China is not a country, which allows free speech. As such, regulations confine people's public opinions and dissidents and it is impractical to believe online content is not monitored. The expressions and attitudes on "A Prosperous Nation" forum are under surveillance as well. Those posts were allowed to be exhibited for years, thus definitely have been approved by the censorship agents.

RQ3: What are the implications of China's media coverage and audience responses to global counter-terrorism and domestic terrorism?

China's media coverage on global counter-terrorism has been intensive. As stated earlier, when Western media and the US government are not pointing fingers to China, Chinese media is trustworthy to perform its journalistic duty professionally around international coverage. International news reporting has always been an essential part for Chinese national TV and newspapers. Since China is dedicated to building an international image of being democratic. When provoked by Western media, China usually takes a defensive–offensive strategy. This is partly due to historical events involving the United States, such as a bombing in China Embassy which killed two Chinese journalists in Belgrade in 1999 and a surveillance plane collision which killed a Chinese pilot in the Southern Chinese Sea in 2001 (Sun and Starosta 2001). Mistrust between the two countries has existed for years. Another important reason is the two countries operate under different political systems. The ideological difference is a significant obstacle hindering mutual understanding on many issues such as national interests, human rights, freedom of speech, and counter-terrorism strategies (Sun and Starosta 2008). Adopting one country's counter-terrorism strategies in another country is impractical.

The Masses Movement to track down and crackdown the potential terrorist's attacks have been a Chinese characterized strategy. With Chinese advanced surveillance technologies available everywhere, it is easier for Chinese authorities to keep an eye on the terrorist suspects. These could be an advantage and disadvantage of Chinese counter-terrorism. This is the area where the Chinese government being criticized by foreign governments, the Western media, and human rights advocates.

RQ4: What are the implications of using an online forum to promote counter-terrorism ideology?

The Chinese national newspaper's online forum is a channel to promote its counter-terrorism ideology. It is netizens who are allowed to make comments freely online; their opinions stand long as soon as their posts followed the core values of the Party. Chinese media plays its role of "the throat of the Party." Criticism often arises that accuses President Xi Jinping and his administration in taking cyberspace entirely under control. It is not unusual for individuals' mobile phones to be tracked. The new Cyber Security Law requires all tech companies to provide individual customer' information to comply with official investigations (Fuhrman 2016). That could create more tension in international cooperation on counter-terrorism.

LIMITATIONS AND FUTURE STUDIES

This study has its limitations. First, it is conducted on one state-owned significant newspaper's archival site, on newspaper coverage, and on Chinese netizens' reactions toward anti-terrorism. It is impossible to know the demographics of these netizens. Second, due to China's cyber-censorship, the posts showing opposing views might have been taken down.

Moreover, for those who post online, registration is required. Moreover, the website will track and publish each computer IP address following the post. That likely forces the netizens to think carefully and self-censor before actually posting anything. Third, the netizens on "A Prosperous Nation" forum may not represent the public's opinion, since gender, age, educational backgrounds, and political beliefs are unclear online. The posts that are available for viewing and analysis tend to be homogenous and likely do not represent the opinions of all Chinese netizens. Future studies should address the above limitations. For example, in-depth interviews might be conducted to further understand the topic.

QUESTIONS FOR DISCUSSION

1. How have China's media policies changed over the last several decades? How have the changes influenced the counter-terrorism policies?
2. What do you think about China's media coverage on counter-terrorism and netizens reactions toward counter-terrorism?

3. What are the implications of Chinese counter-terrorism efforts in international counter-terrorism?
4. Do you think the Chinese government will be eventually enticed by the trappings of the internet and allow its citizens to access social media platforms?

References

Baran, S. J. (2017). *Introduction to Mass Communication.* New York: McGraw-Hill.

Buckely, C. (2015, December 28). Antiterrorism Law Expands China's Surveillance Power. *New York Times.*

Buckley, C., & Bradsher, K. (2018, February 15). China Moves to Let Xi Stay in Power by Abolishing the Term Limit. *New York Time.*

Byman, D. (2015). Beyond Counterterrorism. *Foreign Affairs, 94*(6), 11–18.

Cheng, J. Y. S. (2006). Broadening the Concept of Security in East and Southeast Asia: The Impact of the Asian Financial Crisis and the September 11 Incident. *Journal of Contemporary China, 15*(46), 89–111.

Chesney, R. M. (2013). Beyond the Battlefield, Beyond Al Qaeda: The Destabilizing Legal Architecture of Counterterrorism. *Michigan Law Review, 112*(2), 163–224.

China Network Information Center. (2017). *CNNIC: Thriving After 20 years' Effort, Serving as Cornerstone on the Internet.* Retrieved from https://cnnic.com.cn/AU/MediaC/rdxw/2017/201706/t20170609_69333.htm.

China's People's Congress. (2015). *Anti-terrorism Law.* Retrieved from http://www.xinhuanet.com/politics/2015-12/27/c_128571798.htm.

Chinascope. (2015, November/December). China Should Not Participate in Military Combat Against ISIS, Issue 78, 35–35, 2/3pp.

Cunningham, C. P. (2012). Counterterrorism in Xinjiang: the ETIM, China and the Uyghurs. *International Journal on World Peace, 29*(3), 7–50.

Denyer, S. (2015, March 5). China's New Anti-terrorism Law Provokes Anger in the US, Concerns at Home. *Washington Post.*

Dholakia, U. M., Bagozzi, R. P., & Pearo, L. R. K. (2004). A Social Influence Model of Consumer Participation in the Network- and Small-Group-Based Virtual Communities. *International Journal of Research in Marketing, 21*(3), 241–263.

Duchatel, M. (2011). The Terrorist Risk and China's Policy toward Pakistan: Strategic Reassurance and the 'United Front'. *Journal of Contemporary China, 20*(71), 543–561.

Dunn, E. W., Moore, M., & Nosek, B. A. (2005). The War of the Words: How Linguistic Differences in Reporting Shape Perceptions of Terrorism. *Analyses of Social Issues and Public Policy, 5*(1), 67–86.

Economy, E. C. (2014). China's Imperial President: Xi Jinping Tightens His Grip. *Foreign Affairs, 80,* 93–101.

Fu, J. L., Sun, D. Y., Chai, J., Xiao, J., & Wang, S. Y. (2015, November). The 'Six-Element' Analysis Method for the Research on the Characteristics of Terrorist Activities. *Annals of Operations Research, 234*(1), 17–35.

Fuhrman, P. (2016, February 29). Government Cyber-Surveillance Is the Norm in China—And It Is Popular. *Washington Post.*

Gatson, S. N. (2011). The Methods, Politics, and Ethics of Representation in Online Ethnography. In N. K. Denzin & Y. S. Lincoln (Eds.), *The Sage Handbook of Qualitative Research* (pp. 513–528). Thousand Oaks, CA: Sage Publication.

Gill, B., & Murphy, M. (2005). China's Evolving Approach to Counterterrorism. *Harvard Asia Quarterly, 9*(1/2), 21–32.

Heymann, D. L., & Rodier, G. (2004). Global Surveillance, National Surveillance, and SARS. *Emerging Infectious Diseases, 10*(2), 173–175. https://doi.org/10.3201/eid1002.031038.

IIbiz, E., & Churtis, B. (2015). Trend Setters Trend Followers, and Individual Players: Obtaining Global Counterterror Actor Types from Proscribed Terror Lists. *Studies in Conflict & Terrorism, 38*(1), 39–61.

Janbek, D., & Wiliams, V. (2014). The Role of the Internet Post-9/11 in Terrorism and Counterterrorism. *Brown Journal of World Affairs, 20*(2), 297–308.

Kalathil, S. (2003). China's New Media Sector: Keeping the State in. *Pacific Review, 4,* 489–501.

Keane, S. K., & Kenneth, A. A. (2014). An Integrated Approach to Civilian-Military/Interagency Counterterrorism Capacity Building. *Air Force Law Review, 71,* 1–23.

Lee, C. C. (1990). *Voices of China: The Interplay of Politics and Journalism.* New York: Guilford Press.

Lin, J. (2004). China's Media Reform: Where to Go? *Harvard China Review, 5*(1), 116–121.

Liu, S. D. (2006). China's Popular Nationalism on the Internet: Report on the 2005 Anti-Japan Network Struggles. *Inter-Asia Cultural Studies, 7*(1), 144–155.

Lynch, D. (1999). *After the Propaganda State: Media, Politics and "Thought Work" in Reformed China.* Stanford, CA: Stanford University Press.

McCombs, M. E., & Shaw, D. L. (1972). Agenda-Setting Function of Mass Communication. *Public Opinions Quarterly, 36*(2), 176–187.

Plümper, T., & Neumayer, E. (2014). Terrorism and Counterterrorism: An Integrated Approach and Future Research Agenda. *International Interactions, 40*(4), 579–589.

Rapoza, K. (2014, April 28). By 2016, China Internet Users to Double Entire US Population. *Forbes.*

Ren, J., & Barry, M. (2003). Media Management in a Market Economy. *Beijing Review, 46,* 28–29.

Richard, A. (2015). From Terrorism to 'Radicalization' to 'Extremism': Counterterrorism Imperative or Loss of Focus? *International Affairs, 91*(2), 371–380.

Riessman, C. K. (2002). Narrative Analysis. In A. M. Huberman & M. B. Miles (Eds.), *The Qualitative Researcher's Companion* (pp. 217–270). Thousand Oaks, CA: Sage Publication.

Rubio, M., & Smith, C. (2015). *Freedom of Express in China: A Privilege Not a Right*. Congressional-Executive Commission on China. Retrieved from http://www.cecc.gov/freedom-of-expression-in-china-a-privilege-not-a-right.

Shen, S., & Liu, P. (2009). Perceptions of Anti-terrorism Among Students at Guangzhou University: Misinformation or Misinterpretation? *Asia Survey, 49*(3), 3–73.

Shoemake, P. J., & Reese, S. D. (2014). *Mediating the Message in the 21st Century: A Media Sociology Perspective*. New York, NY: Routledge.

Smith, P. J. (2009). China's Economic and Political Rise: Implications for Global Terrorism and U.S.–China Cooperation. *Studies in Conflict & Terrorism, 32*(7), 627–645.

Sun, D. (2010). China and Jihad Network. *Journal of the Middle East & Africa, 1*(2), 196–207.

Sun, W., & Starosta, W. J. (2001). As Heavy as Mount Taishan: A Thematic Analysis of Wang Wei's Memorial Website. *World Communication, 30*(3 & 4), 61–79.

Sun, W., & Starosta, W. J. (2008). Covering "The Lord of the World": Chinese Sense-Making of the U.S 2004 Presidential Election. *Human Communications, 11*(1), 1–16.

Wayne, M. I. (2007). Five Lessons from China's War on Terror. *Joint Force Quarterly, 47,* 42–47.

Wayne, M. I. (2009). Inside China's War on Terrorism. *Journal of Contemporary China, 18*(59), 249–261.

Wechsler, W. F. (2017). Counterterrorism by Proxy. *National Interest, 148,* 24–33.

Wong, E. (2015, October 30). China Ranks Last of 65 Nations in Internet Freedom. *New York Times.*

Wong, E., & Zhang, T. (2016, February 23). Chinese Leaders New Flash: Journalists Must Serve the Party. *New York Times.*

Further Reading

Cheng, J. Y. S. (2006). Broadening the Concept of Security in East and Southeast Asia: The Impact of the Asian Financial Crisis and the September 11 Incident. *Journal of Contemporary China, 15*(46), 89–111.

Richard, A. (2015). From Terrorism to 'Radicalization' to 'Extremism': Counterterrorism Imperative or Loss of Focus? *International Affairs, 91*(2), 371–380.

Rubio, M., & Smith, C. (2015). *Freedom of Expression in China: A Privilege Not a Right*. Congressional-Executive Commission on China. Retrieved from http://www.cecc.gov/freedom-of-expression-in-china-a-privilege-not-a-right.

Wayne, M. I. (2009). Inside China's War on Terrorism. *Journal of Contemporary China, 18*(59), 249–261.

PART IV

Press Coverage of Regional News: Reconsidering Ethics in Journalism

Media Coverage of the Chibok Girls Kidnapping in Regionally Different African Newspapers

Seseer Mou-Danha

The biggest threats posed by terrorism are the destruction of life, property, and uncertainty regarding security. The democratic rule that emphasizes the protection of rights of the people appears to be the first step in any nations leaning toward counter-terrorism (Wilson 2014). For counter-terrorist actions to be potentially productive there has to be social, political, and economic fairness and justice for all citizens. In Nigeria, the social cleavages—divisions based on differences such as ethnicity, religion, and gender are still a significant national issue. Terrorism within the country is primarily found in religious, tribal, political, and socioeconomic disparities.

Pan-Islamic terrorism is growing on the African continent. Claims of affiliation between international terrorist groups and African extremists like Boko Haram and Al-Shabaab makes some areas in Africa at a focal point of the Jihadi movement. The rise of and growing networks of terrorist groups threaten the social, political, and economic fabric of the societies where they take place (Antwi-Boateng 2017). Instability in

S. Mou-Danha (✉)
Department of Communication, North Dakota State University,
Fargo, ND, USA
e-mail: seseer.mou@ndsu.edu

© The Author(s) 2019
E. K. Ngwainmbi (ed.), *Media in the Global Context*,
https://doi.org/10.1007/978-3-030-26450-5_8

Nigeria caused by terrorism will have serious implications not only for the country or the region but also for the world. Terrorism is not the problem of any single nation or region anymore, but it is now a world problem. Every continent has been affected by terrorist activity in varying capacities, and yet, the war against terrorism is still far from being over. Media carry reports of terrorist activity in large countries as well as remote locations to various parts of the world.

The news media is still the primary source of information about terrorism. The media do not merely report about terrorism but can be very important in determining public perceptions of terrorist groups. Mass media also serves as a reflection of society. Nigeria presents an interesting case study for terrorism because even though it gained independence on October 1, 1960, without war and bloodshed, multiple terrorist groups, most notably Maitatsine (the 1980s), MEND (2004) and Boko Haram (2009) have wracked it. Boko Haram (which translates to "no to western education") is the most severe and dangerous terrorist group in Africa today, and its attacks have been given extensive coverage in the media. This chapter will employ a comparative cross-analysis of prominent newspapers in Nigeria (Thisday, Daily Trust), Sudan (Sudan Tribune, Sudan News Agency), and Egypt (Egypt Independent, Al Ahram), on their coverage of the Chibok girls kidnapping, the most internationally reported Boko Haram activity today.

TERRORISM IN NIGERIA

Terrorism, which refers to the strategic and illegal use of violence to reach goals of either political, ethnic, or religious nature is not new in Africa has been one of the strategies of some of the freedom fighters in Kenya (Mau Mau) and South Africa (ANC) among others. In more recent times, it has taken a religious tone in the insurgent activities of such African terrorist groups as Al-Shabaab in Somalia, Al-Qaeda in the Maghreb, and Boko Haram in Nigeria and Cameroon. Religious terrorism is now one of the most significant challenges affecting peace, stability, and economic development in Africa. Terrorism is not new to Africa. In Nigeria, extremist rebellions as it is known today dates back to pre-colonialism.

In 1841, Christianity missions started in the region, beginning from the interior parts. After the occupation of Europe through colonialism and the accompanying transatlantic slave trade, the political, economic, and social constituents of the region was drastically altered. British protectorates were created to bring different parts of the area under complete British command. Civil upheavals ensured among the south-western peoples, and underground resistance (specifically the Ekumeku resistance) rose up against the British rule (Falola and Heaton 2008). On October 1, 1960, Nigerians claimed the charge for nation-building through independence from the British government. However, the psychological impacts of colonialism, as well as deepening social cleavages, has resulted in an unstable foundation for the new nation (Kalu 2010).

By the early twentieth century, Nigerian journalists such as Herbert Macaulay were criticizing colonialism in the press and by 1944, through the innovation of Nnamdi Azikiwe a National Council of Nigerian and Cameroonians (NCNC) was created, fighting for Nigeria's independence from the British and Abeokuta Women's Union (AWU) actively advocated against the unfairness of colonial rule. Several other anti-colonial lobby groups emerge as well as political parties. A subsequent problem with the political parties developed after Nigeria gained independence in 1960, is that they were formed around tribal groups, leading to multiple coups post-independence about who should rule (Falola and Heaton 2008).

To politically rule the northern region, the British applied an indirect rule system that enabled the local institutional leaders to rule while reporting to the British (Kalu 2010). Not only did this feudal aristocratic structure organize peoples by local leaders, but it also encouraged and supported a classist system based on royal ties. After Nigeria's independence, the indirect rule system remained the most significant challenge for democracy. It gave indigenes of the northern Nigerian hemisphere a sense of superiority and entitlement (Kalu 2010).

The struggle for power eventually led to the nation's civil war, popularly referred to as the Biafra War. Even after the deadly conflict is alleviated, the battle for power continues as the presidential seat switches from military to civilian rule. Building and sustaining a nation out of a "collection of (different) tribes" is a problem Nigeria still has to grapple with. By 1965, Nigeria already had a population of about fifty million people (and today that number is reported to be over one hundred and seventy million), with over two-hundred and fifty distinct languages, complicating multi-tribal issues. Before 1960, there was no specific Nigerian governmental body (or individual) that ruled the whole territory of Nigeria. Not only was English (British colonial master's language) the only standard language, but Nigerians did not have a common faith; there was Christianity, Islam, and a rich spectrum of Animism (Schwarz, Jr. 1965).

In the years since independence, greed, corruption, and weak governance (Kalu 2010) have characterized Nigeria's political rule. In 2007 however, Nigeria marked a milestone in its democratic election with the handing over of power from one civilian president (Olusegun Obasanjo who had served the allowed maximum of two terms) to another through popular vote. Despite the political and national promises of stability and justice that the 2007 election of Yar'Adua brought about, or the cut in corruption due to the increased vigilance of the Economic and Financial Crimes Commission (EFCC) and other similar agencies in bringing corrupt elite to justice, Nigeria still has many challenges to address (Falola and Heaton 2008).

History of Boko Haram in Nigeria

When Boko Haram first emerged, it did not seem to be a significant threat to the West African region and specifically Nigeria, where it originated. In 2010 however, the organization's growth in the magnitude of attacks, geography, and some members could no longer be ignored. Boko Haram is already tagged as a transnational terrorist organization, and the organization has claimed ties with more prominent. (By 'bigger' do you intend to describe the size of the terrorist group or strength?) International terrorist groups, rhetoric that expresses their desire for continued expansion (Pham 2012). Their attacks have targeted civilians, including children and Muslim and Christians alike. They have also targeted public officials and public organizations. Attention to Boko Haram began with a chain of attacks on public institutions, including a police station in Nigeria in 2003 (Pham 2012).

Although many point to the early 2000s when tracing the inception of the organization, other arguments of its inception date back to the 1980s revolts of Maitatsine that caused thousands of death in northern Nigeria. Maitatsine (a Hausa word meaning "the one who damns"), the nickname of Muhammed Marwan, a Cameroon born Islamic preacher in Nigeria of the late twentieth century who spoke actively about the state of Nigeria. Maitatsine was sent to Nigeria by a Christian organization five years before Nigeria gained independence from the British, but his speeches were about the Quran. Muslims found his teaching of the Quran very controversial. He called himself a prophet and rejected Muhammad's (Islam's founder) prophethood.

The British exiled him for his teachings, but he reemerged in northern Nigeria after the country became independent and was able to rally up military disciples. His followers comprised mostly of Nigerian youth and unemployed migrants to Nigeria. Despite continually being arrested, Maitatsine and his followers continued to vocally and violently attack religious figures and the police. In 1980, the Nigerian military stepped in, and several violent clashes ensured between Maitatsine military following and the Nigerian army resulting in the death of 5000 people, including Maitatsine. Post Maitatsine's death, followers of his movement emerged again in northern Nigeria several times between 1982 and 1985. The connections between Boko Haram and Maitatsine can be drawn along the lines of what they have in common. Both groups are pugnacious, extremists, and hold Islamic views that are controversial to the popular beliefs in Islam. Both groups oppose the "secular Nigerian state, invariably described as...evil" (p. 2) and condemn Western civilization. Both groups believe in replacing Nigerian governance with a "purified Islamic" (p. 2) rule, and uprisings from both groups required military interventions (Pham 2012).

The primary concern of this chapter is how the mass media in various African countries report news about terrorism in Africa. The research questions guiding the study are:

RQ 1: How have media reports about Boko Haram activity changed over time?
RQ 2: What are the effects of media on the locals?
RQ 3: Is terrorism localized in Africa even when it occurs in a foreign country?
RQ 4: How is news about terrorism reported?

To adequately address these questions, frame analyses were conducted. The following sections discuss the theoretical framework of frame analysis and the methodology applied.

Theoretical Framework—Frame Analyses

The mass media is influential in shaping public opinion (Connor and Wesolowski 2004; De Vreese 2005). However, this influence—as addressed in this study—is not the one that Mass Society theorists since the nineteenth century feared. It is not assumed that the mass media can undermine social order, or that media reports directly transform the minds of people and average citizens are vulnerable to the manipulation of the press (Baran and Davis 2012). Instead, the interest in this study lies in how news is presented through the media that plays a crucial role in most democratic societies. The coverage of **negative** events in the media has the potential to influence whether such activities are perceived as having high or low intensity, like a crisis or emergency, and a personal or/and public risk. The presentation of news stories can also show the audience whom to blame in the context of the news. Newsmakers can cause even the most mundane matters to seem immediate and extraordinary, and they sometimes do so. The process through which this is done is news framing.

Framing is the way that journalists give news reports a desired and planned value by connecting them to other incidences and ideas (McQuail 2010). De Vreese (2005) describes framing as the way "a communication source presents and defines an issue" (p. 51). It is nearly impossible to present information in a logical, coherent, and comprehensible manner without some relatable context or framing. Goffman (1974) is credited with identifying the concept of framing and its benefit to organizing information. Reportages would be mere isolated "items of facts" without framing. However, with framing comes "unintended bias" since information is inevitably presented with "built-in-frames that suit the purpose of the source" (McQuail 2010, p. 380).

According to Li (2007), the primary focus of news reports during a crisis is to inform about the progression of the problem, and the known and anticipated effects for the benefit of the public, and relevant officials and agencies. The role of crisis reporters also includes educating and enlightening the populace for present and future occurrences, as well as dramatizing reports to achieve these ends (Li 2007). In an analysis of 247 news stories, An and Gower (2009) found that 95.1% of all crisis reports could be group into categories of human interest, conflict, morality, economics, and responsibility. Responsibility has to do with who is to be blamed for a crisis, morality involves the social, religious, and moral tenets of the problem, economic relates to the cost procured by individuals, groups, organizations, or the country as a whole that results from the crisis, conflict has to do with disagreements between parties, and human interest is the emotional angle of the story (An and Gower 2009).

METHOD

Quantitative and qualitative content analysis was applied to examine how media reports about Boko Haram activity over time, the effects of media on the locals, and how news about terrorism reported.

Sample

One thousand two hundred and eighty-six (1286) newspaper reports were collected from Lexis Nexis using the search terms "Boko Haram AND Chibok girls, and "Boko Haram" where the first search terms yielded no results. Reports search selected from 6 African newspapers, with two being Nigerian, two being Sudanese, and 2 being Egyptian newspapers. Reports were pulled from a timeline of April 21, 2014 (when the Chibok girls were kidnapped) to December 31, 2017. Inevitably, there were more Nigerian reports. Out of 1286 reports, 48% were from Thisday, 39.9% were from Daily Trust—both of which are Nigerian papers. For the Republic of Sudan, 4.3% were from Sudan Tribune and 1.1% from Sudan News Agency. Finally, 5.7% of the reports were from Al Ahram, and 0.5% were from the Egypt Independent.

Procedure

In other to answer the research questions: How have media reports changed over time? What are the effects of media on the locals? Is terrorism localized across Africa? How is news about terrorism reported? The first two frames were newspaper ($n=6$) and region/country ($n=3$). Next was the dominant religion of the country/region (Christian, Muslim, Other, Significant Mix). In consideration of the first research question (how media reports changed over time), the year of publication was included (2014, 2015, 2016, 2017).

The other frames were 'skew' (positive or negative), 'intensity' (crisis/ ongoing or emergency/immediate attention), frame (economic, human interest, morality, conflict), blame and hero (individual, government, foreign country, company, army, none). The blame and hero categories, unlike the other frames, evolved after coding had begun. The style was another frame (opinion or news) that emerged as coding began. Finally, whether or not a report was localized to the country of publication was examined.

Qualitative and quantitative processes were utilized to conduct cross-analysis of the stories. Using the frames, reports were coded, assigned a numeric value, and statistically analyzed. Open coding and writing memos were done throughout the process to provide detailed information on other evidence in the reports. Results of quantitative analyses are discussed first followed by discussion within the context of the qualitative findings.

RESULTS

To answer the question of whether reports changed over time, several analyses were carried out to determine if the year of reports affected how news stories were reported. Specifically, the Chi-Square test was calculated to determine the association between year ($1 = 2014$, $2 = 2015$, $3 = 2016$, $4 = 2017$) and frame ($1 =$ economic, $2 =$ human interest, $3 =$ morality, $4 =$ conflict). Results showed a significant difference ($X2$ $(9) = 26.006$, $p < .002$). In 2014, the economic frame was 2.9%, human interest was 25.8%, morality was 24.8%, but the highest was conflict at 46.4%. In 2015, economic was 3.4%, human interest was 19.6, 12.8%, but the highest was conflict at 64.2%. In 2016, economic was 0.8%, human interest was 25.2%, morality was 17.1%, and the highest was conflict at 56.9%. In 2017, economic was 1.9%, human interest was 23.0%, morality was 18.6%, and the highest was conflict at 56.5%. However, the year of the report did not significantly affect the intensity of the story.

To answer the research questions, what are the effects of media on the locals, is terrorism localized in Africa even when it occurs in a foreign country, and how is news about terrorism reported? A series of Chi-Square tests were conducted. Chi-Square test was calculated to compare the region and skew of the report ($1 =$ positive, $2 =$ negative). Results showed a significant difference ($X2$ $(2) = 24.036$, $p < .00$). In the Nigerian newspapers, 52.0% of the reports were skewed positively while 48.0% were negative. In the Sudanese newspapers, 37.7% of the reports were skewed positively while 62.3% were skewed negatively. Finally, in the Egyptian newspapers, 26.3% of the stories were skewed positively while 73.8% were skewed negatively.

Chi-Square test was calculated to compare the region and blame. Results showed significant difference ($X2$ $(10) = 329.498$, $p < .00$). In Nigerian newspapers, blame on government was 11.4%, blame on the group was 72.6%, blame on the military was 6.7%, and blame on political leader was 4.7%. In Sudanese newspapers, blame on a foreign country was 30.4%; blame on the group was 69.6%. In Egyptian newspapers, blame on a foreign country was 12.5%, and blame on the group was 87.5%.

QUALITATIVE RESULTS

The way that newspapers from different regions presented reports varied in several ways. From the quantitative analyses, these differences were in the areas of the frame, the positive and negative skew of the report, as well as the different parties that were blamed in each report. This section will shed more light on those findings.

The frame of conflict was the predominant frame across newspapers, albeit in varying percentages. The conflict was the primary frame across different years. This reflects clashes and disagreement among individuals, groups, or organizations. When used in the news report, the group Boko Haram was usually at one end of the conflict with other entities. Examples include,

As the brutal, gory violence of terrorists in the North-east continues to impact negatively on the lives of the people, counter-terrorism experts and researchers are coming together to seek a way out of the menace. —Thisday

Today, not only I am asking the President and government of Nigeria to take action, but I am also asking that Boko Haram to stop misusing the name of Islam. Islam is a religion of peace. Islam allows every boy and every girl to get an education by going to school. Moreover, education is compulsory in Islam. The word 'Islam' means peace. Islam gives a message of prudence, patience, harmony, and humanity. —Daily Trust, citing Malala

In May 2016, Sudan proposed the establishment of joint forces to monitor the border between Sudan and Libya to fight the Boko Haram group, which is accused of sending fighters to Libya and control the movements of Darfur rebels in the troubled country." —Sudan Tribune

He argues that organization like Boko Haram (which operating simultaneously in three or more countries) has a membership that cut across a broad spectrum and extends to former university lectures, bankers, graduates and undergraduates, and political elites. —Sudan Tribune

57 girls were able to escape, and one of them was found during a routine search by the Nigerian army. Later, the group released a further 21 girls who then met with Nigerian President Mohamed Bukhari. Presidential spokesman Mallam Garba Shehu said that the Swiss government and the Red Cross had mediated an agreement between Abuja and Boko Haram to bring about the girls' release. —Al Ahran

Another category of interest was the positive and negative skew of the news reports. Surprisingly, while Egypt and Sudan newspapers framed their reports as unfavorable, the majority of Nigeria news reports about terrorist activity were skewed positive. Nigerian newspapers focused more on the goodwill, and strategic actions carried out by the Nigerian president, government, international aid groups, and other entities while reporting over half of the selected news. Whereas, Egypt and Sudan focused on the damage and loss of lives and property. Examples of stories about Boko Haram activity skewed positively are as follows,

President Goodluck Jonathan has promised to sponsor the education of the abducted schoolgirls of Chibok, Borno State, in other parts of the country. —Daily Trust

President Muhammadu Buhari on Friday assured Nigerians that his administration would address rising concerns of corruption, insecurity, and injustices in various parts of the country. —Daily Trust

Dickens Sanomi Foundation has offered $48,000 (N17.5 million) for the treatment of a wounded Chibok boy, Ali Ahmadu in Dubai, United Arab Emirates. —Daily Trust

Abia State yesterday joined in the ongoing chain of prayers across the nation for divine intervention in the release of the over 200 school girls of Chibok still in captivity following their abduction by the Boko Haram Islamic insurgents. —Thisday

It has been one month since mothers were separated from their daughters in Chibok by the Boko Haram militants and the outrage has been massive. The atmosphere in the country has become so rambunctious with jumbled conversations. So I decided to move away from the rambunctious state of our country a few days ago on my fact-finding mission. —Thisday

QUESTIONS FOR DISCUSSION

1. Terrorism and communication are concepts that we encounter in interdisciplinary discourses. Choosing any three fields of study, suggest some of the intellectual and practical questions that can involve terrorism and communication in these subjects.
2. Strategic communication can be said to be prescriptive (pre-planned) or emergent, i.e., adjusting and adapting to emerging situations without preplanning. Show how these two approaches can apply to the activities of terrorist groups. Provide specific instances that you are familiar with.
3. Terrorism can be widely defined to include the violent activities of different groups that may consist of sovereign states. Give some examples of historical (past) incidents and some recent cases that may qualify as state-sponsored terrorism.
4. Explain how our knowledge of crisis communication management strategies can be useful in preventing and managing terrorism today. Outline the known steps in crisis communication planning.
5. If terrorism is understood to be communication, how can changes in the nature and uses of communication in society have implications for terrorism? Provide some concrete examples.

REFERENCES

An, S., & Gower, K. K. (2009). How Do the News Media Frame Crises? A Content Analysis of Crisis News Coverage. *Public Relations Review, 35*(2009), 107–112.

Antwi-Boateng, O. (2017). The Rise of Pan-Islamic Terrorism in Africa: A Global Security Challenge. *Politics & Policy, 45*(2), 253–284.

202   S. MOU-DANHA

Baran, S. J., & Davis, D. K. (2012). *Mass Communication Theory: Foundation, Ferment, and Future* (6th ed.). Boston, MA: Wadsworth Cengage Learning.
Connor, S., & Wesolowski, K. (2004). Newspaper Framing of Fatal Motor Vehicle Crashes in Four Midwestern Cities in the United States, 1999–2000. *Injury Prevention, 10*(3), 149.
De Vreese, C. H. (2005). News Framing: Theory and Typology. *Information Design Journal & Document Design, 13*(1).
Falola, T., & Heaton, M. M. (2008). *A History of Nigeria.* Cambridge, UK: Cambridge University Press.
Goffman, E. (1974). *Frame Analysis: An Essay on the Organization of Experience.* Cambridge, MA: Harvard University Press.
Kalu, K. A. (2010). Nigeria: Learning from the Past to Meet the Challenges of the 21st Century. *Social Research, 77*(4), 1367–1400.
Li, X. (2007). Stages of a Crisis and Media Frames and Functions: U.S. Television Coverage of the 9/11 Incident During the First 24 Hours. *Journal of Broadcasting & Electronic Media, 51*(4), 670.
McQuail, D. (2010). *McQuail's Mass Communication Theory* (6th ed.). London: Sage.
Pham, J. P. (2012, April). African Security Brief: Boko Haram's Evolving Threat: A Publication of the African Center for Strategic Studies. In F. A. O. Schwarz, Jr. (1965). *Nigeria: The Tribes, the Nation, or the Race—The Politics of Independence.* London, England: The Massachusetts Institute of Technology Press.
Wilson, S. F. II. (2014). *Terrorist Experts' Perceptions of How the Internet Has Shaped International Terrorism* (Order No. 3668962). Available from ProQuest Dissertations & Theses Global (1648432400). Retrieved from https://ezproxy.lib.ndsu.nodak.edu/login?url=, https://search-proquest-com.ezproxy.lib.ndsu.nodak.edu/docview/1648432400?accountid=6766.

Further Reading

Greenberg, B. S. (Ed.). (2002). *Communication and Terrorism: Public and Media Responses to 9/11.* Cresskill, NJ: Hampton Press.
Norris, P., Kern, M., & Just, M. (2003). *Framing Terrorism: The News Media, the Government, and the Public.* New York: Routledge.
Ryan, M. (2004). Framing the War Against Terrorism: US Newspaper Editorials and Military Action in Afghanistan. *Gazette, 66*(5), 363–382.
Woods, J. (2011). Framing Terror: An Experimental Framing Effects Study of the Perceived Threat of Terrorism. *Critical Studies on Terrorism, 4*(2), 199–217.

CHAPTER 9

The Complexity of Issue-Attention and International Media Reporting of Africa's Protracted Wars and Conflicts

Adebayo Fayoyin

INTRODUCTION

The way in which international media and advocates draw attention to wars, political conflicts and humanitarian crises at the global level remains the subject of significant professional and academic interest in a variety of disciplines. In a critical analysis on the impact of media reporting on policy and humanitarian response, Soderlund et al. (2010, p. 65) has concluded that the relationship between news reporting and international humanitarianism is significantly complicated and does not lend itself to simplistic generalization. An assessment of local and foreign correspondents' coverage of the Darfur crisis shows that different journalists had different understandings of their roles in the coverage of political crisis (Bunce 2001, p. 3). Journalists have also played a critical part in keeping alive the narrative about wars in different parts of the world. While some commentators consider the practice of embedded

A. Fayoyin (✉)
School of Public Health, University of Witwatersrand,
Johannesburg, South Africa

© The Author(s) 2019
E. K. Ngwainmbi (ed.), *Media in the Global Context*,
https://doi.org/10.1007/978-3-030-26450-5_9

journalists as helpful to understanding the complexity of military operations during wars, others consider such frontline reporting as mere public relations gimmicks (Tuosto 2008, p. 1). Thus, issue-attention and media reporting of conflicts and wars is a complex subject that requires continuous investigation to inform contemporary international reporting and humanitarian advocacy.

This paper is a critical examination of the complexity of issue-attention and international media reporting of wars and political conflicts in Africa. Many countries in Africa have been affected by wars and political crises. The list includes Angola, Algeria, Burundi, Central Africa Republic, Mauritania, Congo, the Democratic Republic of Congo, Cote d'Ivoire, Eritrea/Ethiopia, Nigeria, Liberia, Somalia, Kenya, Rwanda, Sierra Leone, Sudan, South Sudan, Libya, Egypt, Tunisia, Mali, Uganda, and Zimbabwe. The International Crisis Committee also lists examples of rebellion and terrorist's activities on the continent, such as Al-Shabaab in Somalia; Boko Haram in Nigeria; the Lord's Resistance Army (LRA) in Northern Uganda; and the Al-Qaeda in the Maghreb region, which are yet to be resolved. Such crises have resulted in decades of deaths and tragedy for the population. Despite the remarkable toll of human suffering from the conflicts and wars, Shan (2014) concludes that media attention to such humanitarian disaster is poor and scant. The author suggests that if the scale of the destruction and fighting in Africa were taking place in Europe, it would have been called the Third World War.

This article is situated within the broader context of issue-attention dynamics and the nature of humanitarian reporting and advocacy. Through this prism, the paper examines some of the concepts that have emerged in the study of international reporting of humanitarian crises, such as *The CNN Effect, The Al Jazeera Effect, Embedded Journalism, The Twitter Effect and Facebook Revolution*. Next, the paper turns to the challenge of promoting sustained media engagement and social action to wars and conflicts in Africa. Using two case studies of protracted crises—the multiple wars in Sudan and the LRA uprising in Northern Uganda—the paper reflects on how the crises were covered in the media and approaches by humanitarian advocates for keeping them on the agenda. The analysis shows that media attention to humanitarian crisis tends to be episodic and deficient in galvanizing political action for the prolonged humanitarian crisis. It also tends to oversimplify the complex root causes of the conflicts. Although humanitarian advocates play a critical role in promoting public attention to wars and military conflicts, unfortunately, they are often embroiled in local and aid politics, which influence their media engagement and capacity to achieve sustainable change. Suggestions for improving media attention and public action for addressing such chronic humanitarian crises are also provided.

ISSUE-ATTENTION AND GLOBAL HUMANITARIAN CONFLICTS

The literature on issue-attention is vast and its application extensive. However, the common thread of the discourse is the question: How and why issues attract or do not attract attention in the social-political space? As will be demonstrated below, the model also helps to explain the ability or otherwise of essential media coverage and social action to address intractable social issues and the role of different actors.

An Overview of Issue-Attention Dynamics

In a pioneering work on issue-attention, Downs (1972, pp. 40–45) theorizes that public issues go through a five-stage attention cycle: the pre-problem stage, alarmed discovery, euphoric enthusiasm, gradual decline, and the post problem stage. Although the analysis was based on the environment issue of the day, its lessons are applicable to the humanitarian context. While Downs does not propose that all issues proceed in a linear progression through the stages, the author argues that issues may recapture public interest once they have reached national prominence. This is an essential consideration in view of the critical role of news media in filtering issues, mobilizing public enthusiasm for various policy options, and assisting in constructing social reality.

Peterson (2009) applies the issue-attention cycle to international terrorism and public opinion in the United States. While lamenting the lack of public understanding of terrorism issues among the populace, the author maintains that the trajectory of issue-attention proposed by Downs for environmental issues would not apply only to terrorism issues. This underscores the need for a nuanced application of existing paradigms for explaining complex humanitarian dilemmas.

Jones and Baumgartner (2006) examine the politics of attention in the policy space and concur with the notion of scarcity of attention and competition of social problems to attract policy and public attention. They also identify the challenge of intra-issue competition in which various strands of an issue (such as policy alternatives or solutions to a problem) compete within a specific social problem. However, they underscore the role of practical information and emotive images in securing attention to social issues. Thus, it is clear that attracting adequate attention to social issues involves the manipulation of symbols, deployment of appropriate policy images and leveraging the multiplicity of information avenues.

From a sociological perspective, Hilgatrtner and Bosk (1988, pp. 60–67) studied how social problems become objects of public attention. They argue that public attention is a scarce resource and only small groups of social issues attain celebrity statuses of being considered for social and political action. In addition, they propose a framework for issue selection that highlights the invaluable role of drama, novelty, culture and politics, institutional capacities and advocacy groups in attaining attention to specific issues or problems. In their opinion, "many social problems that are largely unsuccessful in most areas can be kept alive by small persistent advocacy groups" (Hilgatrtner and Bosk 1988, p. 66).

The concept of issue-attention continues to be relevant in explaining the relationship between the media and issue positioning. Several factors constrain public attention of issues including lack of understanding or knowledge of the issue, the nonexistence of the demand for knowledge, the high cost of policy options for issue resolution or limited interest of policy communities. Conversely, factors such as how the issue is framed and eventually portrayed, the role of policy communities in making the case, the articulation of the actions required, and how policy communities and entrepreneurs pursue the issue, help to sustain attention to issues. Although the notion of issue particularity or valence is also essential, lessons from social constructionism clearly show that "material reality" is less important than "constructed reality." The role of advocates and critical actors is thus critical for issue portrayal and issue positioning. All these considerations are essential within the context of humanitarianism and development.

Issue-Attention and International Reporting of Wars and Conflicts

One of the avenues of attracting attention to global humanitarian issues and political conflicts is foreign reporting. Yet, as evidenced by the literature, international reporting is constrained by different challenges that affect its effectiveness.

In an analysis of how mass media reporting of humanitarian crisis influence policy action, Robinson (1999) developed the concept of the "CNN effect." This relates to how real-time communication technology can provoke major responses from domestic audiences and political elites on global issues (p. 301). While there is no consensus among academics on the exact meaning of the theory, it is generally perceived as "a novel type of media role that is different in nature from the media's traditional role because it is rapid in its transmission, transcontinental in its reach and qualitatively richer than the past media formats" (Bahador 2007, p. 3). However, a significant challenge of the CNN effect is the impact of such coverage on policy action. Using specific case studies as anchors for the analysis, Robinson (1999) could not find any conclusive evidence that news media would always provoke intervention in the humanitarian crisis. In the end, the author wrestles with the conundrum of how in some cases media coverage would seem to cause intervention while in some cases it does not.

> The question raised is why intervention occurs in some instances but not in others, focusing on the CNN effect as an issue of media control does not explain why media coverage of humanitarian crises appear only to cause intervention. (p. 307)

Situated within the domain of agenda setting, the study helps to understand the role of media in humanitarian response and policymaking. However, it does not provide any certain resolution of the impact of media on humanitarian intervention decisions. In a follow-up study, Robinson (2005, p. 344) reaffirms the proposition that media intervention could drive foreign policy action. However, the assumptions and findings of the **CNN effect** have also been questioned in several studies and analysis. Van Belle (2008, p. 6) notes that media impact on disaster aid response in the United States is not as simple as earlier expected. In the end, the author considers the CNN effect as an illusion.

Similarly, Soderlund et al. (2010) tested five independent variables in establishing the impact of news media on humanitarian response. (1) The variables are the severity of humanitarian crisis, (2) the perceived risk associated with the intervention, (3) the national interest of the intervening power, (4) the volume of coverage, and (5) the content of news stories. They found little evidence to support the idea that media coverage shapes policies and programs in the humanitarian context. This suggests that the relationship between media coverage and humanitarianism is indeed complicated.

In examining the configuration of international news reporting of humanitarian situations in the American media, Moeller (1999) established four patterns of coverage as follows: the stereotypical characterization of the structure of news, sensationalized language, and the use of analogies, metaphors, and images for rhetorical effect, and the dominance of American strategic interest. The author maintains that American media apply the American lens; the "political, strategic, commercial and historical considerations" (p. 5) to reporting international affairs and global crises. It also highlights how framing, particularly the language used in constructing reality and the use of oddity as a criterion of news selection, can influence media and public attention to specific humanitarian issues.

The emergence of global news agencies from non-Western countries has given rise to the optimism of a different worldview of international events. In particular, Seib (2008, p. xii) explores how the rise of Al Jazeera, a station that prides itself as the voice of the Middle East and Southern hemisphere, is serving as a counterforce on international news reporting—*the Al Jazeera Effect*. Furthermore, studies have found increased interest from China in reporting the world through her own eyes. China had become a significant player in the world today and is interested in expanding its international media system chain of media organizations to advance her strategic foreign policy interests and global economic agenda. According to Si (2014, p. 10), there is a significant move by the Chinese government to expand the coverage of its presence and position for the international market and audience. The proliferation of international media institutions from Asia and in particular from China on the global scene offers an alternative to the Americanisation of international news reporting.

Wilesmith (2011, p. 4) investigated how international media institutions report the wars in Afghanistan and Iraq and the tactics used to influence media reporting of the wars. The analysis demonstrated the diversity of interests in the wars—strategic, military, geopolitical, and diplomatic interests—that compounded international media reporting. Some of the findings include the use of misleading information and intelligence to justify the war and gap between rhetoric and reality in the political discourse on the war's success. Finally, the study revealed both media and public fatigue over time. The critical lesson from the study is the manner in which geopolitical and strategic interests influence international media reporting.

A new variant of journalism in global reporting of conflicts and military operations is embedded journalism, rooted in need to understand the media–military relationship and war reporting. It entails integrating journalists or war correspondents with army operations to cover wars from the frontlines. It has been extensively used in the Iraq and Afghanistan wars, but for both wars, it has been criticized for its distraction and distortion of reality. Tuosto (2008, p. 20) is of the opinion that embedded journalists in the Iraq and Afghanistan wars were part of the pro-war propaganda disguised as objective reporting. Largely, it is seen as a public relations tactic for the army or the combatants in question. A BBC analysis on media ethics and society affirms that embedded journalism suffers from bias and compromise of independent reporting (BBC News, 22 October 2014). A *New York Times* commentator describes embedding journalists in the Iraq invasion and military drawdown as "soda-straw view of war" (Myers 2010). Thus given the multiple interplay of forces in media–military dynamics, the challenge to inform and influence public perceptions about wars, the political justification for going to war, the need to demonstrate success of military operations and adherence to professional journalism ethos, embedded reporting is another dimension to the complexity of attracting attention to conflicts, wars, and humanitarian crises.

The advent of new media and their subsequent deployment for real-time communication in society has created what has been called *"The Twitter Effect"* and *"The Facebook Revolution"* in public communication and media reporting of humanitarian issues. Forces of globalization and the digital revolution have transformed the contemporary practices of news agencies and international news reporting. Technological and economic developments have affected, globally, media institutions and news agencies, resulting in advancements in digital media and communications technology for war reporting. Our digital age is characterized by increased levels of internet penetration and extensive social media use with a high level of interactivity, genuine dialogue, speed, multimodality, user-generated content, mass customization, horizontal communication, and multidirectionality of information (Fayoyin 2016, p. 2; Keung 2017, p. 7). The availability of digital devices and platforms has prompted what is now called citizenship and networked journalism. Thus, the changing media landscape that has created a 24-hour news cycle, 24/7 imposes new demands and challenges on international news reporting. Clearly, this has led to dwindling exclusivity of international reporting by an elite corps of foreign correspondents while the strict traditional gatekeeping function is no longer adequate (Sambrook 2010, p. 24).

Twitter and Facebook are changing the nature of political discourse, policy engagement and social change on various issues, including development and humanitarianism. Bruno (2010, p. 7) examines the use of Twitter in the coverage of worldwide crises, with particular reference to the Haiti humanitarian crisis. The author found that social media (especially Twitter, amateur videos, pictures, Skype, Facebook, new storytelling formats, including interactive maps, multimedia visualizations, live blogs, etc.) played a phenomenal role in the coverage before the traditional international media got on the scene. Social media were also integrated into the coverage by foreign correspondents, enabling immediate, decentralized, real-time and citizens-based coverage of the earthquake.

The role of aid agencies in reporting disasters and attracting attention to humanitarian crises has also come into focus. Dirjkzeul and Moke (2005, p. 673) argue that in an age of sound bites, it is difficult to convey the complexity of humanitarian activities including the identities of the players such as warlords, militia, peacekeeping, local organizations, and humanitarian institutions. In a similar vein, Kalcisc (2011, p. 6) examined the role of aid agencies in influencing international reporting and how to make disasters newsworthy. The author highlights the increasing role of aid agencies and institutional reporting and has become 'more savvy' in influencing international reporting to their advantage. Aid agencies now function like reporters churning out information and stories that sell their interventions and humanitarian responses. However, it is affected by political complexities, organizational politics and interagency efforts for visibility.

From the foregoing, it is established that the politics and dynamics of issue-attention affect public and media attention to humanitarian issues. Geopolitical interests also drive the nature of reportage, especially by Western media. Different actors also play critical roles within the global development and humanitarianism landscape. Communication is also driven by sound bites. This clearly reflects the complexity of global reporting of wars and the challenge of sustaining attention to protracted political conflicts. In the next section, we examine similar complexities with respect to reporting wars and conflicts in Africa.

ISSUE-ATTENTION AND HUMANITARIAN CONFLICTS IN AFRICA

For over 50 years, media scholars have been interested in the way Africa is covered in international news reports. Notably, in the seventies and the eighties, scholars and government officials were exasperated by the poor, limited or biased reporting of Africa and called for new World Information and Communication Order (NWICO). The underlying premise of the debate was 'the sovereignty of information' and in particular international news reporting by Western countries, which was considered as "elite-focused, conflictual, and sensationalist". The information order was accused of being "Western-dominated, colonial/imperialist-based" (Richstad and Nnaemeka 1980, p. 5). However, with a recent analysis of international media coverage of Africa, this pattern of representation does not seem to have changed. Bunce et al. (2017, p. 38) lamented that US media have been prone to sensationalized headlines that pivot on "troupes of paranoia, racism, and xenophobia."

Similarly, Hawkins (2008) investigated international media reporting of global conflicts and berated the limited attention devoted to the protracted political crisis in Africa. The author makes the case that if Europe has a similar scale of fighting and destruction, it would have been called the Third World War. Yet, Western mainstream media paid 'little and occasional' attention to these crises. To the author, the crises in Kosovo, Iraq and Palestine/Israel have received far more attention in the Western press than Africa, where the toll of the conflicts was higher.

Other studies have uncovered different dimensions in the complexity of reporting wars and conflicts in Africa. For example, Baum and Zhukov (2015, p. 5) analyzed data from 113 countries on the coverage of the Libyan civil war by international newspapers and affirms the existence of reporting biases in its coverage. Their study revealed that media coverage in non-democracies underreported the protest and non-collective action by regime opponents. Government atrocities were largely underreported while activities by rebels were overreported. To them, reporting bias was driven by how news agencies navigate the political context in which they are based. Thus they hypothesized that where political constraints on reporting were more onerous, especially in non-democratic regimes, the scope for reporting should reflect general media preferences toward "novel large-scale dramatic development that challenge the conventional wisdom" (Baum and Zhukov 2015, p. 19). The study also highlights the critical role of geopolitical context and political orientation in international reporting. Overall, media coverage of the Libyan issue ended up as a "filtering" of the revolution in the country.

Selim (2011) compares the coverage of the Egyptian revolution in three countries—Egyptian, American and Israeli—press. The author found that both traditional and social media played a critical role in the coverage of the event. However, there were significant differences in the angles to the event. For the Egyptian press, it was a revolution and a turning point for the country, while American and Israeli press considered it merely as an event that might affect American and Israeli interests in the Middle East. The priority of the America and Israeli press was the implication of the revolution on their strategic interests. This study underscores how different international interests determine the frames adopted by international journalists to interpret and report events.

African coverage of African issues is also constrained by different challenges. For example, Owens-Ibie (2016, p. 80) examined the media narratives of the Boko Haram abduction of the Chibok girls in Northern Nigeria, and highlights some "conflicts in the reporting of the conflict." Aspects of conflicting communication include the incidence and prevalence of the crisis. The newspapers investigating—*the Punch* and *the Guardian*—at various times published different data on the number of girls abducted, the number rescued, and the actions being pursued by the government. From the analysis, the author raises many questions on the impact of shoddy reporting, especially in relation to what the audience would believe and how the public could respond to the situation. The study thus underscores the institutional and professional challenges around reporting conflicts and the crisis in Africa.

In the next section, we will present two case studies to illustrate the imperative and processes of attracting attention to the crisis and the pattern of media representation. They are the multiple conflicts in Sudan and the LRA rebellion in Northern Uganda. The conflicts manifest a significant level of complexity and do not lend themselves to simplistic interpretation.

SUDAN—BLUE NILE, DARFUR, AND SOUTH SUDAN CONFLICTS

Sudan is not a stranger to conflict. In nearly 35 of the 46 years since independence, the country has experienced two civil wars 1955–1972 and 1983–2005 and several other conflicts on various frontiers. Most of the conflicts in the country are around self-determination of ethnic groups or entities that protest the position and policies of the Arab-controlled Northern Sudan. Doane (2010) maintains that some of the conflicts originate from the attempt by the central government in the north to centralize power; Arabize and Islamize the entire country, and divide the south. Brief descriptions of the various frontiers of the crisis and implications for issue-attention, humanitarian advocacy and media reporting are presented below.

BLUE NILE STATE AND SOUTHERN KORDAFON CRISES

The Southeastern and western parts of Sudan have been engulfed in a number of insurgencies for self-determination against the north, for over two decades. The roots of the conflicts are broad, but it boils down to the oppressive policies of the central government. However, these two fronts are now considered the forgotten frontiers of the Sudan crisis because they have been eclipsed by the crisis in Darfur and the South Sudan war of independence. The International Refugee Rights Initiative calls the Blue Nile 'a crisis normalized' because war has become the norm in the region (IRIN News 2018). Apart from occasional spotlights from media, the crisis and its impacts have been largely unnoticed for decades. They rarely made it into severe headlines and sustained CNN or Twitter effect. The impact of the crisis has also not received any primary public debate and international outrage. Thus, we have two frontiers of war in Sudan forgotten by the international public or considered inconsequential because of the scale of the crisis in Darfur and the South Sudan conflict. Yet, according to the 2017 Human Rights Watch Report, civilian populations are suffering under the continuous attacks of government forces on different targets and actors in Southern Kordofan and the Blue Nile.

WESTERN SUDAN—DARFUR CRISIS

The crisis in Darfur began in 2003 and is still currently unresolved, according to Human Rights Watch (2017, p. 16). There are conflicting accounts of the crisis, its history, and its media coverage. This case also manifests unparalleled complexity, such as contradictory narratives of its raison d'etre, competing roles of the various actors in the conflicts including government, a pro-government militia, international observer groups, and the multiple constraints to its reporting. Its impact is also heavily contested. While the United Nations estimates that 300,000 people were killed, the government puts the figure at 10,000.

Bacon (2004, p. 1) examines international media performance on the conflict and establishes that the Khartoum government manipulated the crises in order to delay international media attention. The author claims that thousands had died before the world noticed there was any major crisis in Darfur, as a result of how the President controlled media access and immigration policies to the country. In another study, Bunce (2001, p. 16) compared how local, national stringers and global news covered the Darfur crisis. While the author found some similarities and differences in their style of reporting, overall, the study demonstrated how western media practices influenced the writing and reporting styles of local and foreign journalists. A study by Reporters with Borders established that journalists violated rules of journalism including corroboration of facts, use of different sources and objectivity (Gazette 2007, p. 13).

Unfortunately, the Darfur crisis is yet to be resolved, but it is no longer in the headlines and rarely in the news, apart from a smattering of occasional reports. The International crisis Groups reporter chaos in the region in 2015 *The Telegraph* in the UK reported chemical attacks in 2016, in which hundreds of children were gassed to death. The Human Rights Watch (2017) revealed that government forces including the Rapid Support Force and allied militia launched ground attacks on civilian populations in 2014–2015 and successfully blocked access of AU and UN Peacekeeping Missions and other humanitarian advocates. Unfortunately, the level of public and media attention compared to when the crisis started has plummeted. The noise from activists and humanitarian advocates has equally waned. Celebrities no longer compete for photo opportunities in Darfur. Yet, the population continuously endures the most of militia attacks and government military operations. The challenge is how to get the crisis back on the front burner of media reporting and global attention?

SOUTH SUDAN—THE WAR FOR INDEPENDENCE

Of all the frontiers of the war and conflicts in Sudan, the South Sudan war of independence was the most noticeable. It took nearly 27 years of civil war with the North that resulted in an estimated 2 million South Sudanese civilian deaths. Analysts believe that the war and its horrific consequences did not receive attention at the right time. Doane (2010) observes that despite the fact that the crisis claimed more lives than conflicts in Bosnia, Chechnya, Haiti, Rwanda, Kosovo, and Somalia combined, the crisis was mostly unnoticed for a significant amount of time. South Sudan became an independent country on July 2011, but the war had so many angles and narratives, which complicated media reporting and humanitarian advocacy. Some of the significant elements are summarized below.

International Media Coverage

For the length of the crisis and even during the implementation of the Comprehensive Peace Agreement, which preceded the referendum and the eventual election that ushered in the new nation, there was no shortage of foreign media coverage. The diversity of the South Sudan crisis provided juicy coverage of 'fly in fly out' correspondents of the international media. Some of the media reports on Sudan, including the celebrated photographs of the famine, won international awards. Examining the coverage of the second civil war by international media, Hoile (2003, p. 50) found instances of stereotypical reporting, oversimplification, information filtering, misrepresentation, and misinterpretation of complex political issues.

Transnational Advocacy Networks

A plethora of organizations was also involved in transnational advocacy for South Sudan, with the focus on keeping the issue on the international agenda and motivating key countries and institutions for action. Such agencies include Amnesty International, UNHCR, Human Rights Watch, and the Anti-Slavery Group that ran campaigns to highlight the horror of the war. International institutions and individuals also developed projects to make the horrors of the civil war visible. An NGO, **The Enough Project**, ran campaigns on the war and generated information to highlight the plight of South Sudanese. However, institutions like the European Sudan Public Affairs Council also published materials, monographs, and documents that were not supportive of the cause. Global and regional intergovernmental institutions played a critical role in the diplomatic and advocacy efforts that contributed to influencing critical actors in the process. The UN was a platform for discussion of the various ramifications of the issues. The complexity and multidimensional nature of the crisis resulted in the engagement of many developed countries 'speaking out' and advocating for different issues and solutions to the conflict.

The Slavery, Famine, and Genocide Narrative

The crisis had different storylines, but some of the most impactful were genocide, persecution, and slavery. Religious advocates marketed the crisis as a form of religious persecution of the South for their religious beliefs and slavery of the South by the North. In the United States, Christian lobbyists petitioned power structures—The White House, the Senate, and the Congress—to intervene in the situation. Tactics deployed to generate international momentum and decisive actions from their governments were "publicity, protests, grassroots mobilization, divestment pressure, direct humanitarian aid, and legislative sanction." The alliance of different religious groups on the issue created a major push for decisive government action. In 1996 the National Association of Evangelicals carried out a coordinated campaign (including public gatherings, media coverage, private meetings with critical influentials) to pressure the US President to change its policy on Sudan. In 1999, 200 Christian leaders petitioned President Clinton on what they called the genocide policies of the North against the South. Subsequent presidents—President Bush and President Obama—were also lobbied for policy change on the crisis. The pro-Israel lobby group played a significant role in changing government attitude to the Sudan peace process.

Celebrity Advocacy

Several celebrities were involved in advocacy for South Sudan during and after the referendum. The engagement was for media attention, fundraising and leveraging their influence change. South Sudanese issues featured prominently in charity projects supported by Hollywood celebrities. The roll call of celebrity advocates and goodwill ambassadors on Sudan includes: Baroness Cox who has carried out different campaigns on the platform of slavery and genocide, International Actress Mia Farrow who undertook multiple missions to the front lines, John Prendergast, former basketball player and co-founder of the Enough Project with George Clooney, and Angelina Jolie with UNHCR. Overall, celebrity advocacy assisted in mobilizing the influential voices of artists and local people in keeping the South Sudan issue on public attention.

From a media and advocacy perspective, the South Sudan war of independence presented considerable opportunities and challenges. It resulted in significant humanitarian advocacy efforts to promote international outrage for war, its consequences and the need for a peaceful resolution. There were multiple actors with different interests that played significant roles in mobilizing actions, influencing government and increasing attention on the conflict. However, it also led to a lack of coherent messaging among activists. Furthermore, analysts believed that the crisis experienced significant disinformation, misinformation, and misinterpretation. Misrepresentation of Sudanese issues through poor, sensationalistic and sometimes politically partisan reporting by elements of the international media; publication of unverifiable and dubious claims on the practice of slavery and redemption of slaves by several reputable newspapers and journals; regurgitation of information from reports by advocates and interested parties; bias in reporting by North American and Western European newspapers and other media and academic outlets; appalling media reporting characterized by a mixture of bad journalism, misinformation and deliberate disinformation (Hoile 2003) were rampant. It is also argued that such poor journalism enflamed public opinion among powerful constituencies, fuelled by crude stereotyping of some of the actors, and prolonged the crisis.

Four years after independence, South Sudan hit the headlines again because of political conflict based on the power struggle between the President and Vice President. The crisis resulted in gender-based violation, sexual exploitation, and massive international displacement. However, the attention and response of the international community to the crisis seems fatigued.

UGANDA—THE CRISIS WITH THE LORD'S RESISTANCE ARMY (LRA)

Since 1987, the LRA has been involved in an armed struggle against the government of Uganda. Led by Joseph Kony, the LRA started as a military rebellion against the administration of President Museveni following the assassination of the first president who was of the Acholi tribe like Kony. For over two decades, the group carried out grievous atrocities, including abduction, rape, mutilation and destruction of the livelihood in northern Uganda, specifically around Kitgum, Gulu, and Pader. At the peak of the crisis in 2000–2005, the internally displaced population was nearly 2 million; packed into camps in Gulu and Kitgum with barely any social services. The concentration of population in camps even served as targets of attack by the LRA. Children, both boys, and girls were mainly targeted to serve as soldiers and wives of the LRA regular members. By 2008, the crisis has taken a regional dimension, with reports of LRA raids affecting Congo, Sudan, and Uganda. Some of the activities implemented to influence media and public attention include the following.

Use of Evidence on the Atrocities

International and national humanitarian agencies such as UNICEF, Amnesty International, World Vision, and ACORD undertook a series of documentation and reporting of the atrocities of the war. The University of California Berkeley—Tulane University Initiative on Vulnerable Populations also conducted a series of studies on human rights violations and how children were affected.

International NGO Engagement

The Invisible Children, a US-based NGO, played a critical role in advocacy for the issue. They produced videos on the crisis and undertook tours around the world drawing attention to how the crisis was affecting children, especially girls. Some of their documentaries metamorphosed into a movement on social justice for the children of northern Uganda. Another story was "Night Commuters," the story of an estimated 30,000 Ugandan children who walk about 20 miles every night and day to avoid the potential of being abducted by the LRA. In 2012, they developed the "Kony 2012 campaign." The objective was to advocate for more international action to bring the leader of the group to justice. The campaign involved a highly popular video that received at least 84 million views on YouTube. The video was also showed to live audiences in several parts of Uganda. However, it resulted in heated and significant controversy and was eventually banned in Kampala and many other locations.

Community Advocacy

Several community advocacy initiatives helped to keep the issue on the national and local agenda. The Northern Uganda Advocacy Partnership for Peace, involving different NGOs including World vision and Conciliation Resources, undertook targeted advocacy for the cause. Civil Society Organisation for peace in Northern Uganda (CSOPNU), Local CSOs, Women Organization Campaign, and the Catholic Church carried out peace missions to different national and international stakeholders. Religious leaders formed an interfaith organization—Acholi Religious Leaders Peace Initiative (ARLPI) in 1997, with the goal of 'bearing witness' for the war and promoting the voice of the community most affected by the war and enhance peaceful resolution. The initiative resulted in a series of advocacy and lobbying activities with sub-national, national and international groupings. The group also called for the internationalization of the conflict in order to find an international solution. Another local grouping, Acholi descendants in diaspora (*Kacoke Madit*), also campaigned for peace.

Media Mobilization

The crisis has attracted intense media coverage at the national and international levels. At different moments of the crisis, and especially during spikes in attacks of the LRA, the media highlighted the crisis and its impacts through individual reports, editorials, news analysis, and news commentaries. Additionally, various advocacy organizations at the national and international levels developed communication packages to tell their stories of the war.

Celebrity Advocacy

A number of international and regional celebrities were also engaged for advocacy on the war. For example, Mia Farrow, the UNICEF Goodwill Ambassador visited Uganda several times for celebrity advocacy on the crisis. Other aid agencies also mobilized their celebrities to carry out similar advocacy, to draw attention to the issue and the role of their organizations.

Diplomatic Negotiations

A raft of open and closed diplomatic negotiations was part of the process of resolving the crisis. Governments around the world passed motions and bills on denouncing the LRA. The US Congress passed a bill on LRA Disarmament and Northern Uganda recovery May 2010. The International Criminal Court (ICC) was requested to investigate the scope of crimes, atrocities, and rights through its prosecution process, which led to the indictment of the leader of the group.

Through some of the activities described above, the war, which was largely ignored at first, attracted national and international attention. The atrocities committed by the LRA changed the attitudes to and perceptions of the war. There was increased awareness of the crisis and the brutality of the situation, and a demand for more action. The Government of Uganda was forced to initiate talks with the LRA. A national Amnesty Act was passed in 2000 that granted amnesty to LRA members who willingly returned. By 2004, over 5000 former LRA members had applied for the amnesty. Despite the peace taking place in Northern Uganda, the war is yet to be declared officially over, and the leader of the group is yet to be arrested or killed. In 2017, the US Army and Uganda military discontinued the search for Kony. Yet, the group still attacks countries in the region. The challenge is how to keep the issue alive in a time of relative peace.

EMERGING ISSUES

From our review of the context for international media reporting of Africa and the case studies, we identify four critical issues in explaining the complexity of attracting public and media attention to Africa's humanitarian crisis, especially its protracted conflicts.

The Complex Root Causes of Wars and Conflicts

Wars, conflicts, and rebellions in Africa are products of complex, broad, political, national, and sometimes personal interests. The continent is also riddled with various protracted conflicts that have led to decades of suffering and impoverishment of the population. Africa continues to be fertile ground for violent extremism and radicalization, with many countries described as failed or fragile States. Many countries are either failed states or extremely fragile. They fall within the ambit of "wicked problems," which according to Rittel and Webber (1973) are those for which there is "no solution in the sense of definitive and objective answers".

Such problems manifest six features as follows: multidimensional, multiple stakeholders, multiple causes, multiple symptoms, multiple solutions, and continually evolving (Watkins and Wilber 2015, p. 16). In their complexity, the conflicts evince several elements of wicked problems, partly due to the role of foreign powers in the affairs of the countries and partly to complex political and historical contexts. In some cases, the role of colonial powers contributed to some of the political crisis and conflicts, as seen in countries like Cameroun, Chad, Central African Republic, Congo, DRC, and Cote d'Ivoire. In some cases, the crisis originates in disagreements over politics, power, natural resources, and religious differences. Many of the crises are complex and ill-understood by the foreign governments and agent who want them resolved.

The Roller Coaster Public Attention to Conflicts in Africa

Media coverage and solutions from humanitarian agencies have tended to oversimplify the complex context. Crises experience a roller coaster issue-attention. At the beginning of any crisis, it is sometimes difficult to attract attention, as has been the case for most conflicts in Africa. Even simmering political conflicts in different parts of the continent do not get the level of media attention that necessitates regional or global attention at the right time. However, as the impact grows, almost to the point, they get out of hand; more attention is drawn to the crisis. After reaching the public euphoria stage in the issue-attention scale, attention shifts. While this is the natural dynamic of issue-attention, it has significant implications for the societies and individuals caught in the crisis. The crises are also affected by an oversimplification of complex contexts. For example, solutions by international NGOs, especially their communication interventions, have tended to be simplistic. In the case of South Sudan, Hoile (2003) argues that all media were victims of reporting deliberate state-sponsored and private sector propaganda. In the search for scoops, journalists did not verify claims from pressure groups, Sudan's government, American institutions and European activists (p. 107). The Kony campaign implemented by the **Invisible Children** on the LRA crisis was also accused of oversimplification and celebrating Kony.

The Curse of Newsworthiness

Within the context of media reporting, we observe the "curse of news-worthiness." The inherent values of news (such as change, prominence, conflict, and immediacy) necessitate that only issues that meet those criteria attract media attention However with time, issues lose their news-worthiness and the level of attention drops. This phenomenon can be linked to the gradual decline stage of issue-attention dynamics and compassion fatigue for the protracted humanitarian crisis.

Beyond the pathetic attitude of international media to the protracted crisis, we shudder that the same level of poor reporting is currently affecting simmering conflicts in other parts of the continent, and particularly the crisis in Western Cameroun. To say the least, the attention of the mainstream media is unacceptable, while the response of global humanitarian actors is unconscionable. It does feel that unless an effective level of attention and response is devoted to this crisis, it might become one of the forgotten crisis of the Continent. In addition, largely, the market-driven American approach to reporting is to blame.

The Competition for Attention from Humanitarian Advocates

The aid environment is a competitive and fragmentary terrain (Easterly 2002; Kalcsics 2011) during humanitarian situations, advocates and agencies implement programs and communication interventions in response to the crisis. However, this results in competition for attention and visibility. The fragmented nature of aid delivery reflects in the media and other public communication activities. Every agency wants its "noise" around specific issues to be heard through the media and its flag waved, which compromises the needed attention to the crucial issues. An editorial from *The Lancet* (2010) captures this phenomenon as follows:

> Media coverage as an end in itself is too often the aim of their activities. Marketing and branding have a high profile. Perhaps worst of all, relief efforts in the field are sometimes competitive with little collaboration between agencies, including smaller, grassroots charities that may have better networks in affected counties and so are well placed to immediately implement emergency relief. (p. 10)

CONCLUSION

Wars, political conflicts, and insurgencies in Africa have attracted some level of national and international media attention and ultimately public interest. Beyond the initial headline of the crisis, many of them end up being protracted and prolonged, resulting in plummeting public and media attention. Although several media effects have been bandied around in the discourse on humanitarian communication (CNN Effect, Aljazeera Effect, Twitter Effect, Facebook Effect), they tend to be short-term, episodic and deficient in sustaining interest in protracted humanitarian conflicts in Africa. Therefore, we call for a new philosophy of humanitarian communication, which promotes continuous strategic engagement and mass mobilization until humanitarian crises are finally resolved. Such an approach should also help in building the resilience of the affected and peacebuilding for sustainable change. This will involve a coherent communication agenda that connects humanitarianism with development programming.

WAY FORWARD

The world conflict survey of the International Institute of Security in 2017 suggests that Africa is likely to experience at least 10 conflicts in the years ahead. This implies that political conflicts and wars on the continent are not likely to go away. In outlining the way forward, we revert to the notion of bad solution offered by Watkins and Wilber (2015, p. 15). These include a mapping of the problem, mapping of the network, mapping of crucial stakeholders, engagement of stakeholders, and coherence of action. Applied to how to promote public and media attention to protracted African political crisis, it is essential to understand the reporting challenge being confronted, promote partnership and coherent engagement among communication stakeholders, develop an integrated process for knowledge-based reporting of the issues, and the active mobilization of networked journalists in the process.

Strategic coordination of humanitarian agencies in continuous advocacy during a humanitarian crisis is critical. While it might be assumed that political conflicts and wars should attract the right level of attention at the right time, this is not the case. Most wars and conflicts in Africa did not attract the right level of public attention before they got out of hand for various reasons. A strategic communication is early warning and early actions need to be developed by humanitarian agencies. This will also help ensure that peacekeeping and peacebuilding approaches are in place not after too much damage has been done.

We also need a journalistic philosophy that promotes continuous engagement with the mass media and the affected communities. Currently, humanitarian reporting is influenced by the market-driven American philosophy of journalism. The weaknesses of this mode of reporting have led to the call for the Africanization of the media practices in African countries. Neither the CNN Effect nor the Twitter Effect has been able to keep Africa's protracted issues on the agenda. A new modality of reporting and communication would be essential.

Third, the role of disaster-affected communities in the communication around humanitarian issues need to be prioritized. This will help to continuously highlight the voice of the affected population in humanitarian crisis.

Finally, stronger media engagement must become a significant component of humanitarian responses. While individual aid agencies have their processes and approaches for communicating in humanitarian issues, media engagement needs to be integrated into the global discourse of the humanitarian community. The Action Plan from the 2016 Humanitarian summit does not include any recommendation on how to ensure effective media engagement and mobilization. Media and communication structures must be an integral part of the global processes and arrangements for engaging stakeholders around humanitarian response.

QUESTIONS FOR DISCUSSION

1. Why is it important for communication scholars and students to understand the complex context that drives international news reporting?
2. Discuss the concepts of "CNN Effect" and "Twitter Effect." How do they help or hurt the representation of Africa in the global context?
3. What are the shifts that need to take for an equitable representation of emerging countries in a polarised media world?

4. According to this chapter, examine the value of applying an inter-disciplinary lens to the analysis of international news and global representation?

5. How do international agencies reinforce the stereotypical "roller coaster" reporting of international correspondents of critical emergencies in developing countries?

References

Bacon, K. (2004). Hiding Death in Darfur: Why the Press Was so Late. *Columbia Journalism Review, 43*(3), 9–10.

Bahador, B. (2007). *The CNN Effect: How the News Media Pushed the West Toward War in Kosovo.* New York: Palgrave Macmillan.

Baum, M., & Zhukov, Y. (2015). Filtering Revolution: Reporting Bias in International Newspaper Coverage of the Libyan Civil War. *Journal of Peace Research, Journal of Peace Research.* sagepub.co.uk/journals. https://doi.org/10.1177/0022343314554791.

BBC News. (2014, October 22). *Pros and Cons of Embedded Journalism.* http://scrippsmediaethics.blogspot.co.za/2014/10/pros-and-cons-of-embedded-journalism.html.

Bruno, N. (2010). *Tweet First, Verify Later? How Real-Time Information is Changing the Coverage of Worldwide Crisis Events.* https://reutersinstitute.politics.ox.ac.uk/our-research/tweet-first-verify-later-how-real-time-information-changing-coverage-worldwide-crisis.

Bunce, M. (2001). *The New Foreign Correspondents at Work: Local-National Stringers and the Global News Coverage of Conflict in Darfur.* London: Reuters Institute for the Study of Journalism. https://reutersinstitute.politics.ox.ac.uk/our-research/new-foreign-correspondent-work.

Bunce, M., Franks, S., & Patterson, C. (2017). *Africa's Image in the 21st Century: From the 'Heart of Darkness' to 'Africa Rising'.* London: Routledge.

Dirjkzeul, D., & Moke, M. (2005). *Public Communication Strategies of International Humanitarian Organisations.* https://www.icrc.org/en/international-review/article/public-communication-strategies-international-humanitarian.

Doane, S. (2010). Responding to Genocide in Sudan. *Stanford Journal of International Relations.* https://web.stanford.edu/group/sjir/3.2.10_doane.html.

Downs, A. (1972). Up and Down with Ecology: The Issue Attention Cycle. *The Public Interest, 28*(Summer), 38–50.

Easterly, W. (2002). The Cartel of Good Intentions. *Foreign Policy* (July–August), 40–49.

Fayoyin, A. (2016). Engaging Social Media for Health Communication in Africa: A Synthesis of Approaches, Results, and Lessons. *Journal of Mass Communication and Journalism, 6*(6). https://doi.org/10.4172/2165-7912.1000315.

Gazette. (2007). *Darfur: An Investigation into a Tragedy's Forgotten Actors.* Paris: Reporters Without Borders.

Hawkins, V. 2008. *"Conflict Death Tolls" Stealth Conflicts.* https://stealthconflicts.wordpress.com/category/conflict-death-tolls/.

Hilgatrtner, S., & Bosk, C. L. (1988). The Rise and Fall of Social Problems: A Public Arenas Model. *American Journal of Sociology, 94*(1), 53–78.

Hoile, D. (2003). *Images of Sudan: Case Studies in Propaganda and Misrepresentation.* London: European Sudanese Public Affairs Council.

Human Rights Watch. (2017). *Sudan Events of 2016.* https://www.hrw.org/world-report/2017/country-chapters/sudan.

IRIN News. (2018). *Blue Nile: Sudan's Forgotten Front.* http://archive.irinnews.org/multimedia/BlueNile/.

Jones, B. D., & Baumgartner, F. R. (2006). *The Politics of Attention: How Government Prioritise Problems.* Chicago: University of Chicago Press.

Kalcisc, M. (2011). *A Reporting Disaster. The Interdependence of Media and Aid Agencies in a Competitive Compassion Market.* https://reutersinstitute.politics.ox.ac.uk/our-research/reporting-disaster-interdependence-media-and-aid-agencies-competitive-compassion.

Keung, L. (2017). *Going Digital: A Roadmap for Organizational Transformation.* https://reutersinstitute.politics.ox.ac.uk/risj-review/seminar-report-digital-transformation-organisation-challenges.

Myers, S. (2010, August 20). *Embedistan: Embedding in Iraq During the Invasion and the Drawdown.* https://atwar.blogs.nytimes.com/2010/08/20/embedistan-embedding-in-iraq-during-the-invasion-and-the-drawdown/.

Moeller, S. (1999). *Four Habits of International News Reporting.* http://frameworksinstitute.org/assets/files/PDF_GII/four_habits_of_news_reporting.pdf.

Owens-Ibie, N. (2016). Conflicting Communication in the Communication of Conflict: Chibok and the Narratives on Media Representation. In O. Esan (Ed.), *Taking Stock: Nigerian Media and National Challenges* (pp. 69–83). Toronto, Canada: Canada University Press.

Peterson, K. (2009). Revisiting Downs' Issue-Attention Cycle: International Terrorism and the US Public Opinion. *Journal of Strategic Security, 2*(4), 1–17.

Richstad, J., & Nnaemeka, T. (1980). Structured Relations and the News Flow in the Pacific. *Gazette, 26*(4), 235–258.

Rittel, H. W., & Webber, M. (1973). Dilemmas in General Theory of Planning. *Policy Sciences, 4,* 155–165.

Robinson, P. (2005). The CNN Effect Revisited. *Critical Studies in Media Communication, 22,* 344–349.

Robinson, P. (1999). The CNN Effect: Can the News Media Drive Foreign Policy. *Review of International Studies, 25,* 301–309.

Sambrook, R. (2010). *Are Foreign Correspondents Redundant?* http://reutersin-stitute.politics.ox.ac.uk/our-research/are-foreign-correspondents-redundant.

Seib, P. (2008). *The Al Jazeera Effect: How the Global Media Are Reshaping World Politics.* Washington: DC, Potomac Books Inc.

Selim, H. (2011). *The Coverage of Egypt's Revolution in the Egyptian, American and Israeli Newspapers.* http://scrippsmediaethics.blogspot.co.za/2014/10/pros-and-cons-of-embedded-journalism.html.

Shan, A. (2014, September 14). *Conflicts in Africa.* Global Issues. http://www.globalissues.org/issue/83/conflicts-in-africa.

Si, S. (2014). *The Expansion in International Broadcasting: The Growing Global Reach of China Central Television.* http://reutersinstitute.politics.ox.ac.uk/our-research/expansion-international-broadcasting.

Soderlund, W., Biggs, D., Hildebrandt, K., & Sidahmed, A. S. (2010). *Humanitarian Crises and Interventions: Reassessing the Impact of the Media.* Sterling, VA: Kumarian Press.

The Lancet. (2010, January 23). Growth of Aid and Decline of Humanitarianism, Vol. 375.

Tuosto, K. (2008). The "Grunt Truth" of Embedded Journalism: The New Media/ Military Relationship. *Stanford Journal of International Relations, X*(1), 1–21.

Van Belle, D. (2008, May 29–31). *Agenda Setting and Donor Responsiveness to Humanitarian Crisis and Development.* Harvard Kennedy School, Paper 2.2 the Role of the News Media in the Governance of Reform Agenda.

Watkins, A., & Wilber, K. (2015). *Wicked and Wise: How to Solve the Worlds' Toughest Problems.* Kent: Urbane.

Wilesmith, G. (2011). *Reporting Afghanistan and Iraq: Media, Military and Government and How They Influence Each Other.* https://reutersinstitute.politics.ox.ac.uk/our-research/reporting-afghanistan-and-iraq-media-mili-tary-and-governments-and-how-they-influence.

Further Reading

Fayoyin, A. (2015). *Analysing International News: Contexts, Processes and Practices.* Delaware: Springboard Communications.

Internews: Reporting on Humanitarian Crises: A Manual for Trainers and Journalists and an Introduction for Humanitarian Workers. https://www.internews.org/sites/default/files/resources/IN140220_HumanitarianReportingMANUAL_WEB.pdf.

Owen, J., & Heather, P. (2009). *International News Reporting: Frontlines and Deadlines.* Chichester, UK: Wiley-Blackwell.

Shaw, I. S. (2012). *Human Rights Journalism: Advances in Reporting Distant Humanitarian Interventions.* Basingstoke, UK: Palgrave Macmillan.

CHAPTER 10

Foreign Correspondents
and the Imagination of Africa

Muiru Ngugi

INTRODUCTION: THE IMAGE OF AFRICA

Africa has become synonymous with its myth. The *shuka*-clad, adult
African male resting on one leg like a stork silhouetted against a backdrop of acacia trees and the setting sun, the women delicately balanc-
ing pots on their heads, and playful urchins chattering in unintelligible
lingo while ogling at white visitors and begging for food: primitive, inca-
pable humanity. The expansive savannas are teeming with a game at the
apex of their annual migration, the beautiful beaches of Mombasa and
Zanzibar with their swaying palms, the tropical rain forests with monkeys
swinging under the near-opaque canopy, the big cats, and the silverback
gorilla: nature. The *Makonde* and *Ogun gun* masks, the images of the
Ashanti, Mangbetu and Swazi potentates, intricate wood and soap-stone
carvings, primitive divinations and juju and voodoo magic, female genital
mutilation, warrior dances, Swazi virgin certification, ancestor worship:
culture. Big Man rule, tribal clashes, genocide, guerrillas, private armies,
irredentism, human rights abuses, corruption: politics.

M. Ngugi (✉)
School of Journalism and Mass Communication,
University of Nairobi, Nairobi, Kenya

© The Author(s) 2019
E. K. Ngwainmbi (ed.), *Media in the Global Context*,
https://doi.org/10.1007/978-3-030-26450-5_10

Collectively, these images of the world's second-largest continent, however bizarre they may seem, are real, but they represent only an aspect of Africa. Western writers, among whom the foreign correspondent has loomed large, have popularized these choice images with the result that Africa has become the symbol of not just underdevelopment but also all that is primitive, backward, and uncivilized (Keim 1999). Only recently has Africa started to be portrayed as a place of hope and as a continent open for business (Pineau 2006).

This chapter examines how a group of influential professionals, namely Western media foreign correspondents, reported and explained Africa through their unique genre of literary and near-literary journalism in the early twentieth century. It is posited that the aggregate discourse of foreign correspondents constitutes a unique non-literary genre that is often rarely studied. Also provided are further examples of the foreign correspondent's coverage of Africa and how such coverage has evolved. The purpose here is not to recreate the Africa of the pre-contact past, the Africa that may have existed before its myriad descriptions began to be inscribed. No original, uncorrupted past can be retrieved and described since such description would invariably rely on prior descriptions and interpretations. It is argued, instead, that this genre of journalistic writing is what needs to be critiqued as it complicates and mythologizes the continent more than that it explains it.

Uses of Foreign News

Global audiences have always derived their knowledge of Africa partly, but significantly, from the output of foreign correspondents. These reporters are sent to far off locations by dominant media houses where they may stay for years reporting on local events. Others parachute into the continent whenever there is a crisis that needs to be reported, and they are airlifted out of location as soon the novelty effect of the event wanes in the domestic audience. These fire brigade-type journalists are the kind that covered Africa in the first half of the twentieth century until permanent foreign correspondents started being posted in Africa in 1955 (Segal 1976, p. 49). Over time, the efforts of these journalists have accumulated considerable descriptive debris that has obviated the view of what Africa was and is. Based solely on their journalistic output and irrespective of the duration of

their stay in Africa, these cadres of professionals have been described
as the "men and women who sit on the edge of history and bring
us the flow of words and images that shape our view of the world"
(Emery 1995, p. ix). Their central role in the education of their audiences on foreign affairs was aptly captured years ago by one American
foreign correspondent:

> These men and women are the eyes of America in the outside world! ...
> Many of them are celebrated; their "by-lines" add vastly to the signifi-
> cance of their dispatches. ...But, whoever they may be, famous or totally
> unknown, theirs are the minds through which the great and small events
> and personalities and movements of our generation have been filtered
> before reaching the American public. In line with the American tradition
> of impersonal reporting, they have tried to be utterly objective. Yet a little
> of the texture of their minds, a little color of their moods, has adhered to
> the events and personalities they have "covered" in these crowded years.
> Millions of their countrymen hold views on world affairs, on economic
> and political experiments abroad, shaped gradually but inexorably by the
> reports of these correspondents. (Lyons 1937, p. 4)

These correspondents interpret African events and culture, giving meaning to them, and conferring status to news actors, events, and trends
(Hawk 1992; Hagos 2000; Hess 1996; Hawk 2003). The image of
Africa is derived from many other sources, including television documentaries, Hollywood movies, and the scholarly products of Africanist
scholars. By and large, however, all these channels of explaining Africa
are either replete with the undercurrents of that mysterious Africa first
described long ago, or are built on it; the Africa of Henry Morton
Stanley, Teddy Roosevelt, Edgar R. Burroughs, and Ernest Hemingway.
The Africa represented in those texts is one that is jungle, plain, moun-
tain, hot, humid, expansive, secret, unfathomable, not to mention its
often presented population of primitive, naked, pitch-black people,
"humans framed like museum-pieces within picturesque dioramas"
of thatched huts, homesteads, cattle, drums, spears (Hickey and Wylie
1993). It is an Africa that rarely changes, in which Africans are caught
in a time warp of a certain admirable pristine primitiveness that is only
interrupted by an occasional Africanist "heretic" arguing the case of
Africa and critiquing this predominant view. The work of foreign correspondents is now assumed to be so powerful that some critics credit it

with the ability to influence not only foreign policy but also the delivery of humanitarian aid through what is called the "CNN effect" (Robinson 1999; Hoge 1997).

THE THEORETICAL CONTEXT

The analysis undertaken in this essay is rooted in the notion that journalism, including the work of foreign correspondents, is a form of "cultural production" (Bourdieu 1993) with considerable influence on the social construction of knowledge. Like all writings, the work of foreign correspondents, particularly the genre of non-fiction writing, attempts to construct, "on its blank space – the page – a text that has power over the exteriority from which it has first been isolated" (de Certeau 1984, p. 134). The effect of this writing, as a scriptural operation, is to produce, preserve and propagate certain notions or "truths" about the "Other" (Clifford 1988, p. 212). These "truths" are revived and further elaborated in subsequent texts, with each reproduction adding a layer of normalization so that they, in the long run, attain the status of the gospel—an unquestionable, sedimentation of bias that assumes the proportions of truth and fact. As has been stated: "The power to narrate, or to block other narratives from forming and emerging, is significant to culture and imperialism and constitutes one of the main connections between them" (Said 1993, p. xiii).

This essay takes the view that describing Africa, telling its story and attempting to foretell its future through journalistic analysis has the consequence, perhaps unintended, of canonizing certain perspectives and crowding out new alternative interpretations. In the case of Africa, this explaining and interpreting have in the past been dominated by Western foreign correspondents purveying their particular ways of seeing Africa to the near-captive market of their own hemisphere's audiences. Owing to globalization, the output of foreign correspondents also often constitutes a significant amount of what Africans themselves read.

The reportage of Africa by foreign journalists, taken together with the voluminous literature that purports to interpret or portray Africa by the West's collective cultural and scholarly output, has engendered an interdisciplinary response, including an African literary theory and criticism. This response is founded on the notion, so aptly captured by the *Cultural Charter for Africa* (1976), that cultural domination has led to the "depersonalization of the African peoples, falsified their history, systematically disparaged and combated African values." It is this misrepresentation of Africa that African writers have often railed against (wa Thiong'o 1972, 1986, 1993; Appiah 1988; Mudimbe 1988). It is also part of what engendered the great media debates in the 1970s and 1980s surrounding what was seen as "cultural imperialism" and imbalances in the flow of information from North to South (Gerbner et al. 1993).

FOREIGN CORRESPONDENTS AND THEIR HISTORY

In order to appreciate the origins of the foreign correspondents and the unique genre that their practice has produced, it is necessary to review the history of journalism and how foreign correspondents came into being. This history goes back a few centuries. Some accounts argue that the ancient Roman *"Acta Diurna"*—"daily acts," like the word "journal" derived from the French word for day, 'jour' (Smith 1854, 1874; Warre Cornish and Smith 1898; Gurgel 2018)—were the first newspapers published before 59 bce. The newspapers mostly recorded minutes of official business of the senators and other matters of public interest. However, until the nineteenth century, news was mainly local because of the limitations placed on newsgathering by primitive technologies of transportation and communication. Indeed even local news sometimes took days to reach outlying areas. When George Washington died at Mt. Vernon on December 14, 1799, a Saturday, it took two days before the *Alexandria Times*, only 30 miles away, reported it and it was not until January 7, three weeks later that the news was reported in Cincinnati (Desmond 1978, p. 83). It took a long time before communication could be genuinely liberated from transportation.

The foreign correspondent was the product of globalization. As nations interacted more and more, particularly during the age of exploration and subsequent colonization, it became imperative to receive foreign news. People needed to hear news about their kin and kith in the new lands or the motherland, and there was a widespread, unsatisfied curiosity about exotic places. To address this challenge, a solution was found in the exchange of newspapers between cities and countries, with news being reprinted from the paper that carried them by the recipient newspaper with little or no editing (Desmond 1978, p. 84). The urgency in the delivery of news became imperative. For instance, to ensure more prompt receipt of foreign newspapers, Boston's *Columbian Centinel* began the practice of sending reporters, using rowboats aboard approaching ships. Such reporters would subsequently gather all newspapers on the ship and interview passengers and crew. They would then rush back to write stories that would subsequently be promptly released to the public (Desmond 1978, p. 87). This process of delivering news was later improved when the carrier pigeons, which had been used with considerable success to deliver continental news across the English Channel in Europe, were introduced in the United States to deliver news from the ships to the mainland in what became known as the "pigeon express" (Desmond 1978, p. 90).

It was not until 1838 that the *New York Herald* became the first newspaper to engage foreign correspondents. James Gordon Bennett, a Scottish immigrant who was also the publisher of the *New York Herald*, attended the coronation of Queen Victoria in London and reported the ceremonies for his newspaper. Before leaving Europe, he engaged six "stringers" for his newspaper in London, Glasgow, Paris, Berlin, Brussels, and Rome (Desmond 1978). Upon his return to the United States, Bennett also arranged for stringers in Canada, Mexico, and the then recently formed Republic of Texas (Desmond 1978, p. 92). The foreign correspondent, thus, came into existence. In 1946, the *New York Tribune* sent Margaret Fuller to Europe as the first American woman foreign correspondent (Emery 1995, p. xi). These journalists were the product both of a new broader concept of news, including the application of the human-interest principle in news selection, and technological advancement (Desmond 1978, p. 169). By the time the US–Mexican (1846–1848) and the Crimean Wars (1853–1856) broke out, the species of journalist known as "foreign and war correspondent" was already well established.

Among the very first foreign correspondents to go to Africa was Frederick Hardman of the London *Times*, who accompanied a Spanish expedition to Morocco, and George Wingrove Cooke, one of *Times* editorial writers, who was sent to Algeria in 1856 (Desmond 1978, p. 184). *New York Tribune's* Bayard Taylor also visited Africa at around this time (Desmond 1978, p. 95). By 1860, the *Reuters News Agency* had an agent in South Africa (Desmond 1978, p. 185). James J. O'Kelly, formerly of the *New York Herald*, covered the attack of Khartoum by British forces for the *London Daily News* (Desmond 1978, p. 271). James Gordon Bennett Jr., who had taken over from his father at the *New York Herald*, sent Henry Morton Stanley to Africa, where in 1871, he discovered the missionary Dr. David Livingstone, who had been missing (Emery 1995, p. xi).

Before the First World War, however, foreign news was of interest largely to the "highbrow" and the "specialist" and was, for the common newspaper reader, something "far-off, eclectic, divorced from his everyday affairs" (Lyons 1937, p. 9). What changed all these was the Great War and the subsequent Great Depression that deepened public interest. Events abroad assumed serious domestic implications, particularly in America. The emergent experimentation with new political systems in other parts of the world is a case in point. There was fear that communist rule, which had been established in Russia, would threaten American democracy and that it had to be contained. The First World War had also proved that America could be implicated in wars in which it had no part in fomenting. Generally, the problems of the outside world—armaments, war, debts, tariffs, dictatorships, ethnic nationalism—were seen as having a bearing on America. Consequently, Americans needed a clear, unobstructed view of the world (Lyons 1937, p. 9). Later, America itself became embroiled in the internal affairs of foreign countries as it sought to contain communism during the Cold War and exported its cultural values in the post-communist era to fashion the world in its image. Increasingly, the foreign correspondent "wrapped the news with the American flag" (Lambe and Begleitter 2002). As the foreign correspondent evolved, the professional journalists operated under a confusing range of names, being variously called, as they were, foreign correspondents, war correspondents, diplomatic correspondents, foreign reporters, foreign news editors, and area correspondents.

THE UNIQUE GENRE OF JOURNALISM PRODUCED BY FOREIGN CORRESPONDENTS

Throughout the years, Western media houses have continued to send their representatives to Africa. Over time, these journalists have come to congregate in three main cities of Africa—Nairobi, Johannesburg, and Cairo. Of these cities, Nairobi has one of the most established corps of foreign correspondents. There is no definite term of duty for the journalist designated to stay in Africa. Some stay for many years and others are parachuted into news hot spots and are recalled back home as soon as the crisis is over.

Upon their return home, foreign correspondents usually author what amounts to a post-mortem of their stay in Africa. Full-length books are normally written by trained and experienced writers. Examples of such books are Henry Morton Stanley's *Through the Dark Continent*, John Gunther's *Inside Africa* (1953), Hemingway's *Green Hills of Africa* (1935), Hempstone's *Africa: Angry Young Giant?* (1961), David Lamb's *The Africans* (1982), Sanford Unger's *Africa* (1986), Blaine Harden's *Dispatches from a Fragile Continent* (1992), Keith Richburg's *Out of America* (1997), Michaela Wrong's *In the Footsteps of Mr. Kurtz*, to mention but a few of the most famous. These works appear to constitute a literary genre of their own, since a genre—if we take journalistic work to be broadly literary, where literary means written, learned and containing an information or knowledge value—designates "the types or categories which literary works are grouped according to form, technique, or, sometimes, subject matter" (Holman and Harmon 1986, p. 212). In order to isolate the kind of texts that this chapter is concerned with, it might serve to make a bold claim that books written by foreign correspondents and having Africa as the subject matter constitute a subject-based or area-based genre. This genre is characterized by a number of discernible qualities: most are written in the tradition of analytical journalism, severe but not scholarly, or in semi-fiction formats, while others still are written like personalized ethnographies or memoirs.

Whatever their preferred style, all the books in this genre aim at, and end up, explaining Africa. They tend to be replete with stereotypes about the continent, using specific recognizable rhetorical devices to present their version of the African story. Although the books may utilize literary devices such the composite style, flashbacks, even suspense, the books, whatever their main style, are primarily non-fiction, being based, as they are, on the realities of the African situation. This genre of non-fiction writing is, almost exclusively, a post-mortem of a single journalists' foray into Africa, and constitutes a brand of journalism that is more opinionated, prescriptive, and explanatory than either academic work or fictional writing on the continent. Strangely, this genre is rarely studied. Schools of journalism rarely teach anything more extended than the "longer article"; departments of literature do not consider these texts to be literary enough; and Political Science and History regard them as being less than definitive, using them only as supplementary texts.

Literary journalism has been called the "The third way to tell the story," with the other ways being traditional journalism and fiction writing (Connery 1990, pp. 3–20). Others think of it as a factual representation of the truth in narrative form (Warnock 1989). In a discussion on a late nineteenth century attempt by an American copy editor and editor to determine if an article written in a literary journalism style could qualify as news, Connery states that the article under discussion presented problems because it did not "seem to be fiction" as the "people in it were real and the events had just happened." At the same time, it was definitely not journalism because "it did not contain the type of facts that made conventional news and because in its presentation it tended to interpret events through its narrative point of view" (1990, p. 5). Journalism students are taught to respect facts, to separate facts from opinion, and to write in order to express, not to impress. Literary journalism stands this wisdom on its head, distinguishing itself, as it does, by its adoption of a particular literary quality while claiming fidelity to the truth as the journalist sees, and elects, to present it. It is journalism aided by substantial creative and stylistic resources that are not available to or allowed in, ordinary journalism. It interprets, weaving details and personal impressions not often considered appropriate for the standard journalistic article into a narrative form that is again often disregarded by conventional journalism. However, works of literary journalism are not limited to full books. A lot of it exists in the form of the longer magazine article (Long form), in features, essays, and commentaries.

This style and language of journalism in Africa can be traced back to the work of Henry Morton Stanley (January, 1841—May 10, 1904), Welsh journalist famous for his exploration of central Africa and his search for missionary and explorer David Livingstone. Stanley is credited with coining the phrase "Dark Continent" (Jarosz 1992). In constructing his textual image of Africa, Stanley was himself building on an existing perception of Africa (Hickey and Wylie 1993). Early explorers, English traders, and missionaries had curved out this perception, and had distorted the picture of Africa during centuries of contact (Curtin 1964). The resulting image of Africa was reinforced and riveted in the mind of the Western audience after later incursions into Africa by entrepreneurs, European administrators, and settlers in that order, who used not dissimilar language to describe the continent. However, Stanley is important because he was the first foreign correspondent to write a full-length book on his travels in Africa after his sojourn in the continent. He is, therefore, the founder of this peculiar Africanist genre of literary journalism of the kind we are concerned with here. He described Africans as "capable of great love and affection, and possessed of gratitude and other noble traits of human nature" and observed that "they can be made good, obedient servants" for Europeans whom he saw as superior because they were the products of a 4000-year civilization as opposed to the African who had "just emerged into the Iron Epoch." He went on to say that Africans "possess beyond doubt all the vices of a people still fixed deeply in barbarism" (1878, pp. 19–20). This highly readable but deceptive explanatory style can still be discerned in modern journalistic writing.

Another key figure in the formation of American notions of Africa was Theodore Roosevelt, an ex-President of the United States, who, although not a foreign correspondent and lacking a direct relationship with a newspaper like Stanley, nevertheless was immensely influential in providing the language for describing and explaining Africa. Like Stanley, Roosevelt occupies that nebulous category of the American writer who went to Africa to explore or experience an adventure and later wrote about that experience. The book that emerged out of his trip to Africa has some hallmarks of literary journalism, so much so that it was eventually serialized in the *National Geographic Magazine* (Tebbel 1975, pp. 2, 654), thus turning President Roosevelt effectively into a foreign correspondent. In it, he described the Africans as "ape-like savages, who dwell in the woods and prey on creatures not much wilder or lower than themselves" and by this supposed backwardness supported the move to convert the Kenyan highlands into land for white British settlers (1919, p. 22). In another example, Jerome Beatty published an article in the *American Magazine* titled: "The Great White Chief of the Congo," which was about Camp Putnam, previously established by Belgium entrepreneurs smack into the heart of Congo to attract tourists interested in seeing Africans in their entire savagery splendor. In the article, Beatty described the locals as "rare, raw, black, fascinating, and unusually friendly specimens of savagery" (1939, p. 20).

After that, writing about Africa started to appear more frequently in the mainstream press as foreign correspondents went to Africa, some to the writer for newspapers, others to retrace the routes followed by earlier travelers. Some early foreign correspondents who covered Africa in the early twentieth century were pioneers in their own right. Collectively, they provided an essential link in the evolutionary path between the Henry Morton Stanley type daredevil adventurer-travelers and the modern-day foreign correspondent. The evidence of this linkage is in the very image captivated by the contemporary foreign correspondent—the rugged looks, the multi-pocketed safari jackets, the cargo pants, and perhaps more importantly, the peculiar language, partly inspired by travel writing, now enhanced with stealthy shock phrases that betray a new arriviste style that hides contempt of the continent beneath a seemingly educated objectivity. The articles of these early foreign correspondents appeared in different newspapers such as the *New York Times* and such favorite magazines of the time as *Scribner's, National Geographic, North American Review,* and *Harpers Weekly.* The articles were invariably about wildlife, missionaries, and quaint African customs described exaggeratedly, as well the exotic exercise of power and the threat faced by the only existing genuine African rulers such as the Ethiopian monarch.

Foreign Correspondents and Africa: Toward a More Sensitive Writing

Foreign correspondents continue to report about the continent, employing catchy, sleight phrases and sweeping generalizations that gloss over African diversity and history, devalue its culture and identity and demeaned its people. However, this style of reporting has improved considerably over the years, abandoning overt racism in favor of not-so-obvious contempt. The metaphors, similes, and other literary devices that foreign correspondents used to employ in their coverage should be placed in the context of their generation as people who were influenced by the prevailing notions of Africa, but this should not be used to absolve them from accountability because it was within their powers to breach prevailing social beliefs and conventions. After all, they were already steeped in the liberal tradition of freedom of expression that presumably allowed unbiased reporting. Instead, they opted to join the bandwagon of prejudiced writers who generalized, stereotyped, and sensationalized. Writing is a conscious occupation, involving active inclusion and discrimination of words, revisions, and rewrites. The writers had as much license to break with the dominant thinking about the "Other" as much as they had to experiment with a new literary style. They appear to have taken the latter while making use of dominant stereotypes. As the expression goes, they did not think outside the box, and for that, they must be held accountable.

The discourse in the literary journalism on Africa perpetuates domination and iniquities of power. Africa and Africans seem frozen in a sort of pre-colonial time, prisoners of the old and the primordial, lowbrow culture, still evolving. The image of Africa has been warped beyond recognition. As a result, a place that does not exist has been created in the Western mind. This is not to say there is a desirable description of Africa somewhere that can be accessed to replace the Africa that has been popularized by Western journalists and other writers. Every narration, every construction, is itself a form of interpretation. With each new interpretation, the possibility for understanding what may have been the "real" Africa recedes further and further into a kind of oblivion of sedimentary ignorance.

No doubt, the genre of literary journalism will continue to exist about Africa, and this is beneficial in certain respects given that literary journalism products have an information value. Like all other forms of journalism, literary journalism pieces, despite their timelessness, have news and human-interest value. Besides, they become part of a vital historical record that we often dredge up to understand areas, subjects, and the present. For this reason, writers need to adhere more to the traditional ideals of journalism—objectivity, and fidelity to facts. We need less of the "texture of their mind" (Lyons 1937, p. 4) and more of the facts. Africa is not a special place requiring special care in reporting; there is no need to report it differently. It is just another ordinary place that does not deserve to be described using unusual words and metaphors, as those reserved for reporting the West would do just fine. The excuse that the story of Africa needs to be written using unique metaphors assumes that Western readers cannot comprehend non-Western events and cultures, and this is apparently an insult to the intelligence of this category of readers. A change in approaches to writing is therefore highly desirable.

QUESTIONS FOR DISCUSSION

1. Define the term "foreign correspondent" and give at least four examples of such professionals that you have encountered in this text as well as two examples of other foreign correspondents.
2. Explain how the reporting of Africa has evolved.
3. How does the content produced by foreign correspondents influence how Africa is imagined?
4. Discuss the unique genre of journalism that is produced by foreign correspondents

REFERENCES

Appiah, K. A. (1988). Out of Africa: Typologies of Nativism. *Yale Journal of Criticism, 2,* 153–178.

Beatty, J. (1939, July). The Great White Chief of the Congo. *American Magazine.*

Bourdieu, P. (1993). *The Field of Cultural Production.* New York, NY: Columbia University Press.

Clifford, J. (1988). *The Predicament of Culture.* Cambridge, MA: Harvard University Press.

Connery, T. B. (1990). A Third Way to Tell the Story: American Literary Journalism at the Turn of the Century. In N. Sims (Ed.), *Literary Journalism in the Twentieth Century.* New York, NY: Oxford University Press.

Curtin, P. D. (1964). *The Image of Africa: British Ideas and Action, 1780–1850.* Madison, WI: University of Wisconsin Press.

de Certeau, M. (1984). *The Practice of Everyday Life.* Berkeley, CA: University of California Press.

Desmond, R. W. (1978). *The Information Process: World News Reporting to the Twentieth Century.* Iowa City, IA: University of Iowa Press.

Emery, M. (1995). *On the Front Lines: Following America's Foreign Correspondents Across the Twentieth Century.* Washington, DC: American University Press.

Gerbner, G., Mowlana, H., & Nordenstreng, K. (1993). *The Global Media Debate: Its Rise, Fall, and Renewal.* Norwood, NJ: Ablex Publishing Corporation.

Gunther, J. (1953). *Inside Africa.* New York, NY: Harper & Brothers.

Gurgel, B. A. (2018, September 6). Rome's "Acta Diurna", the World's First Newspaper. In *Carmenta.* http://www.carmentablog.com/2018/09/06/romes-acta-diurna-the-worlds-first-newspaper/.

Harden, B. (1992). *Dispatches from a Fragile Continent.* New York, NY: HarperCollins.

Hagos, A. (2000). *Hardened Images: Western Media and the Marginalization of Africa.* Trenton, NJ: Africa World Press.

Hawk, B. G. (1992). *Africa's Media Image.* New York, NY: Praeger.

Hawk, B. G. (2003). African Politics and American Reporting. In G. Hyden, M. Leslie, & F. Ogundimu (Eds.), *Media and Democracy in Africa.* Piscataway, NJ: Transaction Publishers.

Hemingway, E. (1935). *Green Hills of Africa.* New York, NY: Scribner.

Hempstone, S. (1961). *Africa: Angry Young Giant.* New York, NY: Praeger.

Hess, S. (1996). *International News and Foreign Correspondents.* Washington, DC: Brookings Institution.

Hickey, D., & Wylie, K. C. (1993). *An Enchanting Darkness: The American Vision of Africa in the Twentieth Century*. East Lansing, MI: Michigan University Press.

Hoge, J. F. (1997). Foreign News: Who Gives a Damn? *Columbia Journalism Review*. [Online] http://archives.cjr.org/year/97/6/foreign.asp. Accessed December 2, 2006.

Holman, C. H., & Harmon, W. (1986). *A Handbook to Literature* (6th ed.). New York, NY: McMillan.

Jarosz, L. (1992). Constructing the Dark Continent: Metaphor as Geographic Representation of Africa. *Swedish Society for Anthropology and Geography*, 72b(2), 105–115.

Keim, C. A. (1999). *Mistaking Africa: Curiosities and Inventions of the American Mind*. Boulder, CO: Westview Press.

Lamb, D. (1982). *The Africans: Encounters from Sudan to the Cape*. New York, NY: Random House.

Lambe, J. L., & Begleiter, R. J. (2002). *Wrapping the News in the Flag: Use of Patriotic Symbols by the U.S. Local TV Stations After the Terrorist Attacks of September 11, 2001*. Paper presented at the BEA Convention April 2002. [Online] http://www.udel.edu/communication/COMM418/begleite/patrioticsymbols/symbolshome.htm.

Lyons, E. (1937). Introduction. In E. Lyons (Ed.), *We Cover the World: By Fifteen Foreign Correspondents*. New York, NY: Harcourt, Brace, and Company.

Mudimbe, V. (1988). *The Invention of Africa: Gnosis, Philosophy and the Order of Knowledge*. Bloomington, IN: Indiana University Press.

Pineau, C. (2006). *Africa: Open for Business* (A Documentary). Online. http://www.africaopenforbusiness.com/. Accessed April 11, 2013.

Richburg, K. (1997). *Out of America: A Black Man Confronts Africa*. New York, NY: Basic Books.

Robinson, P. (1999). The CNN Effect: Can the News Media Drive Foreign Policy? *Review of International Studies, 25*, 301–309.

Roosevelt, T. (1919). *African Game Trails: An Account of the African Wanderings of an American Hunter-Naturalist*. New York, NY: Charles Scribner's Sons.

Said, E. (1993). *Culture and Imperialism*. New York, NY: Vintage Books.

Segal, A. (1976). Africa and the United States Media. *Issue: Journal of Opinion*, 6(2/3), 49–56.

Smith, W. (1854). *A School Dictionary of Greek and Roman Antiquities Abridged from the Larger Dictionary*. New York: Harper & Brothers.

Smith, W. (1874). *A Dictionary: Greek and Roman Antiquities*. London: John Mcrray.

Stanley, M.-H. (1878). *Through the Dark Continent* (2 Vols.). London, UK: Sampson, Low, Marston, Searle, and Rivington.

Tebbel, J. (1975). *A History of Book Publishing in the United States* (3 Vols., 2:654). New York, NY: R.R. Bowker.

"Tracking Hemingway" Flashbacks. *Atlantic Monthly*, July 21, 1999.

Unger, S. J. (1986). *Africa*. New York, NY: Simon & Schuster.

wa Thiong'o, N. (1972). *Homecoming: Essays on African and Caribbean Literature, Culture and Politics*. Nairobi, Kenya: Heinemann.

wa Thiong'o, N. (1981). *Writers in Politics*. Nairobi, Kenya: Heinemann.

wa Thiong'o, N. (1986). *Decolonizing the Mind: The Politics of Language in African Literature*. London, UK: James Currey.

wa Thiong'o, N. (1993). *Moving the Center*. Nairobi, Kenya: EAPH.

Warnock, J. (1989). *Representing Reality: Readings in Literary Nonfiction*. New York, NY: St. Martin's Press.

Warre Cornish, F., & Smith, W. (1898). *A Concise Dictionary of Greek and Roman Antiquities based on William Smith's larger dictionary, and incorporating the results of modern research*. London: Murray.

Further Reading

Desmond, R. W. (1978). *The Information Process: World News Reporting to the Twentieth Century*. Iowa City, IA: University of Iowa Press.

Emery, M. (1995). *On the Front Lines: Following America's Foreign Correspondents Across the Twentieth Century*. Washington, DC: American University Press.

Gerbner, G., Mowlana, H., & Nordenstreng, K. (1993). *The Global Media Debate: Its Rise, Fall, and Renewal*. Norwood, NJ: Ablex Publishing Corporation.

Hagos, A. (2000). *Hardened Images: Western Media and the Marginalization of Africa*. Trenton, NJ: Africa World Press.

Harden, B. (1992). *Dispatches from a Fragile Continent*. New York, NY: HarperCollins Publishers.

Hawk, B. G. (2003). African Politics and American Reporting. In G. Hyden, M. Leslie, & F. Ogundimu (Eds.), *Media and Democracy in Africa*. Piscataway, NJ: Transaction Publishers.

CHAPTER 11

One Culture, Different Perceptions: The Role of Politics in the Work of Journalists in Two Arab Countries

Mahmoud M. Galander

PRESS AND POLITICS: PERCEPTIONS OF JOURNALISTS

The notion of media and politics embraces a tripartite relationship that involves the journalists, the public, and the government. Though the journalists are the significant actors in this relationship, studies on media and politics have focused more on studying the attitude of governments toward media in conjunction with the dominant political system, or, on the other hand, studying the impact of the media on political choices of the audiences (Norris 2010; Christians et al. 2009). The attitude of journalists toward the socio-political system has always been treated as a derivative of government stances and, hence, few studies addressed the opinions of the press corps on their activities and behaviors. Early studies on journalist perceptions were more confined to areas of foreign policy (Cohen 1963), and beliefs and attitudes on their roles toward the public (Willis 2010). Hanitzsch et al. (2017) elucidated, in his introduction to the major global study of journalist's perceptions, the earlier studies on

M. M. Galander (✉)
Department of Mass Communication, Qatar University, Doha, Qatar

© The Author(s) 2019
E. K. Ngwainmbi (ed.), *Media in the Global Context*,
https://doi.org/10.1007/978-3-030-26450-5_11

journalism perceptions and posited that these studies could be criticized for "methodological inconsistencies which made the interpretation of results more difficult" (Hanitzsch et al. 2017).

Attitudes and perceptions of journalists are, no doubt, shaped by the values, beliefs, and norms of society. With the diverse landscape of human societies, theorizing about a global journalist perception or attitude is almost impossible. Studies that aim at establishing a framework for understanding attitudes and perceptions of journalists are however more plausible; the "World Journalism Study" is an academic effort of that sort. With currently the number of countries involved in the project reaching 66 and the methodological approaches of the research becoming less "west-centric," the study provides an agreeable platform for the comparison of regions and cultural entities of the world. In the words of Professor Thomas Hanitzsch (2013, p. 11) the leading figure in the World of Journalism Study:

> Today, the Worlds of Journalism Study is an intellectual community, a platform for the exchange of data, a tool for the sharing of knowledge and experience, and a vehicle to drive comparative research in the field. By now, the project has become the largest collaborative endeavor in the field, and a model for many other, similar studies. For the future, we hope that the study may become institutionalized even more, to the extent that it may conduct similar surveys over time for a longitudinal assessment of the development of journalism cultures.

Earlier works on studies on perceptions of journalists include a famous study by David Weaver (1989) and another by him and several collaborators (Willnat et al. 2013). His first study, "Global Journalists: another followed new People around the World (1989): "Journalist Around the World: Commonalities and Differences" (1998) which provided the first global study of journalists that identified the common grounds that bind journalists, and highlighted the differences in their beliefs and attitudes. The studies systematically surveyed journalists from countries from all continents and focused on aspects of demographics, education, socialization, professionalization, and working conditions of journalists in these countries. The two works, however, suffered from some methodological and conceptual inconsistencies that rendered the generalization of journalist's perceptions around the world uncertain (Hanitzsch 2013).

The third study by Weaver and Willnat (2012) included follow-up studies on perceptions of global journalists and concluded that a need for a comparative perspective that identifies common grounds for such comparison is needed. Today, studies of such interest abound, noteworthy for this chapter are studies that focus on Asia, Africa and the Muslim and Arab worlds (Hanitzsch 2013; Pintack 2011, 2013; Amin 2002).

In his study on media and governance around the world, Laurence Pintack (2008), investigated the perceptions of Arab journalists from 14 countries about their roles, and found that they saw themselves as change agents, and believed that the most urgent task facing governments in their region is political reform; thus indicating that they could spearhead such reform. The respondents also believed that an increased intrusion of governments in the work of the press impeded the useful role of the press. In the words of Pintack in his conclusion (2011, p. 348):

> Arab media are in the midst of a revolution. So too is the relationship between journalists and governments. .... It is for the Arabs themselves, to decide the precise model of media-government relations that will emerge.

An Arab sociologist and professor of journalism, Hussein Amin (2002), sounds less skeptical as he discusses the media–government relationship in the Arab world. He reports governments in the region as being adamant in curbing press freedom and incessantly curtailing the free coverage of politics in the Arab media. Amin believes that though global developments have driven toward more liberalization of the press worldwide, Arab journalists still face harsh laws and ill-treatment from their governments. He explains (Amin 2002, p. 129):

> Arab authorities will not move quickly to offer freedom of expression to journalists. It is not an easy thing, after all, to let go of power and trust that the new freedoms will not be abused. Therefore, Arab journalists and people must fight for it. The public is becoming increasingly critical of media content and more vocal about its desire for the media to respond effectively to the need for reliable information and high quality, meaningful entertainment. Professional Arab journalists cannot work in a censorial environment forever.

PRESS AND POLITICS: JOURNALISM SYSTEMS AROUND THE WORLD

Recognizing the role of government in media operations is essential for understanding the attitude and perception of journalists toward their profession. Given the nature of Middle East politics, no study of journalists' perceptions can claim to be thorough if it overlooks the impact of the governments of the region on the attitude and behavior of the press corps.

Several developments in the last quarter of the twentieth century influenced international politics and affected the practice of journalism around the world. Significant among the development is the spread of liberalism and the prominence of globalization. As a result, the typology of the "four theories of the press" (Seibert et al. 1971), was no more suitable to explain the dynamics of the media-government relationship around the world, even with the later theoretical explanations that accommodated for the diverse worldwide socio-political and cultural changes (Hachten 2016; Rugh 2004). A recent and more relevant study of world media systems is that of Hallin and Mancini (2004). Titled "Changing Media Systems: Three models of media and Politics" (2004), the study focused on media systems of western societies and provided a comprehensive system that responds to the changing realities of the twenty-first century. To provide a better explanation of the dynamics of the media–government relationship, Hallin and Mancini depict four dimensions related to the media, and five related to the political system. The media system elements refer to (1) the media structure: circulation, readership, objectivity and other factors affecting the credibility of the press; (2) media affiliation to political organizations; (3) professionalism in the media: abidance by ethics of journalism, remaining a platform of opinion for the public; and (4) the extent to which the state interferes in the activities of the media through licensing, censorship, gatekeeping, and other control-based activities.

The political dimension in Hallin and Mancini's model depicts the following five elements:

1. The type of political system, and the degree of democratization of the state;

2. The dominant type of democracy, as to whether it is a "majoritarian or consensus democracy" (Hallin and Mancini 2004, p. 50).
3. The distinction between "individualism versus corporatism," in public dealing with the government. This dimension focuses on whether people deal with governments mainly as separate individuals (the United States) or as organized groups or political parties (UK).
4. The degree of liberalization in the social and economic aspects of society. Whether the state interferes in the well-being of people, or whether that is left to the market forces.
5. The "rational-legal" dimension, which explains the degree of political legitimacy that the government enjoys. Rational would reflect institutions that are valued as legitimate, as opposed to a system whose institutional legitimacy is challenged and opposed.

Though Hallin and Mancini's model relates to the Euro-American sphere, the classification and dimensions identified are usable for the explanation of the intricacies of media systems in non-western societies, like the ones proposed in this chapter. As several non-western countries are experiencing political transformations similar to those through which western countries have passed, some features of liberal and democratic societies of the West have influenced the essence of the relationship between the media and the government. As a result, media system analysis witnessed significant adjustments by scholars, like Arnold de Beer and John Merrill, who identified a growing trend of departure, by increasing non-western countries, from the "world order" of media systems, to a new system they called the "critical and non-western press system" (Merrill 2008). The system, according to the writers, is prevalent in Latin America, Africa, the independent states of Eastern Europe as well as some Asian countries. The distinct features of the critical non-western system include press ownership types, media regulations and journalists' practices, which are analyzed and explained within the dominant political philosophy.

Acknowledging the fallacy of identifying a worldwide "media system" that explains the relationship between media, and society, Christians et al. (2009) offered a media type model, and a normative role model, to

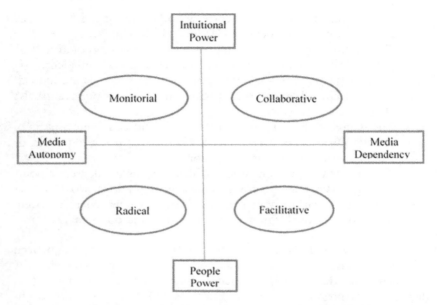

Fig. 11.1 Normative model for understanding media dynamics (*Source* Christians, C., et al. [2009]. *Normative Theories of the Media: Journalism in Democratic Societies*)

explain the media–society relationship. Though the two models offer a healthy perspective for understanding the dynamics of the relationship, we focus on the normative role model most suitable for understanding the difference and similarities in the responses of the journalists in both Qatar and Sudan (see Fig. 11.1).

The normative model (Fig. 11.1) identifies the major elements in a four-pane format that represents an interlinked relationship between the horizontal and the vertical extremes. The vertical refers to the role of media as either a representative of institutional power or a reflection of peoples' power. Media owned by the government, or supported by the government, are more apt to act as agents of the government, whereas media free of official pressures would act as representatives of public power. Media autonomy and dependency—the horizontal dimension—is a reflection of the degree to which the media can publish news and information without official restrictions. Under these four dimensions, media may play a monitorial, a facilitative, a fundamental role or a collaborative role (Christians et al. 2009).

A monitorial role involves media being objective, but under the current environment of information control of governmental institutions, the role of the media as watchdogs is somewhat constrained and limited. A facilitative role refers to a situation in which the media are closer to the people and hence embrace public positions on issues. A fundamental role is a reference to the media being agents of opposition to the socio-political status quo. A collaborative role is a reflection of the media being in the service of governments.

The above analysis of a media system that departs from the "four press theories," is more suitable to explain the attitude and behavior of journalists whose culture, and the sociopolitical context, does not mirror that of the "four theories." Explanations of the perceptions of journalists in such places as Sudan and Qatar, can, therefore, be sounder if based on non-conventional approaches like that of Nordestreng.

JOURNALISM AND JOURNALISTS IN SUDAN AND QATAR

Against the background of the above discussion, the current study looks at the perceptions of the journalists of two countries belonging to the Arab World. Though both countries are predominantly Muslim and Arab, their history and political systems are different, thus begging the question whether the journalists are strongly influenced by a similar socio-cultural orientation that would provide similar responses, or whether the different political path of the two will result in different perceptions about the role and place of the press. The following paragraphs provide a brief history of the development of the media in the two countries.

The history of Sudan's journalism dates back to the early years of the twentieth century (1903) when a non-Sudanese under the scrutiny of the British Administration (Salih 1971) published "Al–Sudan." A few years later, several newspapers began to sprout and, by the 1920s, as nationalist movement swept the country, several Sudanese established newspapers and used the press as political platforms for the call for independence. The colonial power responded to these developments by introducing several restrictions to curb the nationalistic enthusiasm by licensing the press, practicing censorship and denying government employees the right to write in the daily press (Abdel Malik 1980).

By independence in 1956, the independent and partisan press mushroomed, and a free press system was operant for a brief period, until a coup in 1958, brought the first military rule which clamped down on the free press. In 1964, a popular revolution restored liberal democracy, and reinstated the free press for only four years, after which another coup brought a military regime. The second military nationalized the press and replaced 40 independent newspapers with two daily government papers. Under this government, a press council was established to guide media operations in the country. In 1985, another popular revolution toppled the military government and brought back a democratic regime that restored press freedom, and lifted restrictions to private ownership of the press. This sudden return of the liberal press led to an unprecedented rise in the number of the independent press and created a situation that bordered journalistic chaos, with increased violations of basic ethics of journalism. Such conditions, some sources believe, helped the next military coup rationalize the takeover by citing unverified corruption and crime stories in the press (Galander 2000).

The oscillation of Sudan between military and democratic governments resulted in disparities in the press systems operant in the country (Galander 2000). In almost all of the regimes, some form of press restrictions were available. Even under the most liberal ones, press licensing existed, and in most of them, press laws were operant, but with varying degrees of application. Government ownership of the press began when the first military government published its newspaper but allowed the private press to operate. The second military nationalized all the private press and published two dailies owned by the single political party. The third military began with a similar scheme of publishing two papers, then allowed the independent press to publish but surrounded it with a barrage of press laws (1994/1996/1999/2004) (Galander 2009). These laws provided several patterns of curbing the free expression of opinion including censorship, closing down papers, confiscation of printed issues and jailing of journalists.

The Qatari press history is rather placid. The earliest publication, the *Gazette*, appeared in 1961 and was dedicated to publishing the Emiri Decrees and other laws of the land (Galander 2016). Daily newspapers did not start until 1972 when *Al-Arab* daily was published; *Al-Raya* started publishing in 1979, *Al-Sharq* in 1987 and *Al-Watan* in 1995. *Gulf Times* was published as the first English newspaper in 1978, and then two more English papers, *Peninsula* (1996) and *Qatar Tribune*

(2006), followed. Radio services were established in 1968 with Arabic, then English and Urdu Services. The TV began a black and white transmission in 1970 but shifted to color in 1974. Satellite broadcast began in 1998.

Several unique features of Qatar media are noteworthy. The country has, since 1996, abandoned the ministry of information (a staple feature of almost all developing countries), and established instead, Qatar Media Corporation (QMC), which deals with the proper operations of the broadcast media. As private companies own newspapers, only the 1979 press law governs the operations of the daily press. Qatar is one of few countries in the region that have abandoned both press censorship, and government funding of the daily press.

Since 1979, a single press law has governed the press in Qatar. The law focuses more on ownership and other administrative issues of the press as private companies; with few punitive measures stipulated against the publication of potentially harmful material. In Qatar, as in most Gulf Countries, the media abide by the social and cultural norms that make loyalty to the royal rulers a social obligation. A remarkable feature of the press in Qatar is that few Qataris choose the journalism career. Currently, almost all newspapers are staffed with non-Qataris, while the Qataris hold only the posts of editors in chief and managing editors. This situation can only be understood when one takes into consideration the fact that journalism in Qatar, as both a profession and an education, is very young, and have always been populated by expatriates residing in the country.

Aljazeera remains the single most crucial feature of Qatar media landscape (Seib 2008). Established in 1996, it is considered the most significant Arab news network that has caught the attention of the world for unusually becoming the voice of the "south to the north," and for not being the official government voice of the country it broadcasts from. Today, Aljazeera has developed into a network comparable to the most significant media corporations of the world; it broadcasts in more than a language and has offices and correspondents around the world that it is seen as a reliable source of information and news about the Middle East (Seib 2008).

Comparing Sudan and Qatar reveals sharp differences in the development of the profession of journalism in the two countries. Whereas the press in Sudan began as a platform for the struggle against colonial powers in the early 1920s, the press in Qatar was established only after it became an independent Emirate in the 1970s. In Sudan, the press was almost entirely populated by Sudanese journalists and writers, whereas in Qatar it remained a profession favored by few Qataris (Galander 2016). In Sudan, political instability has resulted in different forms of government-media relationships that oscillated from an entirely free press to a nationalized press under strict government control. In Qatar, the stability of the government has resulted in a somewhat stable form of a press system, which led to favorable developments like the abolition of official censorship. In Sudan, the press has been subjected, since independence, to seven press laws, and received a myriad of penalties that ranged from direct censorship to shutting down of papers and revocation of licenses. In Qatar, a single press law has rarely been used against the press or the journalists in the country.

THE STUDY

The brief historical comparison of the press in Sudan and Qatar is an essential framework for this study which aims to provide a unique perspective of the perceptions of media practitioners in two sub-cultures of the Arab world. Using a questionnaire that gauged the perceptions of the journalists in the two countries, the study investigated the impact of political and institutional factors on the beliefs and attitudes of journalists. A comparison of the attitudes and perceptions of journalists from the two countries identified the distinctions and departures.

Telephone and face-to-face interviews were conducted in 2015 with a purposive sample of working journalists drawn from news organizations in both Qatar and Sudan. With due awareness of the cultural differences involved, the research design followed closely the design implemented by the global study of the "World of Journalism" (WSJ). The core questionnaire of the JWS was translated into Arabic and validated against another Arabic version of translation, which involved Egypt.

FINDINGS

As the aim of this chapter is to gauge perceptions and attitudes of journalists in Sudan and Qatar about specific aspects of their profession, the focus centered on the data that reveal the differences between the two groups in their perceptions and attitudes. The following paragraphs address the questionnaire items pertinent to this chapter. However, other data related to Qatar or Sudan may be found in the World of Journalism Study website: http://www.worldsofjournalism.org/data/data-and-key-tables-2012-2016/.

Roles of Journalists

In the original study, the respondents were asked to rate—on a Likert scale—21 roles they believe to be fundamental to their profession. Of these, the chapter reports only the following three: (1) playing the watchdog, (2) setting the political agenda, and (3) influencing public opinion, as they are the most relevant to the practice of journalism in the Muslim and Arab region. The following paragraphs reveal the likely impact of the politico-sociocultural environment on the perceptions of the journalists from the two countries.

Media as Watchdogs

Respondents from the two countries showed different perceptions about this function. Whereas almost 84% of the Sudanese reported the function as extremely important, only around 30% of the journalists in Qatar reported the same level of importance.

Setting the Political Agenda Role

When asked about the extent to which they perceive their role as agenda setters, the journalists in both countries reported a low level of belief in this role. Though journalists generally believe themselves to be politically useful, both Journalists in Sudan and Qatar reported, respectively, 53.5 and 36.4%.

Influencing Public Opinion

Influencing public opinion received high percentage from journalists in both Sudan and Qatar. In the two countries, the levels of "important" and "extremely important" received 91% from Journalists in Sudan and 57.9% from those in Qatar.

Ethics of Reporting Practices

Journalists devise different means of obtaining information from sources. In some cases, they may resort to practices that—in some cultures—are ethically inappropriate. When queried on their position on some controversial means of obtaining information, the respondents reported four of these practices as explained in the following paragraphs.

Paying Money for Information
The journalists of the two countries differed on this issue. 59% of the Sudanese respondents reported, "not approve," whereas 90.6% of the Journalists in Qatar confirmed disapproval. Discrepancies in the responses are explained in the following discussion part.

Using Hidden Microphones and Cameras
The respondents in both countries saw using hidden microphones as the most unacceptable aspect of journalist behavior. 69% of the respondents in Sudan did not approve under any circumstances, whereas almost 91% of Qatar journalists reported disapproval.

Publishing Stories with Unverified Content
Publishing unverified contents were not approved or justified under any circumstances by the journalists in the two countries, with both reporting a high level of disapproval (95% for Sudan; 94% for Qatar).

Accepting Money from Information Sources
This item received the highest disapproval from both groups: 96% from journalists in Sudan journalists and 93% from those in Qatar.

Institutional Pressures on Journalism

The respondents were asked to identify the pressures they consider of significant influence on their practice in the two countries. Although in the original survey the respondents were asked to rate 14 types, this study used three that it saw as of high impact on journalism practice in the region. These are media laws, official censorship and the military and police intervention. The following paragraphs report the responses of the journalists.

Media Laws and Regulations
The impact of media laws and regulations on the activities of the journalists was reported as "very influential" and "extremely influential" by

74% respondents in Sudan. The same levels were reported by 50% of the journalists in Qatar.

Censorship
The influence of official censorship on journalists' activities was considered as "very influential" and "extremely influential" by almost 70% of the respondents in Sudan; whereas, in Qatar, the two levels were reported by only 30% journalists.

The Military, Police and State Security
The impact of the military and police in journalistic activities in the region is a common phenomenon in the non-western hemisphere. Though only respondents from Sudan were reported in the study, we chose to report their responses, as we saw it most central to journalistic activities in the area. 73% of the Sudanese reported, "extremely influential" and "influential" levels of army, police, and security intervention in their practices. Reasons for the probable absence of responses of journalists in Qatar will be explained in the discussion section that follows.

DISCUSSION

Before discussing the results of the study, a critical remark must be made. As described in the discussion of the press in Qatar, the overwhelming majority of the journalists working in Qatar are expatriate Arabs and or Asians. Though Qataris occupy the leading managerial positions, few of them work as ordinary people in media organizations. This fact has impacted the current study in the fact that the responses of journalists do not reflect the opinions of "Qatari journalists," but rather of the "journalists in Qatar". This distinction is most important when one is reminded that expatriate journalists are subject to the same regulations that govern expatriate employees and workers in the country. It must also be reminded that the majority of the journalist working in Qatar are Arabs and Muslims, thus making the impact of socio-cultural features valid.

Another critical distinction between Sudan and Qatar is the (comparatively) long history of the press in Sudan, relative to that of Qatar. As described earlier, the press in Sudan has remained a significant element of political activism in the country, even before independence in the 1950s. As such, the role and place of the press in politics may explain some of the differences in the perceptions of the press corps in the two countries.

Several of the responses of the journalists in both countries can be explained within the framework of the model developed by Nordenstreng, as well as within the context of the media and political system dimensions provided by Hallin and Mancini. For example, responses of the journalists in Qatar mostly fall within the collaborative and facilitative roles described by Nordenstreng, whereas some responses of Sudan's journalists fit best the description of the monitorial role. Similarly, Hallin and Mancini's depiction of the political dimension fits best to explain the perceptions of the journalists about the type of relationship between the media and the government in both countries.

A general finding of this study is that, though the two countries belong to the Muslim-Arab context, national politics still exert considerable pressures on the journalists, and shape their perceptions and attitudes. Taking the relatively long history of journalism in Sudan, and the role the press played during the struggle for independence, a stark difference between role perceptions of the two groups is undeniable. When inquired about their attitude toward their role as watchdogs (Table 11.1), 84% of the Sudanese reported their agreement that their role is to be monitors and watchdogs, whereas only 30% of the journalists in Qatar reported the role. The discrepancy in the belief about their watchdog role, which is commonly considered an essential role of journalists everywhere, can only be explained by the fact that in Qatar, journalists as expatriates consider the watchdog function rather inconsequential in a "loyalist press" type, as defined by Rugh (2004). As to their role of influencing public opinion (Table 11.3), 75% of the Sudan journalists confirm that role, whereas 58% of Qatar's journalists see themselves as influencers of public opinion. As agenda setters (Table 11.2),

Table 11.1 Perception of journalists as watchdogs

	N	Extremely important + important (%)	M	SD
Qatar	360	29.7	2.58	1.35
Sudan	270	83.7	4.39	0.97

Table 11.2 Perception of journalists as agenda setters

	N	Extremely important+important (%)	M	SD
Qatar	352	36.4	2.93	1.37
Sudan	271	53.5	3.58	1.41

Table 11.3 Perception of journalists as public opinion influencers

	N	Extremely important+important (%)	M	SD
Qatar	375	57.9	3.66	1.24
Sudan	269	91.4	4.64	0.72

Table 11.4 Attitude toward paying money for information

	N	Always (%)	Occasionally (%)	Not approve (%)
Qatar	339	3.8	5.6	90.6
Sudan	275	13.1	27.3	59.6

journalists in the two countries did not express a certain belief in such a role, though the Sudanese showed a slight increase (53.5%) compared to the 36.4% of those of Qatar. Such decline in confidence goes against the shared conviction of journalists in liberal political systems, thus making valid the assumption that both groups do not see themselves enjoying a liberal environment that would allow them to be setters of the political agenda of the public. It must be noted here that respondents showed a different attitude when reporting their influence on public opinion, as compared to the agenda-setting role. While they reported higher confidence their impact on public opinion, they reported lower confidence in their role as agenda setters. This can be explained within the cultural context of the Arab/Muslim society, where leaders are socially and politically the unquestionable vanguards of society on whose hands the fate of society is put. Thus a facilitative press role, as suggested by Nordenstreng, can be applied to the role of media in such regions of the world.

There was a slight difference between the two groups on ethical issues that relate to the practice. A clear difference between the two was in their belief whether specific practices were accepted or not. Whereas 59.6% of

Table 11.5   Attitude toward using hidden mics and cameras

	N	Always (%)	Occasionally (%)	Not approve (%)
Qatar	358	2.0	7.0	91.1
Sudan	275	11.6	19.6	68.7

the journalists in Sudan view paying money for information from sources as somewhat acceptable, 90.6 of the journalists in Qatar do not condone such a practice (Table 11.4). On the other hand, when asked about using hidden microphones, 68% of the Sudanese said they would not do that, whereas 91% of the journalists in Qatar expressed disapproval of the practice (Table 11.5). This difference in attitude may be explained by the more widespread practice of journalism in Sudan, where the practitioners have come to believe that, in pursuit of truth, they may occasionally resort to unconventional methods. Taking the Nordenstreng model, Sudanese journalists' belief in a monitorial role would permit the use of such unconventional methods of information collection.

The impact of culture on the perception of the journalists in the two countries is evident when one considers their responses to the questions related to their techniques of gathering news and information, what the study calls "reporting practices." It is evident that the issues of ethics in the practices of journalists were conceptualized within the religion and culture that binds both groups. In both Sudan and Qatar, journalists confirmed they would not publish unverified information (95 and 94%, respectively) (Table 11.6), and they will not accept money to publish information (96 and 97%, respectively) (Table 11.7). Such position can easily be explained from the standpoint of Islam, as the first would amount to publishing lies, whereas the latter is equivalent to accepting a bribe, two vices that the Islam does not condone.

On the issue of pressures of governments on journalistic practices, 75% of the journalists in Sudan, and 43% of journalists in Qatar believe that media laws exert negative pressures on journalism (Table 11.8). The Sudanese are more aware of the impact of media laws as they have experienced, on several occasions, the governments' use of laws to punish newspapers and journalists. As to Qatar, a single media law, which was promulgated in 1979, is rarely used against the media or the journalists.

Table 11.6   Attitude toward publishing unverified information

	N	Always (%)	Occasionally (%)	No approve (%)
Qatar	351	3.0	3.0	94.1
Sudan	275	2.2	2.9	94.9

Table 11.7   Attitude toward accepting money to publish information

	N	Always (%)	Occasionally (%)	Not approve (%)
Qatar	351	0.9%	2.0	97.2
Sudan	275	1.5%	2.2	96.4

Table 11.8   Perception of the impact of media laws

	N	Extremely influential + influential (%)	M	SD
Qatar	357	42.9	3.08	1.39
Sudan	267	74.5	3.97	1.35

Table 11.9   Perception about impact of censorship

	N	Extremely influential + influential (%)	M	SD
Qatar	331	29.6	2.62	1.40
Sudan	271	69.7	3.88	1.51

Compared to those of Sudan, Qatar media law has less punitive measures against the press or the journalists and, even those are rarely applied.

On the issue of censorship, almost 70% of the Sudanese journalists believe that direct censorship is very influential in deterring their journalistic duties, whereas slightly less than 30% of the practicing journalists in Qatar feel such an impact (Table 11.9). It must be reminded that the authorities in Qatar have officially abandoned direct censorship since 1995, as part of new arrangements that seek to provide a better environment for media practice in the country. In contrast, the Sudanese authorities occasionally use direct censorship under the excuse of insurgency

Table 11.10   Perception about impact of military, police and security

Security	N	Extremely influential + influential (%)	M	SD
Qatar		25	2.3	1.24
Sudan		72.7	3.87	0.87

activities in western and eastern districts, which necessitate scrutiny of press content to safeguard against undesirable information leaks.

Though it was not reported in the study, it must be emphasized here that "self-censorship" is the most dominant style of media control in socially disciplined societies like those of the Arab and Muslim world. As discussed in several sources (Galander 2015; Rugh 2004), social obligations lead to uniformity of opinion and require abstention from expressing different positions. Thus, editors and writers tend to either water down, or kill, positions or opinions that do not conform to those of leaders. Thus, taking Nordenstreng model, one may conclude that Qatar journalists do not believe they are heavily censored because they practice self-censorship as part of their facilitative role.

In many non-western countries, the role of police and the military in media operations is actively present. When the perception of the respondents in the two countries about the impact of police and the military in press activity was investigated, the respondents reported a level equal to what journalists in each country reported about censorship (73% Sudan, 25% Qatar) (Table 11.10). A plausible interpretation of the similar responses is that whereas censorship—in the case of Sudan—is a result of military and or police actions relating to the publication of unauthorized information, in Qatar, almost no military or police intervention is needed as self-censorship renders it unnecessary.

CONCLUSION

The impact of politics on the role and place of the press in the two Muslim Arab countries is confirmed, despite the existence of "different worlds of journalism." Though cultures may color the practices and affect the perceptions of the practicing journalists, the central element that decides the role and place of the press in the political orientation of the country. This is not to deny the fact that socio-cultural realities affect the practices, and affects the relationship between the press and society. In the case of Qatar and Sudan, though they both have similar cultural coloration, the difference in the perception of journalists rests in the political structure that is present in the two countries, as well as the historical evolution of the political system. Such structure and historical developments have not only influenced the practice of journalism, but also the perceptions and beliefs of the journalism practitioners in the two countries.

QUESTIONS FOR DISCUSSION

1. How should a journalist function in an environment where there is religious persecution?
2. Under which circumstances should the press serve as a watchdog?
3. Should the press run its operations based on the political orientation of the country from it received its credentials or it should follow the internationally known ethics of journalism? Support your arguments with published examples in Europe, the US, Africa, Middle East, Asia, or your country.
4. If you were a journalist would rather work in your country, Sudan, the Emirates, Germany, US or anywhere else in the world? Give concrete reasons.

WORKS CITED

Abdel Malik, M. (1980). *Press and Politics in Sudan*. Khartoum: University of Khartoum Press.
Amin, H. (2002). *Freedom as a Value in Arab Media: Perceptions and Attitudes among Journalists* (pp. 125–135). Published online: 10 November 2010. Accessed: http://dx.doi.org/10.1080/10584600252907407.
Christians, C., Glasser, T., McQuail, D., Nordenstreng, K., & White, R. (2009). *Normative Theories of the Media: Journalism in Democratic Societies* (pp. 139–218). Urbana, IL: Illinois University Press.
Cohen, B. (1963). *The Press and Foreign Policy*. Princeton: Princeton University Press.
Galander, M. M. (2000). *Mass Media in Sudan* (p. 2000). Kuala Lumpur: IIUM Press.

Galander, M. (2009). Press Laws and Press Councils in Sudan. In M. Y. Husain (Ed.), *Media Laws and Ethics in Selected Muslim Countries*. Kuala Lumpur: IIUM Research Center.

Galander, M. (2015, February 20). Towards a Media System Predictor for the Arab World. *AUSACE 21st Annual Conference*. Qatar University.

Galander, M. (2016, in Arabic). Necessary Illusions: The Role of Press in Politics in Sudan. In Haydar Ibrahim (Ed.), *Sudan's Independence: 60 Years of Trial and Error*. Cairo, Egypt: Dar al-Hadara.

Hachten, W. (2016). *The World News Prism*. Sussex, UK: Wiley.

Hallin, D., & Mancini, P. (2004). *Changing Media Systems: Three Models of Media and Politics*. Cambridge and New York: Cambridge University Press.

Hanitzsch, T. (2013). Comparative Journalism Research: Mapping a Growing Field. *Australian Journalism Research, 35*(2), 9–19.

Hanitzsch, T., Muchtar, N., Hamada, B. I., Hanitzsch, T., Galal, A., Masduki, & Ullah, M. S. (2017). Journalism and the Islamic Worldview: Journalistic Roles in Muslim-Majority Countries. *Journalism Studies, 18*(5), 555–575. http://www.tandfonline.com/doi/abs/10.1080/1461670X.2017.1279029. Accessed 23 April 2017.

Merrill, J. (2008). *Global Journalism: Topical Issues and Media Systems*. Boston, MA: Pearson.

Norris, P. (Ed.). (2010). *The Public Sentinel*. Washington, DC: The World Bank.

Pintack, L. (2008, July). The Mission of Arab Journalism: Creating Change in a Time of Turmoil. *International Journal Press/Politics, 13*(3), 193–227.

Pintack, L. (2011). *The New Arab Journalist: Mission and Identity in a Time of Turmoil*. New York: Tauris & Co.

Pintack, L. (2013, December). *Islam for Journalists: A Primer on Covering Muslim Communities in the U.S.* (Digital Newsbooks, Reynolds Journalism Institute).

Rugh, W. (2004). *Mass Media in the Arab World*. Westport, CT: Praeger.

Salih, M. (1971). *Half a Century of the Sudanese Press*. Khartoum: Khartoum University Press.

Seib, P. (2008). *The Aljazeera Effect*. Dulles, VA: Potomac Books.

Seibert, F. S., Peterson, T., & Schramm, W. (1971). *The Four Theories of the Press*. Urbana: University of Illinois Press.

Weaver, D. H. (Ed.). (1989). *The Global Journalist: News People Around the World*. Cresskill, NJ: Hampton Press.

Weaver, D. H. (1998). Journalist Around the World: Commonalities and Differences. In D. H. Weaver (Ed.), *The Global Journalist: News People around the World*. Cresskill, NJ: Hampton.

Weaver, D. H., & Willnat, L. (Eds.). (2012). *The Global Journalist in the 21st Century*. New York: Routledge.

Willis, J. (2010). *The Mind of a Journalist*. Thousand Oaks, CA: Sage.

Willnat, L., Weaver, D. H., & Choi, J. (2013, April). The Global Journalist in the Twenty-First Century: A Cross-National Study of Journalistic Competencies. *Journalism Practice, 7*(2), 163–183.

Further Reading

Hafez, K., & Paletz, D. (Eds.). (2001). *Mass Media, Politics and Society in the Middle East.* Cresskill, NJ: Hampton Press.
Himelfarb, S. (2011, April 11). *Social Media in the Middle East.* US Institute for Peace. https://www.usip.org/publications/2011/04/social-media-middle-east.
Lockman, Z. (2016). *Field Notes: The Making of Middle East Studies in the United States.* Stanford, CA: Stanford University Press.

INDEX

About the Editor

Emmanuel K. Ngwainmbi is Chair of Instruction with the Global Listening Center. He also serves on the editorial boards of 15 peer-reviewed social science journals and holds memberships in 12 international organizations in media and communication, including IAMCR, IAICS, and ICA. A senior communication consultant who has worked in regional and international American multinational financial services companies such as Bank of America, Wells Fargo, African Development Bank, also at UNESCO, UNDP, UNECA, UNFPA, and other United Nations agencies, he is passionate about promoting adaptive thinking—helping companies and institutions change how they assess human progress. He has been acknowledged by Nobel Laureate Desmond Tutu, Pulitzer Prize winner Gwendolyn Brooks, and the Hawaii International Conference on Arts and Humanities for his contributions to the humanities. Professor Ngwainmbi has also lectured in Asia, Africa, Europe, and the US. He has held faculty positions in ten institutions, including Jackson State University and the University of North Carolina, Charlotte, where he currently teaches global media studies. He was Director of International Education Programs and Head of the Department of Communication at Elizabeth City State University and Graduate Professor at Jackson State University. His academic honors include the Distinguished Professor award from the Chinese Academy for Social Sciences, Who is Who Among America's Teachers, and the Departmental Teacher of the Year. He is listed on the rosters of Communication for development professionals with various United Nations agencies. He has published 17 books, including *Communication efficiency and rural development in Africa* (University Press of America); *Exporting Communication Technology to Developing countries* (Rowman & Littlefield); *Healthcare management and development challenges in developing countries* (Lexington Books); *Citizenship, Democracies, and Media Engagement among Emerging Economies and marginalized communities* (Palgrave Macmillan), and produced over scholarly 200 articles and white papers with some in trade magazines journals; translated into Mandarin, French, Spanish, Afrikaans, and German. His other writings have been published by the Washington Review; Lynne Reiner; Routledge; Sage; Greenwood Press; Yaoundé University Press; Howard University Press; and many newspapers. Through his writings and lectures, Prof. Ngwainmbi hopes to bring awareness to the intellectual and practical forms of globalization and multiculturalism and their impact on society.

CPSIA information can be obtained
at www.ICGtesting.com
Printed in the USA
LVHW020026031220
673230LV00005B/237